MINDING MY OWN F   ESS"

The inside story of Leicester City's success in the 90s

Enjoy
Best wishes
B Pierpoint

By Barrie Pierpoint
Leicester City's first Chief Executive
with Mathew Mann

Foreword by Steve Walsh

This book is a truthful recollection of actual events, all of which are portrayed to the best of Barrie Pierpoint's knowledge.

The conversations within the book all come from Barrie's recollections, although they are not written to represent word-for-word transcripts; rather, Barrie has retold them in a way that evokes the feeling and meaning of what was said and in all instances, the essence of the dialogue is, in Barrie's opinion, accurate.

The stories within the book have been researched and described as accurately as humanly possible.

The book includes views and opinions from multiple contributors. The stories told by the contributors were provided in good faith and in the spirit of the book.

First Edition.
ISBN: 978-1-8382329-0-0
First published 2020
email: info@morganlawrence.co.uk
website: www.mindingmyownfootballbusiness.co.uk

Published by:
Morgan Lawrence Publishing Services Limited
71-75 Shelton Street
Covent Garden
London
WC2H 9JQ
www.morganlawrence.co.uk
Company number: 12910264

Printed and bound in the United Kingdom
by Swallowtail Print Limited, Norwich.

Contents

Introduction from our sponsors, Champions (UK) plc

We are very proud and pleased to be sponsoring Barrie Pierpoint's new book of his life and times at Leicester City Football Club in the 90's.

I have known Barrie since 1991 when he joined the Club as its first Director of Marketing and then two years later was promoted to be their first Chief Executive.

I was a boxholder and sponsor at Leicester City and both witnessed and experienced the tremendous transformation from his early days to over the years, taking the Club from a small and sleepy professional club to a Premiership giant, always ahead of its time, innovative, forward-thinking, progressive and successful. Leicester City Football Club became a household name.

Barrie always looked after people, was friendly, had time to speak to you, made you feel welcome, with nothing ever too much trouble for him to ensure that your experience at the Club was first-class.

His particular strength was developing the commercial and business side, where his attention to detail, the service, standards, quality and value for money for everyone made it a real pleasure to be a supporter.

I particularly remember all the new branding, the introduction of the new club logo, Fox Leisure – the new retail operation with its own kit, leisurewear and merchandise, the conferencing and banqueting operations - where the food, service and ambience was second to none, the community activities, events, sporting dinners with Barrie and his team continually bringing new sponsorship business into the Club.

He achieved the impossible, building a new Carling stand and growing a business very rapidly off the back of that new facility.

He turned a loss-making football club into a profitable success and thriving business.

He achieved so much in a short space of time that when he departed the Club in 2000 he left a legacy for the Club to continue to build upon his success.

Champions is a leading brand agency, a family business with traditional family values and has been growing at a rapid pace since it started in 2003. We are a full service agency, with an offer consisting of creative, digital, marketing, PR, media, events, publishing, advertising, celebrity, sport and web.

We pride ourselves that we work as part of our clients' business, understand their requirements, then produce quality work, offer a Premiership service, value for money and ensure that all our clients receive more than their expectations.

We have a huge affinity with sport as our Sports Division organises many events with sporting celebrities in attendance. We have after-dinner speakers at some of the UK's top prestigious events, as well as providing artists, musicians, celebrities and entertainment for all types of events and occasions.

For further details of all our services see www.championsukplc.com

May I wish Barrie and his new book every success, very best wishes and good luck for a successful launch.

John Hayes
CEO
Champions (UK) plc

Foreword by Steve Walsh

I first met Barrie during the summer of 1991. I had been at Filbert Street for five years by then and had witnessed the sad demise of the club from a First Division side to a team who had only just avoided relegation to the third tier.

Barrie was a flamboyant character, with his big cigars, flash suits and multi-coloured glasses, but what most stood out was his vision for Leicester City. While he didn't know a lot about football, he understood football clubs needed money – and making money was something he knew a lot about.

Brian Little came in around the same time with a three-year plan to win promotion to the Premier League. This meant that we had two ambitious individuals working tirelessly to take us to the next level. It was the beginning of a renaissance period for Leicester City.

As Captain for the bulk of the nineties, I spent a fair bit of time with Barrie to see how we, the players, could help him to develop the commercial side of the club. We were fully on board with what he was trying to achieve and supported him by helping to promote Leicester City and spending more time within the community. We enjoyed it and did as much as we could.

He needed to make changes; some people were not pulling their weight and he had to flush them out and bring in the right people. Barrie was thoughtful and kind, but he could be tough too when he needed to be. The improvements at the club were quick and impressive as a new era began for Leicester.

Barrie brought Prince Charles to Filbert Street and I had the honour of introducing him to the players. It was a brilliant and bizzare occasion. There was also the event that Barrie organised at the Grand Hotel with George Best in attendance – that was the first of many cracking nights which Barrie arranged.

Filbert Street was an old ground and the Carling Stand showed that we were going to the next level and helped improve the stature of the club and bring in valuable revenue.

In parallel to the off-field transformation, Leicester achieved unprecedented success on the pitch with seven Wembley Finals in a decade. I got on well with Barrie; while he kept out of the way of the football side, he was always there for us if we needed him. Barrie helped to organise some events for my testimonial year and I remember he always kept some goodies, like golf bags and umbrellas, in his office to give to the players.

It is sad the way that it ended for him after all he'd achieved at the club. Looking back now, Barrie was an integral part of that golden period in Leicester City's history.

This book chronicles and celebrates the story of Leicester City's achievements, on and off the pitch, during the nineties, the best days of my career.

Enjoy.

Preface

Do you believe in love at first sight? I do. On Boxing Day 1989, my dad took me to Filbert Street where two goals from loanee Kevin Campbell gave City a 2-1 win over Bournemouth. I fell in love immediately. With Leicester City, not with Kevin Campbell, though he was a good player.

Over the next decade, I witnessed many incredible games, top-class players and enjoyed some wonderful moments. As a young boy growing up in the nineties, Filbert Street was my Disneyland – it was such a magical place.

I am still fascinated by everything 'Leicester City' and have a thirst for knowledge. I have devoured everything I can get my hands on, from DVDs and VHS to club history books and autobiographies. They are all delivered from a journalist, player, manager, or fans' perspective. What has never been written about in detail is a boardroom view of City.

In June 2019, I wrote *What If? An Alternative History of Leicester City* and had set up a Facebook page to help promote the book. When reviewing my 'Likes' I spotted a familiar name – Barrie Pierpoint.

I knew that Barrie was the Chief Executive who was voted off the Board in 1999 and I remembered the 'Pierpoint Out' banners. But I did not know anything else about him, so I did some research.

I discovered that he had introduced – amongst other things – Fox Leisure and Family Night Football – two things that evoke happy memories from my childhood. I was surprised I did not know this and wondered what else Barrie had achieved while at Filbert Street and an idea began to develop in my mind.

I arranged a meeting with Barrie to pitch an idea for a book. Ahead of the meeting, I felt nervous. I had not met him before and did not really know what to expect. Would he be the power-hungry monster I had read about in the press? Was he really the man who had tried to ruin my football club?

What I found was the opposite. Behind his imposing six-foot five-inch frame and booming voice was a modest, generous, friendly businessman who was instrumental to the success that Leicester City enjoyed in the nineties.

The more we spoke, the more I realised that his was a story that needed to be told. Barrie agreed to do the book on two conditions. "I don't want it to be the Barrie Pierpoint Appreciation Society and I don't want it to be controversial," he told me.

So, we agreed to write a light-hearted, nostalgic tale of a struggling football club who defied the odds to compete with, and beat, the best – on and off the pitch – told by those who were there. Former directors, players, managers, staff, journalists and supporters have contributed to this book which gives us a remarkable view of that era through their various lenses.

I have spent many hours interviewing players and managers – many of whom were my childhood idols – and what surprised me was that they continue to hold Barrie in high esteem.

It is a credit to Barrie that he refuses to dwell on his torrid last few months at the club, preferring instead to look back on his time at Leicester as the best days of his life. As I collated my interview notes, trawled through the archives at the Leicestershire Records Office and began to shape the story, I realised just how much Barrie had done for Leicester City and how lucky we, the fans, were to have him at our club. I have so much respect for him, what he accomplished and how resilient he was during those awful events leading to his departure.

Barrie will be the first to admit that he would not have achieved all that he did without the support of the hundreds of staff, directors, managers and players who worked at Filbert Street during his tenure. This story celebrates them, especially the unsung heroes. There are many people who made a huge contribution to the success of Leicester City in the nineties, but you will not find their names in any history books.

I really hope that you enjoy this read, but more importantly, I hope that it does justice to the work which Barrie and his team, along with the various directors, team managers and players, carried out during that glorious decade.

Mathew Mann
Ghost writer.

Introduction

When I first arrived at Filbert Street in April 1991, as Leicester City's first Director of Marketing, I was determined to make my mark and turn this giant loss-making dinosaur into a successful, modern football club and business.

I knew that I had the business acumen, drive, vision and leadership off the field with my professionally selected team and the Team Manager, who had joined a few weeks after me – Brian Little – was the proven professional football specialist to make it happen on the pitch.

This club was a sleeping giant which lacked affinity with the community, had an identity crisis with businesses and also lacked ambition with the regular paying fans who thought that the Club was too dictatorial and distant.

I knew that to make this club great again I would have to work hard with the Team Managers and my off-the-field team by introducing standards, quality and service in all areas that we were responsible for – the business side of the Club.

I don't think anyone, myself included, could have predicted just how much success we would enjoy over the next nine years. Thirty have passed since I walked through the doors of the crumbling Main Stand at Filbert Street, during which time I was promoted to Leicester City's first Chief Executive and I look back on those days as the best of my life.

When approached about this book by Mathew Mann – a loyal and dedicated City fan – I agreed that I had a story to tell, but I had always been too busy to put pen to paper. When I looked back through my files, I was reminded of all the great moments, memories, achievements and successes that we had enjoyed; the amazing people I had met, worked with and the fun and experiences that we shared. I realised just what a story there was to tell, but I also realised that it wasn't just my story, so we invited memories from those who were there – fans, staff, players, team managers, Directors, journalists and some of our corporate customers. I was overwhelmed by the response; over forty people have taken the time to contribute to this book that chronicles a glorious period in Leicester City's history.

This is the first time that someone has written about the behind-the-scenes stories of the Club – both the good and bad times too.

As in all clubs and organisations you get troublemakers, internal politics, individuals who are above their station with egos bigger than the Club, whose only ambition is to cause rifts, create bad feeling and contribute nothing but negativity and problems. We had our fair share of those people during my time at the Club! However, there were many others who contributed positively to the Club, pulling and working together for its best interests and success.

I had an amazing journey and I was proud to play my part in the Club's success in the nineties as Leicester City rose from a struggling Division Two side to one of the top Clubs – on and off the pitch – in the country. It is a great shame that it ended so abruptly for three other Directors and myself, who were blamed for being too professional, caring, business-like and not being afraid to challenge other Directors who worked alone and outside of their remit.

I hope that you enjoy my story as it unfolds and that it evokes some memories of that golden era of the nineties. Thank you to everyone for so kindly contributing your memories, both of the Club and working with or knowing me during my time there too.

Mathew, thank you for making this book possible.

Happy reading and thank you for your support.

Barrie Pierpoint

Chapter one - Selling a dream

A brief history of Leicester City

Filbert Street, Leicester was a bleak place to be in 1991. Twenty-two years had passed since the club's glory days in the swinging sixties when Leicester City were established as a force to be reckoned with in the top division of English football. During a glorious decade, City won the League Cup in 1964, were runners up in the same competition in 1965 and also reached three FA Cup finals.

The seventies began with Leicester winning both the Second Division Championship and the Charity Shield in 1971. Bloomfield's Boys, despite being unable to add further silverware to City's trophy cabinet, produced some of the most exciting and entertaining football that the Foxes' faithful had ever seen.

In contrast, the eighties were unremarkable as the Foxes became known as a yo-yo club – not quite good enough for the First Division, but too strong for the Second. To make matters worse, support for the club was dwindling. Home attendances during the eighties averaged just 11,000 – a huge reduction from the 25,000 who flocked to Filbert Street during the sixties and early seventies. With match-day income being City's biggest revenue source, it was no surprise that the club were struggling financially. The fans grew accustomed to losing their best players as the Board of Directors resorted to selling their stars in a bid to balance the books.

The 1960s were a golden era for Leicester City.

At the end of the 1986/87 season, following relegation to the Second Division, top scorer Alan Smith was the inevitable big-name departure. Supporters were expecting an immediate return to the First Division, but results were not good enough and the manager, Bryan Hamilton, was dismissed.

In a move designed to bring top-flight football back to the Filbert Street faithful, David Pleat was named as Leicester's new manager on Christmas Eve 1987. Pleat was regarded as a real coup as he had enjoyed a successful season the previous year with Tottenham; reaching the semi-final of the League Cup, finishing runners up in the FA Cup and achieving a third-place finish in the First Division. His time at Spurs ended abruptly following tabloid allegations about his private life.

Pleat introduced an attractive, passing style and reversed City's fortunes immediately. At the time of his appointment, the Foxes were without a win in five. However, during the second half of the season, Leicester lost just four times and gained more points than eventual champions, Millwall, did during the same time frame and City finished in a respectable thirteenth.

Optimism was, therefore, high for the 1988/89 season, with most bookies installing the Foxes as promotion favourites. A big blow was the loss of former England international, Russell Osman, who joined First Division Southampton for £350,000. Alan Paris and Tony Spearing were brought in to bolster the defence, the prolific Jimmy Quinn was signed to provide the firepower up front and Martin Hodge joined from Sheffield Wednesday to replace Ian Andrews in goal.

Despite the pre-season excitement, Leicester endured a disappointing season and finished in fifteenth place – twenty-one points away from a play-off position. Since Pleat's appointment, there had been a high turnover of players, the issue was that the new boys were not of the same calibre as those who were leaving.

One of the few exceptions was Gary Mills, a European Cup winner in 1980, who signed for City in 1989. Gary explains that Leicester was not the only club after him at the time. "I'd enjoyed eight seasons with Nottingham Forest playing for the great Brian Clough before moving to Notts County in 1987. I won the Player of the Year award in my first year at County as we narrowly missed out on promotion to Division Two. The following season, our manager, John Barnwell was replaced by Neil Warnock. I got on well with Neil, but his style of play did not suit me and was not what I had been brought up with, so it was only a matter of time before I left.

I was in advanced talks with West Brom – who were hunting promotion to Division One – when I received a call informing me that Leicester were also interested, and from that moment it just felt right. I knew David Pleat liked to play my type of football, so I wanted to speak to him. Although, the contract I was offered at Leicester was not as good as the one on offer from West Brom, it was not about the money, so I signed for City."

The summer of 1989 was a busy one for the Foxes, beginning with the departure of Mike Newell – City's top scorer the previous season – who moved to First Division Everton. In came Tony James, Rob Johnson, Pat Gavin, Tommy Wight, Kevin Russell, Wayne Clarke and Allan Evans as Pleat looked to completely rebuild the

Gary Mills in action for Leicester City.

team. David Oldfield and David Kelly joined the Foxes later in the season. As Leicester's league campaign progressed, Pleat handed debuts to several youngsters who would enjoy long careers in the game; notably Paul Kitson, Richard Smith, Scott Oakes, Ian Barraclough and Des Linton.

With a huge array of players at his disposal, it is no surprise that Pleat was unable to figure out his best eleven. A staggering twenty-two different players were used in the first seven games, but they could not gel and Leicester sank to the foot of the table. The loan signings of Paul Moran and a young Kevin Campbell, from Spurs and Arsenal respectively, rejuvenated the side, but when the pair returned to their parent clubs City tumbled back down the table, eventually finishing the 1989/90 season in midtable obscurity yet again.

While the league table did not give cause for any players to smile, there were the occasional funny moments as Gary Mills recalls. "We did have some fun on the training pitch. Every so often David Pleat would take training and we would usually end with a game of eight versus eight. We would be in the middle of the game and, suddenly, David would blow his whistle to stop the match to ask Steve Walsh a random question. The exchange would play out like this:

'What is the capital of Sweden?' David would ask Steve.

'Oslo,' Walshy would reply, inevitably getting nine out of ten wrong.

David would respond, 'You silly boy,' before resuming the game. Fifteen minutes later, he'd ask him another question."

With the formation of the Premier League on the horizon, it was imperative for the Foxes to quickly retain their place back in the big time. Ahead of the 1990/91 campaign, Pleat reminded supporters that four teams would be going up this year instead of the usual three. But any advantage gained by the additional promotion spot up for grabs was lost when Gary McAllister became the latest big-name player to depart for pastures new, as he joined Leeds United for £1,000,000.

In contrast to his previous pre-season transfer activity, Pleat made just two signings, both midfielders. Former England international, Ricky Hill was first in followed by Billy Davies, but neither were good enough to fill the McAllister-shaped void in midfield. By September, Davies had played his fifth and final game for the club.

Leicester-born goalkeeper, Carl Muggleton began the season as City's number one, before he found himself, unexpectedly, on the move. "I came through the ranks at Leicester and enjoyed loan spells at Chesterfield, Blackpool and Hartlepool before I eventually made my City debut in January 1989, deputising for the injured Martin Hodge. I played three games that season and then went back on loan, this time to Stockport County. It was August 1990 when I made my next Leicester appearance. After keeping goal for the next three matches, Martin came back into the side and I was relegated to the reserves where I played against Liverpool's second string. The next day, David Pleat phoned me and told me I was going to Anfield on a loan exchange, with Mike Hooper coming to Filbert Street.

Carl Muggleton was a product Leicester City's youth team.

I could not believe it. Liverpool were the Champions of England at the time and full of stars like Ian Rush, Peter Beardsley, and Alan Hansen. They were also managed by the great Kenny Dalglish. I didn't play for the first team, but it was a fantastic experience and I learnt a lot."

After eight games, City were rooted deep within the relegation zone with twenty-four goals conceded. Pleat attempted to shore up the defence by recruiting the experienced trio of Lawrie Madden, Colin Gibson, and Terry Fenwick; however, at the mid-way point of the season Leicester were staring relegation in the face. Third Division football was now a very real possibility.

Off-field matters were no better with the club losing over half a million pounds a year and with a turnover of just £2,000,000. The recently published Taylor Report required the Board of Directors to transform Filbert Street into an all-seater stadium. Things were not looking good and this was a wake-up call to the directors. They knew that radical changes were needed on and off the pitch.

John Sharp had been a Leicester City supporter since boyhood – his grandfather had been chairman pre-war and his father had acted on the board from 1946 until his death in 1983, twice acting as chairman, once in the Matt Gillies era and again when Jimmy Bloomfield was manager. John joined the Board as a Director in 1990 and remembers football was in a vastly different place back then. "It was a time of flux in the football world. Following the Bradford City fire and the Hillsborough disaster, which precipitated the Report by Lord Chief Justice Taylor, standing areas, at least in the upper divisions, were phased out and this chimed with a general realisation that British football grounds were past their sell-by date and were in need of modernisation. The public had to be treated as they would be at a theatre or cinema and not like cattle being processed through a turnstile.

We did not have any great benefactors, so we needed to find a way of generating additional income. Although Leicester City had been relatively good at introducing commercial operations in the past there was still much potential to exploit. The Captains Club in the Filbert Street Stand was a small, but good restaurant and there was a very popular carvery open on match days in the Debenture Holders' Lounge inside the main stand. There was clearly a lot of potential to exploit and it was soon apparent that we needed someone with a special remit to carry this policy out."

**The Taylor Report required City to
replace the terracing with seating.**

Roy Parker, a successful businessman, joined the board at the same time as John Sharp. Roy was drafted in to help steer the club through the recommendations outlined in the Taylor Report and to boost the commercial operation. He recalls his first impressions of the club, "It was obvious that John and I had to liven it up. There was so much negativity and every time someone made a suggestion, the answer was always, 'No, you can't do that.'

During my first board meeting, I was asked for my thoughts on the club. I replied that the club lacked diversity and was weak in sales and marketing. I said that we needed to run the football club as a business, and that to do so, we needed someone with a strong marketing background, someone to come in and make things happen."

Showing great ambition, the Board of Directors placed a job advert in the National press for an experienced marketing professional.

`I later received a phone call that changed my life . . .

Behind the scenes

The success that I had brought to various companies had been brought to the attention of the Leicester City Chairman, Terry Shipman who, in September 1990, invited me to attend an interview for the newly created Director of Marketing role.

'But I don't know anything about football,' I said.

'We aren't interested in your football skills. It's your marketing and business prowess we want,' I was told.

I was living in Somerset at the time, so days later I drove a 320-mile round trip to the Midlands. I whiled away the hours by thinking about what lay ahead of me at my interview. As I pulled into the car park, I saw Filbert Street – famous for launching the careers of Peter Shilton and Gary Lineker – for the first time. I was not impressed with the deteriorating state of the ground.

I was met in the reception of the dilapidated Main Stand and escorted to the boardroom where I was introduced to Terry Shipman.

The Shipmans' love affair with Leicester began in 1939 when local businessman, Len Shipman, lent the club £1000. With Leicester unable to pay back the debt he was instead invited to join the board. Terry, his son, was a lifelong City fan who followed in his father's footsteps, joining the Board of Directors in 1966 and becoming Chairman in 1981. In total the Shipman family served the club for fifty-nine seasons.

'So, lad' – I was almost 40! – 'You're here for the salesman's job then?' Terry asked.

'Erm, no. The role is for Director of Marketing,' I replied, wondering if I was at the right job interview.

'Same thing ain't it?' Terry replied.

Over the course of the next sixty minutes it was apparent that the club had previously attached little importance to marketing and were commercially naïve. The role would involve me having autonomy over the commercial operation which genuinely appealed to me. I was excited by the opportunity to create and implement a marketing strategy from scratch within a business that had such huge potential. I shared my ideas and sold them a dream.

I travelled back to Somerset feeling positive, but two months passed before I was told that I had been shortlisted and invited to a second interview. On a cold morning I set off on another road trip to Leicester.

This time the interview was with Tom Smeaton, a straight-talking Aussie who had become a director at Leicester City in 1979. They say that first impressions count, so I did my best to create a good one. In those days I was a flamboyant dresser – my trademark big, bright Elton John style spectacles always matched the colour of my tie, socks and even my underpants! During the meeting I answered Tom's questions and repeated my vision for the club's off field activities.

After almost three years of living in the South West, the idea of moving closer to my family in the Midlands was appealing. After a while, I had not heard back from Leicester, so I started to apply for other jobs. What I did not know at the time was that several changes were afoot at Filbert Street.

A 3-1 defeat at home to Blackburn Rovers in front of just 8000 fans was the final straw for the Board of Directors who sacked Pleat shortly after that match.

My big glasses becam[e] my trademark.

John Sharp provides the rationale behind Pleat's dismissal. "After such a disastrous season we wanted a complete fresh start. The board decided that David Pleat should leave the club. David was a very knowledgeable football man and a very courteous and delightful person, but there comes a time, and at football clubs it can be fairly frequent, that a change of leadership is the right course of action – both for the club and for the individual. Public sentiment had been critical of both the manager and, indeed, the chairman. So, Terry Shipman stood down at the same time and we appointed Martin George, whom I had been at school with, as his replacement."

Gary Mills was sad to see Pleat leave. "We had some good players, and I enjoyed working with David, but as a team it just wasn't happening. David wanted us to play a certain way and it got to the stage where, regardless of results he stuck with that system. We were not picking up enough points and he lost his job. I know David was disappointed, though not surprised, that the managerial change was made."

Shortly after Pleat's departure, I received a phone call from Leicester City inviting me to yet another interview.

'Has everyone else dropped out?' I jokingly asked.

'We put the role on hold until we had made a decision about the future of the team's manager. We have done that and are now ready to fill the vacancy. Will you come and speak to us again?'

After so many interviews, my car could practically drive itself to Filbert Street. I arrived sporting a new colour scheme of glasses, tie, socks, and underpants combo and met with the new chairman, Martin George.

'Good morning, Barrie.'

'Good morning. May I call you Martin?' I asked

'Try me,' replied the chairman.

'Ok. Good morning, Martin.'

'It is Mr George or chairman to you,' I was told in no uncertain terms. Martin – sorry, Mr George – explained that the recently published Taylor Report required all First and Second Division clubs to play in all-seater stadiums by August 1994, so the club were looking for a marketing professional to raise the money to replace the crumbling Main Stand and to fund the necessary development for the rest of the stadium.

Over two hundred applications had been received, the directors had created a shortlist and now Mr George wanted to quiz the remaining potential candidates himself before making his decision. After explaining what I could bring to the club we shook hands and I was told they would be in touch.

Weeks later I was offered a General Manager and Marketing role within Top Rank where I would be based in London, much closer to my family than my current Somerset base. I had not heard from Leicester and did not expect to, so I accepted the position and began my new role in March 1991.

Just days into my new employment I picked up my phone and was greeted with a familiar Australian voice.

'Barrie. Tom Smeaton here. I have some good news. I would like to offer you the job as Director of Marketing at Leicester City Football Club.'

'I am really sorry, Tom, but I have just started a new job and I do not want to mess them around.' As I placed the receiver back into its cradle, I thought that was the end of my brief dalliance with Leicester City.

However, there was to be one final twist in the tale a few days later when I received another telephone call, this time from my boss at Top Rank.

'Have you read today's *Leicester Mercury*?' he asked.

'No. I'm in London and I do not read that paper,' I replied cautiously.

'Well, I am in Melton Mowbray and it says here that you are the new Director of Marketing for Leicester City. Is that true?'

'No. They offered me the position last week, but I said no.'

'I do not like this, Barrie. I need people who are committed to this company and you, obviously, are not. I have no choice – you are fired,' he said before hanging up.

I phoned my boss back to explain. 'I am not going to Leicester City. I am staying here.'

'Barrie, this has just been officially announced in the newspaper, so as far as I am concerned you are leaving,' I was told and that was that. From having two jobs on the table I suddenly found myself unemployed.

Whether deliberate or a genuine error I still do not know, but on 12th March 1991 an article appeared in the *Leicester Mercury* announcing that I had been appointed as the club's first Director of Marketing.

I immediately called Tom Smeaton. 'Tom, I have got to come to Leicester City now as it has been made public and I have just been sacked from my job.'

'Sorry about that, Barrie. We will send you a formal offer in the post.'

Roy Parker recalls how I almost missed out on the job – because of my coloured glasses! "Barrie excelled at the interviews and it was clear that he had all the attributes we needed. However, three board members were concerned that Barrie was an extrovert because of his large, blue framed spectacles. I argued that this was exactly what we needed – someone who was self-assured with a big presence. I convinced the others and we offered Barrie the job. It was one of the best decisions the club ever made."

Days later I received two letters from Leicester City. One signed by Martin George offering me a salary of £35,000 a year. The other from Terry Shipman offering £30,000. Guess which one I accepted?

This article in the Mercury cost me my job.

'Money man' at Filbert Street

CITY were today making a new appointment – but not team manager.

The Filbert Street club named 39-year-old Barry Pierpoint as their Marketing Director – a man charged with attracting major investment.

With the prospect of revamping the ground, and the cost likely to run into £millions, Pierpoint, a Nottingham-born businessman, will be a key figure in City's next few years if they are to get the necessary cash backing from industries and businesses throughout the area.

Pierpoint, who lives in Somerset, but works in London for a management consultant company, is set to start his job in a month's time and was being introduced at a Press conference later today.

A former local referee, he he used to watch Notts County.

Chapter two - The dawn of a new era

On the pitch - 1990/91 season

At the time of Pleat's departure in January 1991, City were sitting just three places away from the relegation zone. Leicester had a proud history. Since being elected to the Football League in 1894, they had only ever competed in the top two tiers, but the Third Division was now beckoning. The Board of Directors were desperate to retain their Second Division status, so they opted to promote Gordon Lee from coach to team manager on a short-term contract until the end of the season. It would prove to be an inspired choice.

Lee had spent the bulk of his playing days at Midlands rivals, Aston Villa, before he became a manager. His vast experience – Newcastle, Blackburn and Everton amongst the teams listed on his CV – was just what Leicester needed. He also knew the club and players well, having joined City as a coach under Pleat in 1988.

Lee was confident that his squad were capable of pulling the Foxes out of the mire and, astonishingly, he did not sign anyone, or hand anyone a debut during his half season at the helm. Instead, he focussed on coaching, man-management and lifting his demoralised players.

Gary Mills remembers being pleased with Lee's appointment. "From the moment he got the job, Gordon was relaxed and positive and the feeling around the club improved. He was very approachable and he kept things fun to improve our spirits."

Performances improved, but Leicester's results remained mixed and, following defeat to Ipswich in the penultimate game of the season, the Foxes were second from bottom and just ninety minutes away from the drop.

On 11th May 1991, Oxford United rocked up at Filbert Street for the final fixture of the season. City needed to better the result of their relegation rivals West Bromwich Albion, who faced Bristol Rovers.

Having already secured a mid-table position, the game meant nothing to Oxford but everything for the Foxes. The Blue Army were out in full force, 19,011, which was the biggest attendance of the season.

Lee's pre-match team talk had clearly motivated his players as Leicester began the game with attacking intent, throwing everything at Oxford. With twenty-four minutes on the clock a Tommy Wright corner fell to Player of the Season, Tony James, who stabbed home from six yards. The score remained 1-0 which, with West Brom only managing a draw, was enough to guarantee Second Division football for the Foxes. When the referee's whistle signalled the end of the game, the delighted City fans ran on to the pitch to celebrate with their heroes in blue.

Gary Mills believes that this was a pivotal moment in the history of Leicester City. "The Oxford game is one of the most important games in the club's history. Who knows what would have happened had we gone down. It was ironic that it was West Brom – the team that I had almost joined – who were relegated. Devon White, who is a good friend of mine, scored the crucial goal for Bristol Rovers and Tony James gave us a 1-0 win. Gordon Lee deserves a lot of credit for keeping us up. After the game he took us to Portugal as a treat for staying up. We celebrated a lot on that trip, I tell you!"

Jubilant City fans celebrate the 'Great Escape.'

Young defender, Richard Smith, enjoyed the match, too. "I'd made a few appearances during the 1990/91 season, but I wasn't included in the squad for the Oxford game, so I watched it from the stands with Paul Kitson. There was a lot of belief that we belonged in that division and I was delighted that we stayed up. It got even better for me as I won the Young Player of the Year award and I remember being so excited because Gary Lineker's name was on the same trophy. I was a Leicester fan as well as a player, so that was amazing for me."

Richard Smith shows off his Young Player of the Year award, alongside Alan Paris and Ali Mauchlan.

Gordon was popular with the fans, but he stepped down as the chairman felt that a complete revamp of the managerial and coaching staff was the best way for the club to move forward.

At the dawn of the Premier League era the Board of Directors had to make the right decision in their choice of manager. A host of managers were considered, including Wycombe's Martin O'Neill and John Beck of Cambridge, before Martin George approached Darlington to enquire about the availability of their promising young manager, Brian Little.

As a player, Little had made almost 250 appearances for Aston Villa, winning two League Cups and earning an England cap until a knee injury prematurely ended his career at the age of just twenty-six. He had a short spell as manager of Wolves between coaching spells at Villa and Middlesbrough before he joined Darlington in 1989 to become their manager.

During his first full season in charge, Little led the northeast club to the Conference title and he was celebrating his second successive promotion – and Championship – when he found out about Leicester's interest.

Brian jumped at the chance to join the Foxes and he signed a three-year contract in the summer of 1991. "I had a great relationship with my chairman at Darlington and he had always promised me that I could leave when the right club came in for me. I had won two league titles and a few clubs had made offers, but none of them felt right. Then, one day in May 1991, the chairman phoned me and said, 'I've just had a call from someone you might want to think about.' That someone was Martin George, Chairman of Leicester City, and I was instantly interested.

As a player, I'd had some tough games at Filbert Street and I knew that the fans were great, so everything was in place to build a successful team. It was such an appealing job.

I made sure that I was prepared by assessing the club and analysing their results and statistics. I really did my homework and found that they were a team who leaked a lot of goals. That was right up my street. I wanted to set up my teams to be strong at the back, exactly the type of sides that I would not have liked to have played against.

I knew exactly what I was going to do; build a team that was tough to beat who also played with some flair. I realised that I was going to have to overhaul the playing side, but I was used to that. When I had arrived at Darlington, we were relegated to the Conference and I got rid of twenty players in an hour to allow me to rebuild. I did it and brought them success and I was convinced that I could do the same for Leicester."

Brian Little became Leicester City manager in 1991.

City supporter, Ashley Barratt, considers Brian's appointment was the turning point for Leicester City. "In 1986, a young Steve Walsh was making his Leicester City debut in a 1-1 draw at home to Filbert Street. That match was also my first trip to Filbert Street. I was just a boy, but I remember being overcome with emotion – it is a memory that will live with me forever. Sadly, the next four seasons were unremarkable. We were a mediocre side and a mediocre club. But things changed drastically with the arrival of Barrie and Brian Little in 1991."

In just a few months City had appointed Martin George as the new Chairman, me as the club's first Director of Marketing and Brian as the new manager was considered to be the final piece of the jigsaw.

Behind the scenes

On the 2nd April 1991, a week shy of my fortieth birthday, I officially joined Leicester City. I was allocated an office on the ground floor which had recently been vacated by David Pleat. Well, I call it an office, but the room could have been used by the police to interrogate criminals! Tiny, windowless and reeking of gas from the old kitchen next door – it was hardly a creative environment. There was even a dead plant in the corner! As I made my way to the wobbly desk, I bashed my head on the shadeless light bulb dangling from the ceiling and thought, not for the last time, 'what have I let myself in for?'

Later that week I met with the Board of Directors to agree my objectives which were to:

• Generate the funds (thought to be circa £5,500,000) to build a new stand to replace the crumbling Main Stand.
• Build bridges and improve Leicester's standing in the community.
• Increase the profile of the club.
• Make Leicester City more accessible for fans and to increase attendances.
• Raise money to be invested into the playing squad.
• Develop the existing and research new commercial ventures.

I left the meeting in no doubt that I was facing the biggest challenge of my working life, but I thrive under pressure and could not wait to get started. I sat in my drab office with a blank piece of paper to write my own job description and produced a strategy for achieving my objectives.

My first home match in the Director's Box was a league game versus Portsmouth and I was also in attendance for the famous 'Great Escape' against Oxford. What really struck me was that City had some of the most passionate fans around and I felt that they deserved a club – on and off the pitch – that they could be proud of.

Seven-year-old Clare Storey received this wonderful Easter egg on behalf of the children in the Leicester Royal Infirmary.

CLUB CALL 0898 12 11 85 • TICKET CALL 0533 555000 • CLUB CALL 0898 12 11 85

28

The dire financial situation at the club became immediately apparent when I was told that I could not use the photocopier because of the cost of ink, electricity and paper! So, I had to sneak in early on a Sunday morning to do my paperwork and to produce some marketing flyers for me to send out to businesses and organisations in order to generate money and to raise awareness of the club.

My exploration into the 1990/91 accounts told me that Leicester had a turnover of £2,200,000; the commercial avenues contributed just £736,000 and City had recorded a loss of £638,000. I discussed this with the Directors and discovered that this was the norm. Leicester had consistently made a loss on operations, excluding incoming transfer fees. The only way that the club had managed to survive was by selling their best players. Gary Lineker, Gary McAllister, Mike Newell and Alan Smith were some of the big names who had moved on as the Directors balanced the books. The club were stuck in a cycle. Finish a season in debt, sell a player to get out of the red, repeat the following year. This had to change.

Roy Parker, who joined the board in 1991, describes his eye-opening experience that highlighted one of the reasons why the club were struggling financially. "The club was leaking money

**I had to sneak into Filbert Street
on Sundays to print marketing fliers like these.**

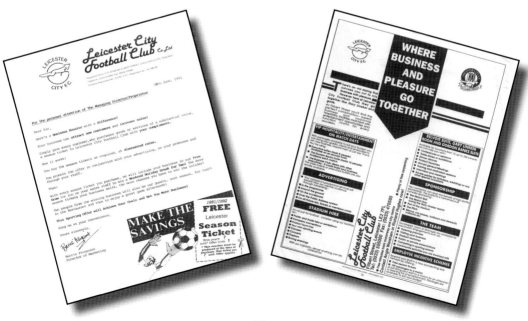

and it was not surprising. I joined Barrie for some of his introductory meetings with the senior staff. One of the lottery scratch card managers entered the room, introduced himself and then sold us some scratch cards. We then had a short general discussion before he left the room. A few minutes later, Barrie and I noticed that the manager had left his money bag which contained a considerable sum. We put the bag in a safe place and waited for him to report it missing, but he never did. It was no wonder that the club had no money."

Before I implemented any changes, I wanted to fully understand how Leicester City operated, so for the next few months, I immersed myself in the club, working sixteen-hour days, learning and absorbing everything that I could about the club and Leicester as a city. It was clear that, business wise, little had changed since the club's inception in 1884 when the aim was purely to make enough money to field a team.

Staff morale was incredibly low and I was shocked by the melancholy that engulfed Filbert Street. There were a lot of people working hard, but they were doing it in isolation and without understanding their purpose.

My initial reflections were that our catering was practically non-existent, except on match days; our facilities – if you could call them that – were small, out-dated and under-utilised, while our poor-quality merchandise was not popular with the fans or making any money. It was a huge culture shock for me as the commercial operation was stuck in the Dark Ages.

It wasn't all bad, though. I could see that the club, as a business, was a real sleeping giant with enormous potential and I was determined to bring it into the twenty-first century. The question was, would the existing staff be willing to adapt and come with me?

The commercial set up that I had inherited was led by a Catering Manager, a Lottery Manager and a Commercial Manager. I held individual meetings with each to hear their suggestions, share my thoughts and vision and to develop a professional working relationship. Sadly, I found them unhelpful; they were negative, resistant to change, reluctant to share information and they dismissed my ideas saying things like, 'We've tried that before,' or 'It won't work.' I felt that they were more interested in protecting their own interests when they should have put the club and our supporters first. They made it clear that I was not wanted.

"We're doing alright here and we don't need a marketing whizz-kid," I was told during one meeting.

Being completely honest, I found it tough. But I am a strong, resilient character and I had confidence in my ability to turn things around. I had no choice but to persevere.

To be blunt, the club had no vision, it lacked leadership and direction and the staff did not know why they were doing whatever they had been asked to do. They had not received adequate training and many were sitting in roles that did not suit them. It was like playing your goalkeeper up front!

My earlier fact-finding mission identified several opportunities to improve the club's off-field fortunes and I was not afraid to take risks and stand by my judgement. I formed a business plan, drew up a twelve-month marketing roadmap and created a strategy and vision for the club. I agreed these with the Board of Directors and gained support of the staff.

Ensuring that everyone understands their purpose is so important to me. One person who understands the rationale behind their task is more powerful than a hundred who do not, so I explained to my staff the aim of the commercial operation and how this would contribute to the club's overall success. This was essential as they were the ones who would be working with me to achieve them.

I knew immediately that there were people who did not share my dream. I was persuasive and ruthless in outing those who could not, or would not, change with me and I surrounded myself with good people who shared, and could deliver, my vision.

For my first signing I brought in Richard Hughes as the Business Development Manager. Richard's role was to score sponsorship and advertising contracts by helping me to sell the matchday packages and general commercial activities to local businesses.

Charles Rayner joined us from the Burton Group to head up the retail operation. Charles, my creative man in the middle, was instrumental in completely overhauling our merchandise operation, as you will read later.

My third acquisition was Michelle Newman, who I brought in to be my Personal Assistant. Michelle was the rock in defence; orchestrating my time and managing my diary; making every minute count so that I could get on with my core tasks of engaging our customers and making the club money.

So, what did my new recruits think of their new boss?

"Meeting Barrie, a six-foot five chap with Elton John style glasses, walking around a run- down football stand with a tin of biscuits in his hands was not what I was expecting for my job interview!" - Richard

"He was nuts! Very charismatic, but also very driven. I'd never met anyone like him before and I haven't since!" - Charles

"My interview was very bizarre. Barrie gave me lots of challenges to test my ability. The final task was dictation to see how accurate my typing was. He spoke so fast,explaining the offside rule. The terminology was new to me, so I struggled to keep up. When I had finished, he told me it was rubbish, but I could try again. Then he dictated an offer of employment and told me that I had got the job!"
                    - Michelle

So, while I was replacing the staff I had inherited with experienced professionals, Brian Little was making wholescale changes to his backroom staff. Brian wanted people around him who shared his view on how the game should be played. So, he replaced the existing coaches with his ex-Villa teammates, John Gregory, Allan Evans and Steve Hunt and he brought in former Leicester player, David Nish, to head up the youth team.

Brian explains why having the right backroom staff was vital to him. "It was crucial for me to surround myself with people that I could trust. We were all different characters, but we worked so well together. Allan and John were very important to me. I would pick the team which could create animosity, but as they were amongst the squad, they were able to bridge the gap between me and the players.

I took a keen interest in all aspects of the club. I attended reserve matches and the three of us even joined in with the training as we could still play a bit in those days. I would not tell anyone to do anything that I would not do myself. Allan, John and I even joined in the pre-season running to show them that we were part of the group, though we did come last!"

Brian was changing the culture on the playing side too. He gave popular defender, Steve Walsh, the captain's armband and placed the previous skipper, Ali Mauchlan, on the transfer list. At the training ground he removed the pool table because he wanted the players to be focussed on football and not distracted by recreational activities. He also made flip flops in the showers and dressing room mandatory and decreed that only injured players were allowed into the physio room as he stamped his authority.

Rules were a key aspect of his management style. "Discipline was important to me, but you can do it in a fun way," Brian says. "When I was at Darlington, I would issue a fine and write them a little poem. So, if they were late because they had missed the train, they would be fined and I would write them a poem about a train.

At Leicester, the fines were five pounds. Some clubs were fining players large sums, but that could be detrimental. A fiver was just enough to niggle them, but it also kept it fun. Some of the reasons for a fine were wearing the wrong shirt, arriving two minutes late, not wearing flip flops in the shower. Little things like that galvanised team spirit. The lads would try to get each other fined five pounds for a laugh! One of the rules we had was that players had to be clean shaven on a matchday, which would certainly not stand nowadays. Some of the players would deliberately come in unshaven just to get a fine and to get a laugh from their teammates. At lots of clubs, the fines pay for the Christmas party. That did not sit right with me. All our fines went to a local charity.

Colin Gibson received a lot of fines in those early days. I had known Gibbo since he was fifteen years old, when he was an apprentice at Aston Villa and we later played together for the Villa first team. The first day of training at Leicester was a nightmare for him as he kept calling me Brian instead of gaffer. It took him so long to get used to calling me gaffer. He got a bit of stick from the lads for that!"

The Directors understood that Leicester needed to modernise and they had shown ambition when they created the marketing post that I now occupied, but I am not sure that they had all understood quite how much change was needed or how radical the changes would need to be.

John Sharp, one of the Directors who shared my vision, explains that some other members of the board did not. "The agreed strategy of the club was to raise the profile of the club and to increase the non-footballing revenue so people were generally supportive of the good work Barrie was doing, though it is fair to say that he always had detractors on the board. There were factions within the club that were always trying to drive a wedge between the football side of the business and the non-football operations."

Like most clubs in those days, Leicester City were owned by a few families. They were predominantly football fans who had an opportunity to sit in the Director's Box, get close to the players and manager and the boardroom was like an exclusive members' club. This was fine. We need football – especially Leicester – fans at all levels within the club. But what they were lacking was someone impartial, who had a marketing brain, someone who did not let their heart rule their head and that was where I came in. I was often criticised by influential supporters because of my lack of football knowledge, but that was why I was so successful.

I had no aspirations to get involved in the football side then, or at any point during my time at Filbert Street. We had a great manager in Brian who was a football specialist who possessed the professional expertise and skills to make it work on the pitch.

My job was to focus purely on growing our commercial operation, running the business side of the club and thus transforming us into a profitable entity.

Alan Birchenall, Leicester City's Club Ambassador recalls his first impressions of me and what I was trying to achieve. "At the end of my playing career, Terry Shipman brought me back to Leicester to be the Club's Public Relations Officer. Terry deserves a pat on the back for that. It was a part time role because I was still involved with my pub and a footwear business in those days.

It was a difficult time, financially, for Leicester and then big Baz – as I call him – joined the club. I remember that he was a big man with a big character. He used to wear glasses with different coloured lenses each day – he stood out a mile! I got on well with him and he made

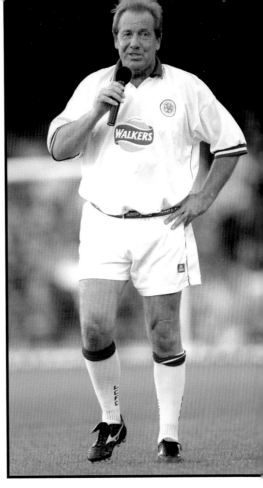

Alan Birchenall became Leicester's Public Relations Officer when his playing career ended.

me smile, probably because we are both extroverts.

I like characters and big Baz certainly was one. He came in at a difficult time. The club was living hand to mouth and a lot of the staff had two or three roles. He was the first person to come to Leicester who had a strong knowledge of commercialism. He was imaginative and had some great ideas. Not every idea worked, but he was never afraid to try something new.

He was terrific at bringing money in and did exceptionally well to be in that job for almost a decade. There were some clashes because you cannot please everyone. Anyone in his position will upset a few people, it is inevitable, because not everyone will agree with all your decisions. Whatever happened, though, he always came in the next day with a smile on his face."

The Leicester City Board of Directors in the early nineties.
From left to right: Roy Parker, John Elsom, Bill Shooter, Brian Little (Manager), Martin George, Barrie Pierpoint (Director of Marketing), Alan Bennett (Club Secretary), Tom Smeaton, Terry Shipman and John Sharp.

It took a lot of time but eventually, we let business folk concentrate on the business and let football people run the football side. This resulted in us making money off the pitch which was ultimately reinvested into the playing side.

I remember sitting in a board meeting and requesting £50,000 for a marketing budget that would enable my team to promote the club to businesses and draw them into Leicester City. With money scarce, one director instantly said, 'Brian could get a new player for that.' Which was true as he did sign several incredibly good players at bargain prices. But I argued that my budget would last me several years and that I would turn it into a much bigger sum, which I did. Some people heard stories like this and cast me as the villain, taking funds away from the team. They did not see the bigger picture which was that I used the money that I was given to generate more cash for the club, some of which was eventually used for players.

Not all fans understood that if we invested all of our money into the playing side, rather than the business, we would eventually run out of cash which would result in the best players being sold. This was the cycle that the club had been trapped in when I arrived and the Directors and myself were determined to break that. I knew that I needed to get the fans onboard, so I invited them in to the club to explain where we were taking the club and to seek their input.

Cliff Ginnetta, the Leicester City Supporters' Club Chairman, was a great ally and helped me to bridge the gap between the club and our supporters. "Barrie was a breath of fresh air at the club. He was the first to see the club's business potential and he quickly identified revenue raisers. He brought the club into the 21st century kicking and screaming. He introduced budgets for everything and recruited people to enable the club to fully utilise the facilities. He was a good businessman.

Barrie's impact was immediate and the fans loved him at the start. He brought in the right people and put them into the right roles. He did things like transforming the ticket office from a pokey little place into a proper ticket office.

Barrie understood the importance of happy supporters. Before he joined, the club was very much a closed shop to supporters, but Barrie opened the doors to the fans. What I liked most is that he recognised that the supporters were an integral part of the club. He talked to us, asked our opinions and included us in important changes within the club. For the first time we were involved and it really felt like it was our football club.

One example is the open meetings that Barrie held with fans. He would pay for our food and talk to the supporters so that we could get to know each other and so that he could find out what we really thought of the club. We often disagreed, but Barrie never took offence. He and I had a few arguments over the years, but he never took it personally. He really listened to us and our suggestions for change and he was good at making things happen.

For example, the Supporters' Club sat in the corner between the Family Stand and East Stands and there was a gap between the Executive Boxes above the North Stand and the roof of the East Stand. This meant that we often got soaked. After one miserable, rainy game Barrie noticed that I was wet and asked why. When I explained that we had no shelter he told me that it wasn't acceptable and he got it fixed straight away at a cost of around £30,000. We had raised it with the board before, but no one had ever been bothered. Barrie didn't know anything about football and he couldn't understand why the supporters put up with things like awful food, broken seats and leaky roofs. He would say, 'You wouldn't accept it at the cinema or theatre.'"

THINGS ARE HAPPENING AT FILBERT STREET

LEICESTER CITY F.C. 100 YEARS AT FILBERT STREET

Plans for future
City are building for the next century

HARD WORK: Chairman Mr. Martin George.

Real chance for the City to make a fresh start

by Martin George, City Chairman

EXCITEMENT: City striker David Kelly challenging for the ball in the match against Oxford United.

Excited by the challenge ahead

by Brian Little, City Manager

DETERMINED: Leicester City Manager Brian Little.

This article appeared in the *Leicester Mercury* and is one example of the media publicity that we were generating in 1991.

The reason that we had so much success in those days was a combination of Brian and his team performing miracles on the pitch and also my people working tirelessly, raising money off the pitch, through our new and existing commercial activities. Brian and I got on well and developed a strong working relationship.

Like me, Brian recalls trying to learn everything about the club. "I really immersed myself in the world of Leicester City. Barrie was great and he spent time with me to explain what he was trying to achieve. I enjoyed the board meetings too and stayed for the duration of the meeting, not just the football part, because I wanted to know everyone and to understand everything that was going on at the club."

Brian and I were completely revolutionising the club. We both encountered resistance to change from people within the club and from the media but, most importantly, we both produced results.

Chapter three - Developing the brand

On the pitch - 1991/92 season

With Brian Little's backroom team now assembled, the cloud that had hovered above Filbert Street for the past few seasons was dispersing. The players were buoyed, supporters had regained their optimism and there was a positive feeling around the club with a sense that their fortunes were about to change.

"The change was immediate and immense," recalls Gary Mills. "Brian created a relaxed atmosphere and we didn't feel any pressure. He was great at building team spirit. Even though a lot of new players came in, we gelled as a group. We spent a lot of time together, ate together, trained together and did so much that we became close, like a family. As our team spirit grew, so did our confidence."

Richard Smith noticed the different atmosphere, too. "When Brian arrived, things changed overnight. There was a lot more discipline and rules than we had had before, but we had so much fun on the training pitch that it brought us all together. It is surprising for a group that big – with so much competition for places – but we all got on well with each other and we would do anything for our mates. Things became much more enjoyable than ever before."

Steve Walsh was impressed with Brian's ambition. "Brian came in and said he had a three-year plan to get us to the Premier League. I remember thinking, 'Wow, that's some claim.'"

Little demonstrated his transfer nous when he overhauled the playing squad. The close season saw the arrival of five new signings (Kevin Poole, Ashley Ward, Paul Fitzpatrick, Colin Gordon and Nicky Platnauer) for a combined sum of just £160,000. As the season progressed classy midfielder, Steve Thompson was brought in from David Pleat's Luton and Little raided his former club to bag the trio of Michael Trotter, Jimmy Willis and Gary Coatsworth.

Coatsworth remembers that he was both surprised and delighted to be linking up with Little again. "Darlington to Leicester was a big step up for me and I was surprised that Brian thought I

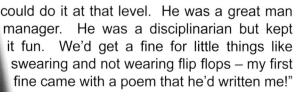

could do it at that level. He was a great man manager. He was a disciplinarian but kept it fun. We'd get a fine for little things like swearing and not wearing flip flops – my first fine came with a poem that he'd written me!"

A revamped Leicester began the league campaign with a five-match unbeaten run. By the end of September, a 3-0 victory over Blackburn Rovers sent the Foxes up to third place. Confidence was high, and just as well, as the First Division champions, Arsenal, were coming to town for a League Cup tie.

The Gunners record £2,500,000 signing, Ian Wright, was making his debut and he gave the visitors a first half lead. Leicester would not quit, though, and in the dying minutes, Steve Walsh scored a bullet header to give City a deserved equaliser and the match finished 1-1. Arsenal won the second leg, 2-0, but it was encouraging to see the progress that had been made.

During the 1991/92 season, Gary Mills was playing the best football of his career and he went on to play every minute of every game, setting a club record of sixty-one appearances in a single season. A feat even more remarkable considering that he had spent most of the year nursing a broken toe. "It was so painful that I had to have an injection before every game. I remember when we played Watford at Vicarage Road in early November and I had to go into the home treatment room to have my injection. The Watford physio had to nip out, leaving me alone in the room. Suddenly Elton John, Watford's owner, walked in and declared, 'You're not one of my players.'

'No,' I replied, 'I'm waiting for an injection.' Now, I was a huge Elton John fan, so I could not let the opportunity pass me by.

'Can I shake your hand?' I asked. 'I'm a big fan and it's a pleasure to meet you,' I said before adding, 'But I hope your team don't win today!' They didn't – we won 1-0."

Later in November, with City occupying a play-off position, they had another opportunity to test themselves against First Division opposition. David Oldfield and Steve Thompson scored the goals that gave Leicester a 2-0 victory over Everton in the Zenith Data Systems Cup (ZDS).

Confidence around the club was growing and at the turn of the year fans realised that City were very much in a promotion race.

The Foxes had not progressed beyond the third round of the FA Cup since 1985 and most pundits were expecting that dismal run to continue when Leicester were drawn against the 1990 runners up, Crystal Palace – another First Division side.

During a very tight match, neither team seemed able to break the deadlock. But as the clock approached the ninetieth minute, City won a free kick a few yards outside the penalty area. I will let Richard Smith, tell you what happened next . . .

"We had played really well and were pushing for a goal when Paul Reid was fouled. It was the last minute of the game and probably our last chance to avoid a replay at Selhurst Park. Gary Mills stood over the ball and I knew he would try and put it on Walshy's head. Mills chipped it, the ball evaded Walsh and fell to me just inside the penalty area. I hit it first time and volleyed the ball into the top corner of the net past Nigel Martyn. I could not believe it! I had spent part of the previous season on loan at non-league side, Nuneaton Borough, and here I was, barely a year later, scoring a goal against an England international goalkeeper!

I floated for the next few weeks. It was a great experience and it was all down to Brian, John and Allan. They gave me the confidence and belief that I belonged at this level and they told me that I had earnt my right to play."

Richard Smith's late goal sent City into the fourth round of the FA Cup.

The next match was the northern semi-final of the ZDS Cup where we were drawn against Notts County. At the time, County were a top-flight side and we fought to another victory. Sadly, our cup runs were ended by Bristol City in the fourth round of the FA Cup fourth round, and Brian Clough's Nottingham Forest in the ZDS cup northern final, but it was clear to all just how much progress Brian and the team had made.

By March 1992 City were sitting just outside the play-off places in seventh and, with a prize in the newly created Premier League up for grabs, they surprised supporters by selling the highly rated young striker, Paul Kitson. Fans did not understand why Kitson was sold, but Brian Little had a plan. "We'd had a little spell where I didn't think we were going to make the play-offs and I needed to do something to push us on. I did not want to ask for more money, so I found a way of generating some additional transfer funds," Brian recollects. "Throughout the season Paul Kitson had been attracting some interest from Derby, but I had told them that I was not interested in selling him. When they rang me again in March to make another enquiry an idea began to form in my head. I felt we lacked a target man, so I arranged to meet Derby manager, Arthur Cox, to see if we could agree a deal. I met Arthur at the Baseball Ground and was told that we needed to be discreet, so I had to sneak in through a side entrance to make sure no one saw me.

The Foxes faithful enjoyed City's revival under Brian Little.

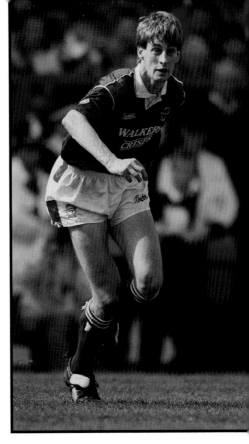

After some tense negotiation, the deal we agreed was that Kitson would join Derby and, in return, Leicester would receive Ian Ormondroyd, Phil Gee and £850,000. I knew that if we failed to make the play-offs, we would lose Kitson anyway and this deal gave us some different options up front.

It was not a popular decision. In fact, the *Leicester Mercury* ran a poll on whether I had made the right decision! I never had any doubts, though. Fans and the media do not always know what is going on behind the scenes and criticism is part and parcel of football. Looking back now, it worked out very well for us."

It wasn't just the fans who were caught off guard by the transfer, it came out of the blue to Ian Ormondroyd, too, as he explains. "I'd had a couple of good

Ian Ormondroyd became a cult hero at Filbert Street.

years at Aston Villa and was part of Graham Taylor's team who finished runners up to Liverpool in the 1989/90 season. Graham then left to manage England and, in his place, came Jozef Venglos, the first foreign manager in the English top flight. It all fell apart at Villa and he was soon replaced by Ron Atkinson. Big Ron signed Cyrille Regis and told me I was off. To be fair, he sorted me out with a new club, and I joined Derby at the start of the 1991/92 season. I was playing well and scoring goals and then, out of the blue, I was told I was going to Leicester – I had only been there for six months!

Phil Gee and I met Brian at his house, had a discussion and that was it – done. At the time, I was happy at Derby and did not really want to move but it worked out well. Although, I played at a higher level with Villa, I had a better time at Leicester. They were a good set of lads right from the off. Leicester had a big squad and you were never guaranteed to play, but the team spirit was brilliant.

Training was top quality and we had experts in each area. Brian would take the forwards, John Gregory the midfielders and Allan Evans the defenders. Our manager and coaching team were all either ex-England internationals or had won the European Cup, so the standard of coaching was extremely high."

With money to spend, Little turned his attention to strengthening the defence. Twenty-two-year-old Simon Grayson was the first signing, joining from Leeds United for just £50,000. What a bargain that turned out to be. Brian had been an admirer of Grayson for a while. "Before I joined Darlington, I had three years with Middlesbrough looking after their youngsters. I remember we played a couple of games against a strong Leeds youth team featuring David Batty, Simon Grayson and Gary Speed. Simon caught my eye and I knew he was the kind of player who would fit into my team. After one match I shook his hand and thought, 'I'm going to sign you one day.' I ended up signing him twice!"

A fortnight later, Leicester gave Leeds £250,000 in return for their left back, Mike Whitlow. Whitlow remembers jumping at the chance to join City and play regular first-team football. "I was a bit of a late starter and didn't turn professional until I was twenty. One weekend I was playing non-league football on a Saturday for Witton Albion and Sunday league with my mates, the next I was making my debut for Leeds at Elland Road in front of 20,000 people!

I was part of the Leeds side who were promoted to the First Division in 1990, but then a year later Howard Wilkinson signed Tony Dorigo – who was playing for England at the time – and I ended up on the subs' bench. Howard told me that he wanted me to be part of the squad, but I just wanted to play football. When Brian came in for me, it was an easy decision for me to join Leicester, even though Leeds were on their way to winning the League title.

I settled in so quickly and within a week, I felt part of the team. The City lads were down to earth, honest and a hardworking bunch. It was a similar situation when I was at Leeds as we also had good players and were a very close group. I had five years at Leicester and enjoyed every day."

The third, and final signing of the season was centre back Colin Hill, a Northern Ireland international, who joined on loan from Sheffield United. Hill explains that he was also in talks with City's promotion rivals, Cambridge United. "I'd spoken to Brian and John Gregory and then John Beck, the Cambridge manager, got in touch and tried to persuade me to join them. It was not long after Paul Kitson had joined Derby and Beck was telling me that Cambridge were on the up, whereas Leicester had peaked and were selling their best players. However, I liked Brian, John and Allan instantly and could sense that they were a tight knit management team. I had a feeling that Filbert Street was the best place for me. I signed, went straight to training and played the next day."

The new signings propelled Leicester to second place and automatic promotion was on the cards, until defeats to Charlton and Newcastle in the final two matches of the season consigned City to the play-offs.

Cambridge were the opponents in the semi-final and they held the Foxes to a 1-1 draw at the Abbey Stadium in the first leg before a remarkable match at Filbert Street. The twenty-one thousand in attendance on 13th May 1992 witnessed one of the most dominant performances in Leicester's history. Tommy Wright bagged a brace with Thompson, Ormondroyd and Kevin 'Rooster' Russell also netting in a comprehensive 5-0 victory that sent City to Wembley. Even today, that match evokes fond memories for Brian Little. "My favourite game as Leicester manager was the play-off semi-final against Cambridge. Night matches at Filbert Street were always special, but that was something else. We'd lost 5-1 to them early in the season, so to win that comfortably in a match of that magnitude really showed the progress we'd made."

It was a sweet moment for Colin Hill to play against the Club he had almost joined. "We absolutely battered them. There are not many games where it is all over and you can just enjoy it

The City players received a ticker-tape reception for the play-off semi-final match against Cambridge United.

because your opponents are not coming back. We were so good that day. It was one of those games that, when I look back, I can remember the euphoria and the fans – they were magnificent!

It is funny because I almost missed the play-offs. My loan period had finished at the end of the regular season. Brian came to see me and asked me if I would stay for the play-offs. I told him that I was enjoying my time at Filbert Street and we came to an agreement that, whatever happened, we would talk about me joining Leicester on a permanent basis. I have a lot of respect for Brian. He always treated people fairly and he stayed true to his word and signed me at the end of the season."

Over twenty years had passed since last the Foxes last trip to Wembley in 1969 and, understandably, demand for tickets was high, with fans snaking around the stadium. Current Radio Leicester presenter, Ian Stringer, was one of the fans desperate to secure a ticket to the big game. "I remember that the tickets were released in stages; season ticket holders, members and then general sale. My family and I were members, so the day the tickets went on sale, my late mother took me to Filbert Street in the hope that we would get a ticket. It was a school day and I stood against the wall of the Main Stand in the queue for hours. When we eventually got to the front, we managed to get four tickets. I was over the moon, it felt like I'd got one of Willy Wonka's golden tickets."

Leicester-born singer/songwriter, Jersey Budd, was another young fan who was lucky enough to go to Wembley. Jersey reminisces about the trip. "I was only eight at the time, but I went down on a coach with my dad's mates. We went to the Wembley Hilton so the adults could have a drink before the match and my friends and I were outside, all kitted out with our faces painted and waving City flags."

Free-spending Blackburn Rovers, managed by the legendary Kenny Dalglish, were the opponents for Leicester's visit to the Twin Towers. Despite the magnitude of the occasion, Gary Mills admits the players were full of confidence. "I felt that we would win. We had already beaten them twice in the league and I really believed we would do it."

Colin Hill shared Gary's confidence. "I grew up around the corner from Wembley and had been there for Northern Ireland's match against England, although I didn't play. Blackburn were the big spenders of the division, but we always had a chance. We were a hard-working bunch of lads who trusted one another and never gave up. John Gregory used to say that we were grinders, but we were better than that."

Mike Whitlow enjoyed his first trip to the Twin Towers. "Brian gave me the best dream ever by signing me and taking me to Wembley. Leeds United had just been crowned champions of the First Division and I had made enough appearances to win a medal and now I was off to Wembley.

At that stage in my career, I always felt like I could run forever. But that game was different because of the adrenaline and the nerves, it takes it out of you. After twenty minutes, I was gone and felt like I was wearing miners' boots!"

Most of the players had not played at Wembley before, so Brian took the team to a hotel in London a few days before the match. The idea was to watch the other two play-off finals to sample the atmosphere and to get a feel for the stadium. A couple of hours before Blackpool took on Scunthorpe in the Fourth Division play-off final, the Leicester players boarded a coach and departed for the Twin Towers. Well, almost all the players. . .

City 'keeper, Carl Muggleton, takes up the story. "The first play-off final of the season took place on the Saturday, two days before we were due to face Blackburn. We had trained in the morning and, after lunch, some of my friends and family came to the hotel to say hello. We were sitting in reception having a nice chat when Brian came over to let me know that we would be leaving soon and he told me that he would give me a shout when it was time to go.

I carried on the conversation with my family and then I looked around and noticed everyone had gone! This was before mobile phones, so we jumped in my friend's car to try and catch up with the coach. We eventually arrived in the Wembley car park and I ran over to the bus. Allan Evans looked at me and said, 'We thought we were a player short.'"

On the day of City's big match, the team – including their goalkeeper – gathered in the Wembley dressing room to listen to Brian Little deliver his final instructions. Ian Ormondroyd recalls one specific message. "Brian explained that the referee, George Courtney, was retiring after the match and he told us that George was renowned for awarding

Over 68,000 fans witnessed the Second Division Play-Off Final.

penalties. 'He will give a penalty in this game, make sure it's not against us,' he warned us. He was right."

There was not much to split the two sides until the stroke of half time when David Speedie tumbled in the box following minimal contact from Steve Walsh. Courtney pointed to the spot and former City star, Mike Newell, converted the resultant penalty. Carl Muggleton maintains that the referee made the wrong decision. "To this day, I do not believe it was a penalty. I gave away another spot kick in the second half, but I managed to save it, becoming one of only a handful of 'keepers to save a penalty in open play at Wembley."

The Foxes were unable to find a breakthrough and an evenly fought game ended 1-0. Blackburn were promoted and City faced another season in the second tier. It was a cruel end to what had been such a fantastic season.

Carl Muggleton was devastated. "It was such a bittersweet occasion. I was a Leicester fan, I had been at the club since the age of ten and to play at Wembley, for my team, was a dream come true. But to lose in that way was devastating. After the game, Kenny Dalglish – who I knew from my loan spell at Liverpool – came up to me, congratulated me on my performance and wished me well for the future."

"We played so well and didn't deserve to lose. It was so disappointing," adds Colin Hill.

Gary Mills concedes that the defeat was hard to take. "It was heart breaking. We had so much confidence going into that game, it knocked us back a bit. It was a tough summer and it took a lot of time to get over it."

Behind the scenes

With the right people now in the right roles, Charles Rayner and I turned our attention to the merchandise and leisurewear that we were offering to our supporters. When I took my first foray into the club shop, I saw it was riddled with poor quality, unappealing tat. But that was nothing compared to the huge quantity of unsold stock gathering dust in the back room, including women's knickers displaying vulgar messages. This was not the image that I wanted us to portray!

There was no strategy at all for retail or merchandise and items were being stocked without any consideration as to what our fans wanted. We were not making any money and we were missing a huge opportunity as interest in football related products was on the up due, in part, to the 1990 World Cup. Italia 90 was memorable for many reasons; England produced their best World Cup performance on foreign soil, Leicester's own Gary Lineker won the Golden Boot and Gazza's tears in the semi-final created an instantly iconic image. It was also the summer where the replica shirt crossed over into the adult mainstream and became fashionable. It was the dawn of the commercial era in football.

We were a year behind other clubs who had capitalised immediately and Charles and I were determined to catch up. It was clear that we needed a complete overhaul of our stock, so I met with some suppliers to see what products were on offer. I was shocked when one unscrupulous trader offered me 'a gift' in exchange for stocking their wares. Needless to say, the club did not ever deal with them again.

Our primary supplier was Bukta who had manufactured the team's kit since 1990, but we had a big problem with the quality of the kit. Each shirt was a different shade, the colours ran, and we had a constant stream of customers returning faulty goods. We later discovered that someone was selling seconds to traders to flog at discounted prices which was affecting our sales and eating into our profits.

There were various sports brands vying for a shirt deal with Leicester City, all proposing slightly different contracts. The one thing that they all had in common was that they were offering us very little. My medium-term plan was for us to manufacture our kits in house, which would increase profits and allow us greater control on the design and quality.

The contract with Bukta ran until the end of the 1992/93 season and they had agreed to pay us £7000 a year in six monthly instalments. However, they didn't stick to the agreed payment schedule and this, along with the quality problems, meant that we could terminate the contract a year early. This presented me with an opening to bring my in-house kit manufacturing idea forward.

It was essential that the playing side felt comfortable wearing our own brand, rather than a recognisable name, so I met with Brian to discuss the possibility of cutting out the middleman and producing our own kit. This was incredibly innovative as no other club in the UK had manufactured their own kit before. Brian, who was always so engaged with off-field activities, thought that it was a great idea and he agreed to be involved throughout the process. "I liked Barrie from the first minute, especially his flamboyance," Brian recalls. "He didn't know much about football, but he was willing to learn. I felt that as manager, I should be involved in all aspects of the club and Barrie was perfect for me in that regard. He had a lot of ideas and he always ran them past me first and involved me in the decision making which I appreciated. I suppose a lot of old-school managers may have said no, but I was very open to trying new things."

To turn the idea into reality we needed to partner an established sports clothing manufacturer who had the means to mass produce our apparel. I interviewed several local companies and was particularly impressed with Alan Ward Sports Limited. Based in the East Midlands, they had a proven track record of supplying all manner of sportswear to football and other sports clubs. Alan Ward himself met with me and promised that he would personally look after us and oversee the development of our merchandise. He offered us a very competitive price and Fox Leisure, a subsidiary company under the Leicester City umbrella, was born. We operated as the supplier, wholesaler, manufacturer and distributor. We were the first UK club to do so, but certainly weren't the last. Portsmouth, Bradford City, Southampton, Sheffield Wednesday and Preston North End are some of the clubs who followed our trend and manufactured their own kits.

We now needed to create a kit that was stylish and durable, one that the players and fans would feel proud to wear. Brian, Charles, Alan and I threw around some designs and eventually settled on something that we were all happy with.

Brian Little had been involved in kit design before. "When Barrie spoke to me about creating our own kit, it was right up my street. I'd designed the Darlington kit, so I knew a fair bit about the process. I wanted us to do something different so decided to change from white to blue shorts. I was really happy with the kits."

The new shirts provided us with a fresh start and presented us with an opportunity to rethink our club's image. It was imperative for us to develop a strong, recognisable brand that epitomised what Leicester City was all about. I didn't feel that the current badge – known as 'the running fox' – introduced during the summer of 1983 was powerful enough. It was not just me who felt this way.

I had been approached by two graphic designers who were also avid Foxes fans, Chris Lymn and Mike Rayns. They had told me that they thought the badge was poor and asked if they could have a go at creating a better one. I agreed to take it to the directors, so during a meeting, I gave them my thoughts on our crest.

'It's terrible and does not represent how we want to be thought of as a club. The fox has only got three legs and it looks like it's limping away from something. This fox creates a slow and steady, plodding along image. This does not represent what we are trying to achieve here. We are a club that is going places and we should have a strong logo that signifies Leicester as both a city and a football club. I'd like us to change this,' I said.

'How much will it cost us?' I was inevitably asked.

'It will cost us nothing,' I explained. 'We have some fans who have offered to design it for us. We'll give them some criteria but it's their club and it feels right that they should be the ones to design it.'

The 'running fox' logo needed to be replaced.

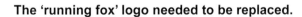

EMPLOYMENT OF THE NEW LEICESTER CITY EMBLEM FROM JUNE 25 1992

Please use the emblem below until further notice

There are two versions:

(A) **THE MAIN VERSION**
Which should be used in all circumstances where the ground is white or light or medium in tone.

(B) If the ground is black or of dark tone then this version should be used.

COLOUR DETAILS (common to either version)
Main colour: PMS Reflex Blue. Interior of fox's head: PMS Yellow 124. Red is no longer featured.

SOME NOTES ABOUT TERMINOLOGY
The nicknames 'Foxes' or 'Filberts' are no longer to be used except for the term 'Junior Foxes'.
Favoured colloquialism is 'the City' or 'City'.
'Leicester' should always be followed by 'City'.

Additional pmt's may be obtained by contacting
MOTIF DESIGN AND ADVERTISING
8 UPPER KING STREET
LEICESTER LE1 6XE.
Tel. 0533 554768
Fax. 0533 547539

We launched our new corporate identity in June 1992.

'As long as it won't cost us anything, you have approval,' I was told.

We made it clear that Leicester City would own all rights to the new badge and we specified that the new emblem must symbolise who we were as a club and a city, but other than that, Chris and Mike were given creative freedom.

They did a great job. The background of our badge was taken from the cinquefoil of Leicester's Coat of Arms. The fox was retained because the county of Leicestershire is widely regarded as the birthplace of fox hunting, but the side-on fox's head that had previously featured was considered too weak, so an imposing, face-on fox's head was chosen. The colour scheme of blue and white was obvious, but Lymm and Rayns opted to add yellow to the fox's face. The badge was launched on 25th June 1992 and, with only minor tweaks, it is still the crest that is now recognised all over the world.

With a new kit – featuring a fresh club badge – in production, we turned our attention to renovating the club shop. Charles redesigned the layout of the store to maximise the space and to allow us to stock a greater quantity of merchandise without the shop becoming cluttered. A local shop fitter, Brian Garrity and his company, offered to carry out the refurbishment free of charge. They were huge Leicester City fans and just wanted to help their club. In return, we agreed that they could fit any subsequent stores that we opened. The existing store was ripped out and refurbished in line with our new design and branding. It took around five months to complete and while the building work was underway, we sold the unsold garbage in bulk at heavily discounted prices and we set our sights on bringing in high-quality products that the fans wanted.

Football branded items became increasingly popular following the creation of the Premier League in 1992 and, using exclusively local companies, we wanted to create a first-rate product whilst also providing great value for money. The quality was as equally important to us as our profits. Customer satisfaction was essential, so we created a fans' retail forum to test ideas for exclusive Leicester City retail products and to gain their honest feedback. The concept was simple – if the supporters did not like it, we would not make or stock it.

The forum consisted of a cross section of twenty to thirty fans ranging from youngsters to adults and from grandparents to families. Everything that we considered stocking had to go through the supporters in order to gain their approval.

On a monthly basis, we reeled out various products on a generation-game-style conveyor belt for fans to view. We canvassed their opinions on everything from clothes, shoes, bedding and, of course, a cuddly toy! We gave them the recommended retail price and asked them if they would buy it at that price. If more than half said they would, we would then stock it. If not, we wouldn't. We gave fans greater control of what was being sold and it was a totally transparent way of purchasing goods. All meetings were minuted, we changed the fans on the forum annually and our retail team could not buy anything without it going through the forum.

Every item we stocked had to be approved at a fans' forum.

PANELISTS NAME: _____

FOX LEISURE CONSUMER PANEL

DETAILS OF PRODUCTS	WORKING NOTES:
1. Sample No. 13	
2. Description FOOTBALL GRAPHICS	
3. R.R.P. £10.99	
4. Minimum Quantity —	
5. Lead Time (delivery timescale) 6 WKS.	
6. Local Supplier? NO – B/HAM.	OVERALL OPINION: NO.
7. Target age group 18+	
8. Size Ranges STD	

PANELISTS NAME: _____

FOX LEISURE CONSUMER PANEL

DETAILS OF PRODUCTS	WORKING NOTES:
1. Sample No. 14	
2. Description CAR HANGER.	
3. R.R.P. £1.99.	
4. Minimum Quantity 50	
5. Lead Time (delivery timescale) 6 WK/.	
6. Local Supplier? NO.	OVERALL OPINION: YES
7. Target age group AU	
8. Size Ranges STD	

PANELISTS NAME: _____

FOX LEISURE CONSUMER PANEL

DETAILS OF PRODUCTS	WORKING NOTES: NOW 5omm. THICK
1. Sample No. 15	
2. Description SOFT CUSHION.	
3. R.R.P. £8.99.	
4. Minimum Quantity 100	
5. Lead Time (delivery timescale) 5 WKS.	
6. Local Supplier? NO – BUKS.	OVERALL OPINION: NO
7. Target age group AU	
8. Size Ranges STD	

**A proud Charles Rayner (centre), Gary Mills and Steve Walsh,
open the newly refurbished Fox Leisure store.**

"Fox Leisure was a runaway success," recalls Cliff Ginnetta, Chairman of the Leicester City Supporters' Club. "Barrie was blessed with a good lieutenant in Charles Rayner. Charles always made time for the fans and often spoke to us in the car park after a game to listen to our ideas for the club shop and merchandise."

Our first Fox Leisure kits were launched in our newly refurbished shop in time for the 1992/93 season and they were a huge success.

Ian Stringer, who is the current BBC Radio Leicester sport presenter, felt Fox Leisure made a statement about the Club. "As a kid you want to wear a fashionable brand like Nike or Adidas but when Fox Leisure came along, there was a change in culture and it became a cool thing to wear, especially as we were a one club city. It was siege mentality; we are Leicester City, we make our own kit, our sponsors, Walkers Crisps, are a Leicester-based company – we are proud of who we are."

City fan, Ashley Barratt, now CEO of Barratt Smith & Brown, remembers wearing Fox Leisure clothing when he was a child. "Fox Leisure became the fashionable item to wear at school. It was such a cool brand because it was manufactured by the club, for the club. One year my brother got a pair of the, now famous, Fox Leisure trainers. He loved them."

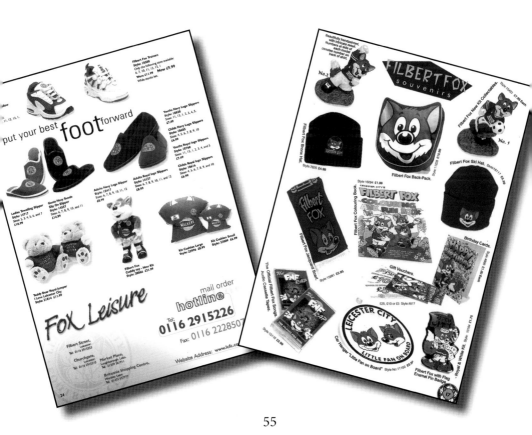

Geoff Peters was a loyal Fox Leisure customer.

Geoff Peters, BBC Radio Leicester sports presenter at that time, was a regular customer at our new-look Fox Leisure store. "I bought loads of Fox Leisure items, not just kits. They really thought outside the box with the new brand. The commercial brains went to town and came up with loads of ideas. Not all worked but you have to credit their boldness in trying something fresh. However, I don't recall ever wearing the Fox Leisure aftershave. But from what others said, I didn't miss out on much!"

Brian encouraged the players to model the kits and leisurewear which was all important to the success of Fox Leisure. So, what did the players think?

Carl Muggleton: "There was so much competition for us 'keepers, I was just pleased to get to wear the shirt, regardless of what it looked like."

Lee Philpott, who joined in November 1992: "Fox Leisure was a very different model to other clubs. The players could see that it was all part of developing the club off the pitch and we embraced it. Tony James and I were asked to model one of the new kits. We got a lot of stick from the other lads, but it was a bit of fun. Even now, almost thirty years later, I still see references to Fox Leisure, especially those trainers!"

Ian Ormondroyd: "In those days, most team's kits were supplied by Umbro and Adidas, but we weren't really bothered that our kit wasn't a recognised brand. It was a different era. When I went to Hull later in my career, they were so skint that we only had one kit for the entire season. After a few months, the socks had holes in them!"

**The Fox Leisure store went to another level
when the Carling Stand was built.**

Mike Whitlow: "I thought Fox Leisure was great. We could see it was helping the club move forward so we were all for it. Everything at Leicester was family based and the kids loved the new kit."

Under the Fox Leisure brand, we designed a wide range of clothing and accessories including ties, pyjamas and even bedding. Leicester City merchandise was now very much in the mainstream.

A huge advantage with Fox Leisure was that we could control costs and quality and we recorded record profits from shirt sales and merchandise. It was hard work and the staff were so dedicated. After office hours and at weekends, Charles would load up his car with boxes of merchandise and drive around the county, visiting sports shops and increasing the number of official Leicester City stockists.

Within two years Fox Leisure had an annual turnover of more than £1,000,000. To put that into context, back in 1991 when I joined, our entire commercial operation was turning over less than £750,000.

In fact, sales were so good that I wanted to open another fans' store, one based in the City centre. Filbert Street wasn't an easy place for supporters to get to and our only customers were those who specifically decided to visit the ground, people who came to buy tickets or to attend games. We needed to attract passing trade and sell to customers who would not normally come to us.

I ventured into the city centre to look for suitable locations, made some enquiries and agreed a deal in principle with Lewis's Department Store on Humberstone Gate. Lewis's was a hugely popular feature of the city centre that attracted thousands of shoppers each week, an ideal outlet for us. I took my proposal to the chairman.

'Good afternoon Mr George. As you know sales in our club shop have increased expectations recently and I think there is an opportunity for us to open another store, one in the city centre so that we can attract customers who are not able to get to the ground.'

'But won't it increase our costs and move trade from Filbert Street to the City centre?' he countered.

'No. Brian Garrity's company can fit the shop at a low cost and my research shows that we would be attracting a different type of customer so there is room in the market for both stores. Filbert Street's location excludes customers who don't drive or watch home games. A city centre store will bring in new customers.'

'I'm sorry Pierpoint' – it was always Pierpoint, never Barrie – 'but I have to say no.'

I was disappointed, but as it was low risk and inexpensive, I decided to do it anyway.

The Fox Leisure store on Churchgate.

So, I opened the club's first city centre based shop. Two weeks later I met the chairman again.

'Mr Chairman, do you remember the new shop I talked to you about?' I asked.

'Yes, why?' replied Mr George.

'It opened two weeks ago.'

'But I told you not to open it.'

'Well, we took £5000 in the first week and £10,000 in the second.'

'That's fantastic,' he said with a smile.

'So, would you still like me close it?' I enquired, tongue very firmly in cheek.

Unsurprisingly, we kept it open and it was so successful that we opened further stores in the city centre on Churchgate, as well as shops in the towns of Hinckley and Loughborough.

As usual our standards were incredibly high and we wanted them to be consistent, so we supported all official stockists with regular visits and a retail pack. The Churchgate site also became a city centre ticket office to make it easier for fans to buy tickets.

It was not just the customers that we had to look after, we had some demanding players, too. Our kitman, Taff Davies, a lovely bloke, sorted out everything that the players would need for a match. The team would turn up with nothing as Taff would have all their equipment laid out. This worked out well when players told the kitman what they needed, but one new signing assumed he could read minds!

Before the first game of one season, Charles received a call from Taff, 'Charles, our new signing has said he can't play today because he doesn't have any ankle socks to wear under his football socks. He won't play without them because he suffers from blisters.'

'Leave it with me,' Charles replied.

'They must be merino wool,' Taff added. This was at 13:55 and kick off was at 15:00. Charles got in his car and drove to Marks and Spencer's at Fosse Park. There were so many different types of socks, but he managed to get some and raced back to Filbert Street.

The problem was that at this time the roads were gridlocked with match-day traffic. He eventually got back to the ground at 14:40, ran into the kitman's office and gave him the socks. Taff passed them to the player and held his breath as he tried them on.

Photonews kicks off with the successful selling of Leicester City

The sky's the limit!

Leicester City's preparations for the new season are not confined to the training ground. Behind the scenes at Filbert Street there is a professional team of businessmen "selling" the club and its image. Richard Brown reports.

FILBERT Street will erupt in a massive Blue Army cheer tomorrow as the club's tills rattle frantically with the start of a new campaign for Football League glory.

While the £5 million three-tier stand is completed and pre-season signings take to the pitch, another battle — to keep cash flowing into the club's coffers — will heat up.

Club bosses feel a new age could be dawning to make it not only a Premier League outfit but also a premier business operation.

Off-field business is booming and making the football club one of the city's biggest money-spinning concerns.

Sales of Leicester City merchandise — anything from old-fashioned scarves to training shoes and perfume — have given the club the sweet smell of financial success.

And cash could be ploughed back into buying the players who can do Leicestershire proud.

Business is booming, with trade 50 per cent up on last year's pre-season rush.

Strips and flags have been snapped up to kit supporters out for a long, hard season, while business brains at Filbert Street aim to adapt sophisticated marketing techniques to rake in the cash.

'There's a terrific buzz around the ground that Leicester can do it and nothing is going to stop them.'

Mr Barrie Pierpoint, director of marketing

Mr Barrie Pierpoint, the club's director of marketing, said: "Leicester City has been boosted into a brand new era and interest is already astonishing."

"The team is determined that this season will prove third time lucky and they are going straight for automatic promotion with no need to go for the play-offs," he added.

"Everything will be finished in early 1994, after which the sky is the limit."

Mr Pierpoint said two visits to Wembley had instilled a new optimism at Filbert Street.

He said: "There's a terrific buzz around the ground that Leicester can do it and nothing is going to stop them.

"Interest has built up around the club as never before, whether in fans' support, business sponsorship and advertising, using facilities for meals, hospitality or functions, or, of course, coming along to the matches."

And once the new stand is completed Leicester City hope they will be miles ahead most of their First Division competition.

NEW ERA: Mr Barry Pierpoint, Leicester City's director of marketing

ON THE BALL: Fox Leisure manager Mr Charles Rayner with some of the products on sale

LEFT: Mrs Beverley Norris, who is in charge of the restaurant and bar, with chef Mr Norman Lee

FORGING NEW LINKS

- A community programme is forging links with areas beyond the football world, including the ethnic minorities, groups for the disabled, OAPs and the jobless.
- The biggest community and business centre Leicester has ever boasted is about to come about, with function rooms and bars for corporate and private hire.
- It will have a 80-seat restaurant and 400-seat conference room.
- The centre will also have a prestige 7,000 square foot health and fitness facility and a sports injury clinic.
- There will be 30 boxes and hospitality suites.

ON TARGET: Mr Dean Simms, promotions manager, and Mr Paul Martin

ON SCREEN, Mr Mark Ingle and head of publicity Mr Paul Mace work on a new match programme

SELLING CITY: Louise Underwood and Mr Richard Hughes in sales and marketing

Police ready for big kick-off

by John Marsden

POLICE began drawing up tactics for the new season as early as City manager Brian Little.

Intelligence work began once the final whistle was sounded on Leicester's promotion challenge.

Chief Inspector Judith Rowden, of Charles Street Police, said every force covering clubs in the First Division had exchanged information with Leicestershire.

She said: "Our policy has not changed a great deal from last season. "Liaison work across the country began for the coming season as soon as we knew City had just missed out on promotion."

Police categorise matches on a a descending basis of C B A.

Chief Inspector Rowden said games rated C are regarded as requiring higher profile policing — perhaps a local derby game or big cup match.

Tomorrow's kick-off match against Peterborough has been rated in the middle B band.

All- ticket

The game has been made all-ticket — with no allocation for Peterborough fans.

Chief Inspector Rowden did not expect supporters from Peterborough to travel without tickets.

She said: "It has been well publicised that they will not get be allowed in."

She said the ground capacity had been reduced because of massive redevelopment of the main stand.

That has led to the closure of the main stand car park.

But Chief Inspector Rowden said she did not anticipate parking problems to be "too bad" because of the reduced ground capacity.

The maximum crowd has been reduced to 14,000 for the match.

And yesterday afternoon there were only 300 tickets left for members and 75 for non- members.

Chief Insp Rowden will be one of the senior officers on duty within the ground on kick-off day.

She said: "We're all wishing City the best for the new season!"

'These are ok. I can play today,' the player replied before joining his team-mates on the pitch for the pre-match warm up. He was that close to not playing.

In two years, we sold over 20,000 of our inaugural Fox Leisure shirts and in 1994, when we launched a new kit in time for our maiden Premier League campaign, we sold 20,000 in the first six week and 45,000 in total. Fans loved it.

"I had the yellow one with 'Walsh – 5' on the back," Jersey Budd, recalls proudly. "All the Fox Leisure shirts were great. I can't remember us ever having a bad kit."

Fox Leisure was so successful that it became a profitable company in its own right.

We later manufactured kits for amateur football and rugby teams and even the Leicester Riders Basketball side which provided the club with a revenue stream that was entirely separate to the football side. By the time I left Leicester City, Fox Leisure's annual turnover had grown to almost £2,000,000.

Chapter four - A club for the community

On the pitch - 1992/93 season

Brian Little's first year in charge had culminated in an unexpected trip to Wembley. As Leicester's season had so very nearly ended with the ultimate prize of Premier League football, expectations were high for the coming season. City made three signings in the summer of 1992; Ipswich midfielder, David Lowe, forward, Bobby Davison, joined from Leeds United and defender Colin Hill made his loan move permanent.

There were concerns from outside the club that the Blackburn game could affect morale, but by the time the pre-season tour began, it was clear that the players were in good spirits and raring to go, as Steve Walsh recalls. "To get to Wembley and lose to a disputed penalty was hard to take, yet it made us even more determined."

Gary Mills was another player who returned from the summer break full of determination. "The disappointment of the Blackburn game was fresh in our minds as we reconvened ahead of the new campaign. There were concerns as to how it would affect us, but I couldn't wait to start the season and put it right."

Brian Little took the team to Scandinavia for pre-season training. It wasn't all football, though, as Ian Ormondroyd reveals. "Brian brought us to a remote part of Norway for our pre-season tour, probably because they didn't want us drinking. We decided to sneak out anyway, so we found the local pub, went up to the bar and ordered some drinks. I could not believe it when we were charged £12 a pint! We then realised that there would not be much drinking taking place on the tour!

Colin Hill joined Leicester on a permanent basis in the summer of 1992.

Instead, the staff arranged other activities for us to enjoy like canoeing, fishing and clay pigeon shooting. I had never been shooting before and did not have a clue what I was doing. I picked up the rifle and moved it around to have a look. The lads all ducked when they saw me waving a loaded shotgun around! It was only when I'd blown two holes in the ground that I was banned from shooting and asked to leave the range!"

Colin Hill and Bobby Davison slotted straight into the starting eleven and City made a decent start to the campaign. The biggest impact, though, was made by a trio of youth team graduates.

City's first ever televised league match, against Wolves, got off to a dramatic start before the game even kicked off! Leicester's number one, Carl Muggleton, was injured during the warm up, and in the days before substitute 'keepers, Little turned to twenty-year old, Russell Hoult, who had yet to make his first team debut. Hoult was actually eating a hot dog in the stands when he was told he would be playing! Hoult performed a series of stunning saves that earned the Foxes a 0-0 draw. Also making his debut in that match was eighteen-year old left back, Neil Lewis, who came on as a substitute.

The pick of the bunch though was teenage sensation, Julian Joachim. Joachim began the season playing for the youth team, but three hat-tricks saw him quickly promoted to the first team and he made his debut in a 2-1 win over Barnsley in September. He scored his first senior goal in the following match, a League Cup tie against his hometown club Peterborough, and he remained in the team for the rest of the season – winning 'Goal of the Season' for his wonder strike against Barnsley.

Little recalls the moment he witnessed Joachim's blistering pace first-hand. "We had a lot of fun at the training ground. Allan, John, and I would play games against the apprentices and try and pass on our knowledge and experience. We also spent hours playing head tennis. I loved it all and often did not want to go home!

I remember when Julian began training with the first team and I realised how quick he was. We did a little session where I joined in the running. I was right at the back, so I thought I would have some fun. I shouted, 'Everyone turn around and race to the goal. If anyone finishes behind me, you'll be fined.' Now, I had a twenty-five-yard head start in a seventy-five-yard race, but within seconds, I saw this flash as Julian ran past me. I could not believe it. What was incredible is that he was just as fast with the ball."

In November, Cambridge winger, Lee Philpott was added to the ranks. He had impressed Little in the four games between the sides the previous season and the left-sided midfielder explains that he was keen to join the Foxes. "Over the summer, there had been lots of talk in the papers about me joining Leicester, but I didn't know if it was genuine interest or just speculation. Once I knew that Brian wanted me, I jumped at the chance.

I had a great time at Cambridge, but our best players were moving on – Steve Claridge joined Luton and Dion Dublin departed for Manchester United – and I felt we had peaked. I found it sad to watch the eventual demise of Cambridge United as they were the club who had given me a chance.

It was a big step up to join a club with the history and stature of Leicester City. The goal was automatic promotion, though the play-off system was a useful safety net. City spent £350,000 on me which was a club-record equalling transfer fee at the time.

A couple of months after I joined, I played one of my best games for the club. We beat Watford 5-2 and I scored twice. I opened the scoring with a right foot finish from a Julian Joachim cross and my second was a twenty-yard screamer. I didn't score too many goals – especially with my right foot – which made the match even more special."

Lee Philpott joined from promotion rivals, Cambridge United.

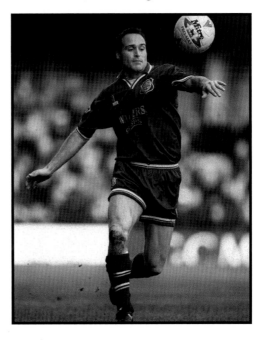

That victory over Watford was followed by a five-match winless run. Leicester's stuttering form meant that as March approached, their automatic promotion dreams were all but over and even a play-off place appeared unattainable. That was when Brian displayed his tactical genius. Bobby Davison had struggled to replicate the goalscoring form he had achieved at Leeds and Derby, so Little opted to move defender, Steve Walsh, to centre forward. The big-man-little-man routine paid immediate dividends as Walsh and emerging talent Joachim formed a formidable partnership. Walsh scored twelve in the final sixteen matches and the pair finished the season with more than thirty goals between them in all competitions. The change rejuvenated City and propelled them back up the table.

With three games left to play, Leicester needed just a single point to qualify for the play-offs. First up was an away trip to Peterborough. The Foxes lost 3-0, but Richard Smith remembers the game for a different reason. "It was a poor performance and we were well beaten. At one stage a long-haired streaker from the Leicester end ran on to the pitch. A Peterborough player caught up with him, pulled his hair and was treating him unfairly. I wasn't having that, especially towards a City fan, so I ran over there and sorted my opponent out."

A top six finish was achieved in the next match, when Leicester drew 1-1 at home to Bristol City. It was the final game played in front of the Main Stand that was demolished shortly afterwards.

The final match of the season was away at Newcastle who had already secured automatic promotion. Mike Whitlow retains strong memories from that game. "We'd already been guaranteed a play-off place, so there was nothing to play for at St James' Park. In the dressing room before the game, Brian said, 'We've got the semi-final next week so don't do anything stupid, don't get injured and don't get booked.'

At half-time we were 6-0 down and we got a right pasting in the dressing room! Brian was usually so calm, but not that day. We lost 7-1 in the end, but at least we didn't get any injuries or suspensions!"

Leicester's play-off opponents were Portsmouth. With Filbert Street under development, the 'home' leg was played at Nottingham Forest's City Ground. Colin Hill remembers it was a peculiar experience. "It felt like an away game. The City Ground was a decent stadium, but it wasn't ours."

Lee Philpott agreed. "It was very strange to play a home game at the ground of our rivals. Julian scored a great goal; he picked the ball up on the halfway line and just ran past everyone before slotting in the only goal of the game."

The City Ground, Nottingham, was the venue for Leicester's play-off semi-final 'home' leg.

The return game was very tense. Pompey took the lead in the first half before Ian Ormondroyd levelled. Ian talks through his goal. "It was probably the easiest goal I ever scored but also the most important. David Oldfield's shot was heading wide and I managed to deflect the ball into the net from six yards. The Portsmouth fans thought that it was offside. It was tight. I turned to Roger Milford, the ref, and the linesman to check. They gave the goal, so I ran off to celebrate. I still get stick about it from Pompey fans who remain convinced that I was offside."

Steve Thompson put City 2-1 up before Portsmouth grabbed a late equaliser. A 2-2 draw was enough to send Leicester back to Wembley to face Glenn Hoddle's Swindon Town. The Foxes had won one and drawn one in the two league fixtures against Swindon, so were considered the favourites going into the match.

The game was evenly poised until Hoddle gave Swindon the lead just before half time. The reds came out the strongest after the break and goals from Craig Maskell and Shaun Taylor gave them a comfortable lead. Swindon had scored three goals in just eleven minutes, so no one gave Leicester a hope in coming back.

However, Just four minutes later, Joachim scored to give City a glimmer of hope. Walsh pulled another back in the sixty-eighth minute and, unbelievably, Steve Thompson equalised one minute later to complete a remarkable comeback. The drama was not over yet, though, as for the second year running, Leicester's play-off final opponents were awarded a controversial penalty when Kevin Poole was judged to have brought down Steve White inside the penalty area. Welsh international, Paul Bodin, slotted home from the spot to break Foxes' hearts and inflict Leicester's sixth successive defeat under the Twin Towers. It was another devastating blow to the players.

Richard Smith: "I had been with Leicester since I was a young lad and I think I had spent more time at Filbert Street than I had at home. It was a huge honour to play at Wembley for my team, especially against players like Glenn Hoddle and Micky Hazzard who were both still class.

At 3-0 down I looked up at the stands and saw my friends and family and it was heart breaking. Some of the more experienced lads were trying to raise our spirits by telling us that we had nothing to lose. I could not believe it when we got back to 3-3, we were in complete control. I honestly thought we'd go on to score four or five but, sadly, it wasn't to be."

Colin Hill: "Even at 3-0, I knew we could come back. We were a hard team to beat and we did not quit. When Joachim pulled one back, I could see Swindon were physically gone, so I was shouting and screaming, 'They've gone, we can get back in this!' We did so well to level the scores and then we lost to another penalty."

Mike Whitlow: "The Swindon game was the hardest one to handle. It took some getting over."

Lee Philpott: "I played at Wembley for Cambridge in the 1989/90 Play-Offs and we won which was a great experience. The Swindon final was tough. It was a great game for the neutrals. I set up a couple of goals and got man of the match, but then we lost to a very soft penalty. Nothing could prepare you for all that emotion. I remember that I collapsed on the floor when the referee blew the final whistle. It was one of the most disappointing days in my career."

It was tough for the fans to take too as Jersey Budd recalls, "I was devastated. To lose in the final was bad enough, but it was made worse by the fact that we had to go back to school the following day!"

Behind the scenes

Leicester City are now known all around the world and are truly a global football club. It certainly was not like that in the early nineties. I remember a conversation with someone when I had just joined the club. They asked me where I worked and when I replied, 'Leicester City Football Club,' they asked, 'Who's that?'

I did some market research and discovered that the club was not too popular in the county, so my mission was to make us more appealing to Leicestershire residents and to put Leicester City on the map nationally. I certainly achieved the latter when I arranged a high-profile visit from British royalty.

One of my first community initiatives was to make the club more environmentally friendly. As well as reducing our bills, this was an opportunity for us to set an example to the local community. I drafted an Environmental Policy Statement for the club and made sure that all of our staff were signed up to it. I introduced recycled water, energy saving lightbulbs and placed a bottle bank outside the ground. I created an Environment Charter that made our 'green' mission clear to all staff who embraced the initiative; Shelia Kent, the club's laundress began washing the kit with environmentally friendly washing powder and Filbert Street's Grounds Manager, Steve Welch, used organic fertiliser on the Filbert Street pitch. I collaborated with Leicester City Council to help Leicester become the UK's first 'Environment City' and Leicester City the first 'green' professional football club.

His Royal Highness Prince Charles was an environmental leader, so I contacted his office, explained what we were doing and invited him to Filbert Street to give his Royal Ascent. This was back in 1991 when we were a relatively unknown club, so I did not really expect to hear from the future King of England. You can imagine my surprise when I received a response informing me that the Prince was planning a trip to Leicester in November and that he would be delighted to start his visit at Filbert Street. I could not wait to tell the Directors at the next board meeting.

'Barrie, do you have anything for any other business?'

'Actually, I do. Prince Charles will be coming to Filbert Street later this year,'

'What?'

'Prince Charles is coming here,' I repeated.

'No, he's not,' Really? Why? How? were some of the responses that I was met with. No one could believe it.

'I invited him and he's coming,' I replied proudly. I then explained about the green initiative and how it would benefit the club. The Directors and Chairman were thrilled. Everyone wanted to meet him. Even Martin George's brother turned up.

The security was incredible. The club staff did a fantastic job of sprucing up the stadium and laying out the red carpet. At 11:00 the Directors and I were standing in the tunnel area of Filbert Street, flanked by the Mayor of Leicester and his entourage, when we first glimpsed the red Wessex helicopter that was carrying the Prince. Excitement rose as the chopper landed in the centre of the pitch and we walked over to make our introductions.

As expected, the Prince was immaculately turned out in a navy suit, with pale blue shirt and decorative tie. In contrast, I was sporting large green-framed glasses in addition to a striped green tie – well, we were showcasing Leicester City's 'greenness'!

At the time of the Prince's visit, the Directors were considering rotating the stadium to build a new stand. John Sharp, Leicester City Director, remembers the moment he described the concept to the Prince. "Alan Bennett, the Club's secretary, and I were designated to explain to the Prince how the plan was to re-configure the Filbert Street Ground at right angles in order to build a new stand along Filbert Street, opposite the Double Decker on the other side of the pitch. We had a scale model of the plan to show the Prince. I remember him asking how we were intending to finance it all. Jokingly, I told him that we would, of course, attract certain grants and hope to win sponsorships. In fact, I said that we had even thought of calling the new stand, the Windsor Stand; at which the Prince quipped, 'What do you think I am, a bloody bank?'"

I proudly explained the club's environmental charter and the progress that we had made. He also met the Chairman, the Directors, the team manager, the players and the other staff. I found the Prince to be a friendly, down-to-earth bloke. Steve Walsh presented him with two Leicester City kits for the young Princes, William, and Harry. He enjoyed his visit and was genuinely interested in what we had achieved. More importantly, we passed the green audit. This visit really put the city of Leicester, and the football club, on the map.

Gary Mills was one of the players who met the Prince. "The visit of Prince Charles made us all realise that things were happening. It was a real positive for him to come to Filbert Street. I remember that the lads were all relishing the opportunity to meet him."

Prince Charles
VISITS FILBERT STREET

His Royal Highness meets some of the team.

Leicester City Football Club was one of the first businesses involved with Leicester's Environment City project. The club has recently undergone an environmental audit and Prince Charles was visiting Leicester to see some of the initiatives that the club have undertaken such as:

▶ Adopting predominantly organic methods of pitch maintenance.
▶ Starting to install low energy lightbulbs.
▶ Phasing out the use of leaded petrol in its company cars and moving to more environmentally friendly unleaded cars.
▶ Setting up an office paper recycling scheme.
▶ Adopting water saving practices in stadium toilets.
▶ Erected a kestrel nesting box on one of the floodlight stations.
▶ Agreed to the placing of recycling banks for use by the community in the Club's car park.

The Club was also host to several international, national and local companies

who made a series of presentations to Prince Charles on how they had implemented environmentally friendly practices within their companies.

Martin George introduces His Royal Highness to head groundsman Steve Welch and Maintenance Manager Gordon Clarke.

ENVIRONMENTAL POLICY STATEMENT

Leicester City Football Club recognises its responsibility to care for the environment and undertakes to identify and implement best possible environmental practice in all its policies and operations.

The Club expects all its staff to accept responsibility for caring for the environment and at all times to support the Club's environmental efforts.

His Royal Highness Prince Charles and Leicester City FC Chairman, Martin George.

69

Prince Charles's visit made people sit up and take notice of what I was trying to achieve, but the biggest success I had in my first year was holding an open day before the start of the 1991/92 season.

Football was trying to shed its reputation as a magnet for hooligans and I wanted to improve the public perception of Leicester City and show people that Filbert Street was a safe, accessible place for fans of all age, races and gender, so I organised an open day to showcase the club and to attract some new supporters.

It was a fantastic, fun-packed day. Fans had the opportunity to visit the home dressing room, musicians from the Thurmaston Scout and Guide marching band serenaded the crowd before children were invited onto the pitch for a coaching session led by our former player, Neville Hamilton. As the exhausted children returned to the stands with smiles on their faces, Brian Little brought the team out and gave supporters a rare glimpse of a first-team training session that ended with players signing autographs for the fans.

The culmination of the day was a Charity football match featuring the cast of Brookside facing a combined Leicester Sound/ Leicester City team featuring Frank Worthington, Lenny Glover and Alan Young. We gave out free goodie bags to kids, offered 10% off everything in the club shop and, while we predicted a decent turn out, the 12,000 people who attended wildly surpassed our expectations. The police had to put diversions in place to prevent traffic driving onto Walnut Street. To put this into context, our average attendance the previous season was just 11,500!

The event was so successful that we held an open day every year that I was at the club. As its popularity grew, we held the events in the summer over three days to allow more people to attend. When we won the League Cup the open days gave fans the opportunity to have their photo taken with the trophy. Although we kept the open days free for fans to attend, they still proved very profitable for the club with us eventually bringing in around £70,000 each summer due to advertising, catering, shop sales, as well as ticket and membership sales.

Gary Mills could see the positive impact that my team were having on the club. "I got on great with Barrie. You could tell that he was making things happen off the pitch by doing more within the city and community. He was a positive man and I could see how the club was growing. He was so positive and if you needed something Barrie would do it. He deserves a lot of credit for what he did. He arranged a lot of events and the crowds started to come back."

With the launch of Leicester's new identity and re-branding, we again set the pace and were one of the first British professional football clubs to create a modern mascot – a fox kitted out in our brand-new Fox Leisure apparel. Leicester's Lottery Department had a fox character and Richard Hughes decided to adopt him as the mascot for the entire club. The idea was to create a character that all fans would love – from children, parents and grandparents to the hardcore supporters in the Kop.

The as-yet unnamed fox was unveiled before a home game against Brentford on 19th September 1992. He was with illustrious company on the pitch, walking out of the tunnel with Alan Birchenall and Gary Lineker. We ran a competition for fans to name our new mascot and from hundreds of entries we picked 'Filbert Fox.'

The kids loved him and his popularity was so great that we introduced his girlfriend, Vicki Vixen and Cousin Dennis. For our younger fans, the trio of foxes were as big a draw as the players. In fact, they were so popular that we had businesses, like Dominoes Toys, asking to sponsor them for £5000 a season. We did not create Filbert to make money, he was to act as a role model, and we exploited Filbert's popularity to spearhead anti-bullying and anti-racism campaigns and free-to-attend cycle safety courses.

Vicki and Dennis have since returned to their burrows, but Filbert is still going strong today and his legend continues to grow. He has won multiple 'Mascot of the Year' awards and rubbed shoulders with countless celebrities, including Cristiano Ronaldo, Ronaldinho, Ricky Hatton, Kasabian, and David Neilson, better known as Roy Cropper from Coronation Street. Filbert even held aloft the Premier League trophy when Leicester were crowned Champions in 2016.

There is a less glamourous side of being Filbert. Wearers of the fox costume were paid £10 a match, but they were responsible for drying and spray cleaning the outfit.

So, who was the person beneath the costume? I will let Richard answer that. "People used to ask me that all the time. My response was always, 'What do you mean costume? He is real!'

My children, Chloe and Daniel, cannot believe that I helped to create Filbert and, despite the fact that this was before they were born, it's the only thing they tell anyone about what I have done for a living!"

As our community programme developed, we decided to bring in a Community Office Supervisor, Ann Sharpe, to orchestrate the various activities that were designed to integrate Leicester City into the community.

Our players were idols to the supporters and, with the agreement of the team manager, we encouraged the players to make themselves available for various public appearances, including new shop openings, charity events, handing out trophies at junior football presentations and visiting children's hospitals. It was a great way for the fans to meet their heroes and to bridge the gap between community and football club.

Carl Muggleton remembers that he enjoyed the community initiatives. "When Barrie arrived, there were more events that the players were expected to attend, but none of us minded. We might occasionally swap, but it was all good fun and brought us closer to our supporters."

Gary Mills also appreciated the opportunity to meet the fans. "I loved the community and corporate stuff. I was a big believer in us players getting involved and interacting with the supporters. I enjoyed my time at Leicester. I have been in the game a long time now, and the people at Leicester City and the fans really are something else. It is such a special club. I won Player of the Year twice in my five years which meant a lot as it was the supporters who voted for me. The community events Barrie organised really bridged the gap between players and fans."

Our community drive made a real positive difference to the people of Leicester and Leicestershire. This was one of the few departments I was involved with where the primary goal was not about raising cash. In fact, most of the time it cost us money, but it was a great investment and brought monies into the football club in other ways.

Jersey Budd fondly remembers a City star visiting his school. "When I was at Primary School in Wigston, we found out that Gary Coatsworth was coming to open the school fete. It was big news and there was a real buzz around the playground. Players were accessible to fans in those days. I lived in Countesthorpe and Julian Joachim lived round the corner. Me and my mates used to go round and knock on his door. He always answered and he signed everything we put in front of him.

Iwan Roberts lived nearby too and I found out that his house was part of my sister's paper round. He was my hero and I was so jealous of her. I used to beg my sister to let me deliver his paper, but she never let me.

I got involved in the community events too and joined the School of Excellence. I was never quite good enough to make it as a pro and I always felt a bit intimidated training Tuesdays and Thursdays at Belvoir Drive. I could not stop thinking, 'Wow, this is Leicester City.' I loved it, though.

There was one day after training when David Nish came into the dressing room and asked, 'Who wants tickets to the game against Manchester City?' I remember being green as grass and thinking we would have to pay. I really wanted to go, but said, 'I'll have to check with my dad.' It took a few minutes before I realised that they were free – I did not know what complimentary meant!

Those tickets were amazing. We sat in the top tier of the Double Decker, right in the middle. The Kop was the best for atmosphere, but you couldn't beat the view from the Double Decker – you could see everything."

All our hard work off the pitch led to Leicester City becoming increasingly popular with youngsters and it was important that we used our influence in a positive manner. Richard created 'The Fox Club', a series of membership schemes exclusively for junior supporters aged from birth to sixteen. For just £15 a year – a percentage of which we donated to Filbert's Leicestershire Child Appeal – we gave members a pack including a scarf, pin badge, birthday card, bi-monthly newsletters, free entry to reserve games, coaching sessions throughout the year, an opportunity to be a mascot , a chance to meet the players and a 10% discount in the club shop.

We split the Fox Club into four different age categories, 'Filbert Tots' catered for the birth to four year olds, 'Filbert Fox Club' was for children aged five to nine, 'Team 10-14' was, as the

An example of the goodies that our Fox Club members received.

name implies, for ten to fourteen year olds and 'First Team' was for our older fans aged between fifteen and seventeen. Splitting the memberships this way meant that we were able to target members with age appropriate membership packs, competitions and special offers. Thousands of members signed up and this attracted Pepsi who paid us £10,000 a year to sponsor the Fox Club.

The incredible uptake in junior memberships highlighted the progress that we had made. Leicester City was now a club that appealed to youngsters, many of whom looked up to our club and our players. My team and I were determined to use our influence to make a beneficial impact upon the community.

In 1994 we joined forces with Leicestershire County Council's Education Department for their truancy programme which was designed to encourage children to regularly attend school. Midfielder David Lowe and goalkeeper Kevin Poole helped us launch the campaign as we presented the scheme to schools across the county. When a school signed up, all children who achieved a 100% attendance record were eligible for a Leicester City themed prize, ranging from a tour of Filbert Street for the entire class, signed photos, reserve team season tickets and complimentary tickets for first team matches. Over one thousand children received an award.

This success led to us teaming up with the local newspaper, the *Leicester Mercury*, to develop a reading passport scheme for Primary school pupils. This was an incentive-based reading scheme that was aimed at encouraging children to read more and to develop their reading ability. The children had fifteen assignments to perform before a teacher could stamp their approval. The pupils then posted their completed passport to Filbert Street for one of our first team players to sign and return with a certificate, two free tickets to a reserve match and an invitation for the entire class to have a free tour of the ground that concluded with a visit by Filbert Fox. This was all free of charge and Ann Sharpe received fantastic feedback from schools, pupils, and parents.

We opened a classroom in the East Stand which was made available free of charge to hundreds of schools in Leicestershire and we produced our own Filbert Fox branded educational material including 'Learn to Read with Filbert' and 'Learn to Spell with Filbert'

This was the first of many projects that we partnered with the *Leicester Mercury*. John Aldridge OBE, DL. was the Chairman and Managing Director of the *Leicester Mercury* Media Group, then the sixth largest regional newspaper in the UK. John recalls our first meeting. "I swiftly learned, when I met Barrie for the first time, that he was a big man. Big in stature, big in drive, big in creativity – and big in friendship

In those pre-internet days, the Mercury enjoyed a huge circulation and was highly supportive of the community that it served. Barrie recognised that a partnership with the Mercury would be beneficial to both parties. He shared with me his remarkable vision of what the football club's off-field activities could look like.

His plans were original, creative and massively ambitious, but no one listening to them could have had any doubt that if anyone could achieve this turnaround he could.

Barrie's objective of raising the commercial profile of the Club, attracting serious sponsorship, increasing the Club's community involvement and creating a much needed revenue flow, fitted the Mercury's objectives too and it quickly became clear that there could be mutual benefits for both operations."

We also put a real emphasis on making Leicester City more accessible to under-represented groups. I persuaded the Leicestershire Co-operative Society to sponsor a Christmas dinner that we held at Filbert Street for elderly people. This event proved so popular that the Co-op later sponsored Bingo nights and tea dances in the Belvoir Suite.

Brian Little was a fantastic ally and he always offered his support. Brian explains why he was so supportive. "I embraced what Barrie wanted to do and was happy for him to try things. I was always happy to attend any functions if I needed to. I enjoyed working with him and never had a cross word against him. The commercial side is prevalent now, but that was the start of it all really. Barrie was ahead of his time.

In those days, the football side was the 'be all and end all' of the club and most people did not recognise that things were changing. The football manager was looked upon as the most important person at the club and some managers used that to become overly involved. I did not and that is probably why we worked so well together. Our personalities were completely different, but we complemented each other and, together, we really turned Leicester City around."

We formed the Leicester City Disabled Supporters Association to gain a deeper understanding into the needs of our disabled customers and we put substantial development into our disabled facilities to make them among the best in the country. The later building of the Carling Stand allowed us to increase our capacity of disabled spaces and we often collected and dropped off disabled supporters who were otherwise unable to attend matches. Through my regular discussions with supporter groups I discovered that we had blind supporters who attended our matches because they wanted to feel closer to the club and experience the atmosphere. We installed a radio link specifically for them so that they could listen to match commentary and feel part of the club.

Within the club we were tremendously proud of our community efforts and we also received national recognition when we beat Wolves in the final to win the coveted 'Jewson Family Football Award for Progress' at a glitzy awards ceremony in London in 1994. The panel of judges considered our impressively strong Fox Club, our innovative pitch side commentary facilities for our blind supporters, the addition of extra wheelchair spaces and our work with schools and the local community. We were awarded £5000 which was ploughed back into the community.

In 1998 we gained international recognition when Filbert Street was chosen to host the final of the INAS (International Sports Federation for Persons with Intellectual Difficulty) World Football Championships – a competition for athletes with intellectual difficulties – which was won by Poland.

That same year we were the runners up in the Ease of Access Service and Employment (EASE) Awards which was an award scheme initiated by Queen Elizabeth's Foundation for Disabled people and the following year we went one step better and won! We were the first professional football club to receive the accolade. The awards were not just based on the quality or quantity of our disabled facilities, toilets, lifts, etc. but also the way that we communicated with and understood our disabled customers and their needs.

The opening ceremony of the
INAS World Football Championships.

Ian Ormondroyd recalls being delighted to see the club grow. "As the commercial department developed, we could see that the club was becoming more professional. Barrie was a good guy, he kept out of the way of the football side, but we could all see the good work that he was doing off the pitch."

Lee Philpott embraced the community work too. "I did a lot more off-field community activities at Leicester than I did at other clubs. We always tried to share it out throughout the squad and most of it was enjoyable and rewarding, like meeting the fans, coaching the kids, and visiting our supporters in hospital."

Racism had been rife in football during the eighties and was still prevalent in the nineties and this meant that football wasn't deemed safe by the some of the ethnic population. This wasn't acceptablee especially for a multi-cultural city like Leicester.

We created numerous initiatives aimed at the ethnic minority population to make the club more inclusive to all. We began by displaying a prominent message in our match-day programme informing fans that we had a zero tolerance of racism in any form. We instructed our stewards to evict anyone making racist chants or gestures.

One third of Leicester's population was from an Asian background, so I met with community leaders to inform them about the changes that we were making at Filbert Street, to promote our facilities and to inform them that Leicester City was a club for all. We designed specific courses to cater solely for ethnic groups. Nev Hamilton, a former player and the Community Development Officer, set up and ran several football courses aimed at Asian youngsters and he also spoke at temples and other community places to encourage young people from Asian backgrounds to play football and become involved with Leicester City. We gave free tours to kids and allowed Asian businesses to use our facilities at a discount so that they could experience them first-hand.

We were delighted that our efforts to integrate Leicester City within the community led to Sabras Sound, formed in 1995 as a commercial Asian radio station covering the Midlands, partnering us. We sponsored their radio show and made our players available for interviews and this gave us a voice to forge closer links with the Asian community. A mutually beneficial partnership. Sabras advertised our upcoming games and events and we provided merchandise for competitions and got an insight into a whole new audience. This partnership led to an Asian company sponsoring a Leicester City match for the first time.

Everyone involved in the Leicester City ethnic minority programme was so dedicated and it is testament to their hard work that by 1996 our home crowds were formed of an average 16% ethnic minorities, compared to the Premier League average of just 1%.

In 1999 Tony Banks MP, Minister for Sport, visited us to praise our work on making football accessible to all races and said, "Leicester has taken the lead and we want to make sure that all other football clubs join in."

Females were another under-represented supporter group that I was determined to welcome to Filbert Street. Leicester already had a lady's football team, although they had quite a low profile. We gave them a bigger platform on which to display their skills and they played on the Filbert Street pitch during our open days and other events which allowed them to shine in front of a larger crowd than they were used to. We increased the number of ladies' and girls' teams to meet the increased demand from female players and we encouraged female supporters to attend our first team and reserve matches. When I left Leicester in 2000, 17% of our fans were female compared to the 5% national average.

I was sometimes asked to sign autographs for young fans.

We also used our standing in the community to promote good health. We recruited a health professional, Ria Harkness, on a three year placement from Leicestershire NHS Trust, Ria's role was to support and promote a healthy lifestyle and to run initiatives like No Smoking Day, healthy eating and encouraging people to get more exercise, within the club and the wider community. I always enjoyed leading from the front and decided to help to promote the scheme.

I'll quit smokes and help folks!

by John Marsden

A SOCCER executive has a burning ambition — to quit smoking and raise cash for charity at the same time.

The New Year resolution is part of a series of pledges by staff at Leicester City Football Club.

Chief Executive Barrie Pierpoint is stubbing out his last cigarette and also plans to lose two stone in weight.

He is joined in the anti-smoking drive by four members of staff.

A number of others plan to lose weight, some have pledged to take more exercise and one has decided to give up chocolate.

Active

Mr Pierpoint will donate to charity £1 for every pound he loses and also for every day he does not smoke.

The club's health promotions project officer Ria Harkess is supporting the resolutions.

She advised people who are stopping smoking to keep busy and active, be careful at social occasions, get the support of family and friends and "expect to feel rough!"

TAKE MY TIP: Leicester City Chief Executive Barry Pierpoint sits in the Filbert Street stand and gives us all his New Year message to give up smoking

GETTING FIT: Barry Pierpont and the club's health promotions officer Ria Harkess, right, exercise with City stars Brian Carey, David Lowe, Lee Philpott, Emile Heskey, Paul Bedder and Kevin Poole

Leicester City received good publicity for our health campaign.

In those days I was a big cigar smoker and I had gained a lot of weight from dining potential investors and sponsors, so I agreed to stop smoking and lose weight. For every day that I did not smoke, I agreed to donate £1 to charity, with an extra quid for every pound I lost in weight. The story made the papers with a cringe-worthy photo of me, Ria and a few of the first team – including Lee Philpott and a young Emile Heskey.

Michelle Newman, my PA at the time, laughs when remembering my attempts to stop smoking. "Every New Year was the same. Just after Christmas, Barrie would proudly announce that he was giving up his beloved cigars. By the fifth or sixth of January, he would leave his office and tell us that he was going for a walk to lose some weight. When he returned, he would stink of cigar smoke. He'd continue with this charade for a week, convinced that we didn't know, before he eventually told us all he'd started smoking again!"

I really enjoyed helping out in the community and having a job that made a real difference. One of the most rewarding aspects of my time at the club was delivering free Marketing and Public Relations' training to charities and voluntary groups within Leicestershire to help them to maximise their fundraising efforts and to attract more volunteers. This was organised by Voluntary Action Leicester.

I was a big networker and I never missed an opportunity to speak to potential sponsors and investors, so most evenings I attended a function or an event to spread the world about Leicester City. It is a good job that I liked to keep busy because I was also a governor at Loughborough College and a non-executive Director at Glenfield Hospital NHS Trust and Leicester Sound commercial radio station.

The staff made this possible, but we could only be inclusive to our customers if our employees were from diverse backgrounds and felt part of a community. There was one director who stated to me that he would not talk to anyone lower than Chief Executive and Managing Director level and would not communicate with the office staff. I was the complete opposite.

We had over two hundred staff and I made a point of knowing every single one of them by name and would regularly speak to them, about them personally as well as about their work. I had a superb relationship with City's employees and treated everyone the same, whether you were the car park attendant or the twenty-goal-a-season striker. I understood that everyone contributed towards the club's success.

No, this wasn't my usual office attire! I was performing at a fundraising event dressed as a hippie.

Chapter five - A new grandstand to mark a grand new era

The history of Filbert Street

One hundred miles north of London, in the very heart of England, sits the modern King Power Stadium, home of Leicester City Football Club since 2002. Just three hundred yards away is a piece of wasteland with a rich history, for it was on this land that Filbert Street stood for over a century. Don Revie, Frank McLintock, Peter Shilton, Gary Lineker and Emile Heskey all launched their trophy-laden careers on this hallowed land.

During their formative years, before election to the Midland League in 1891, Leicester Fosse played their games in five different locations. Keen to abandon their nomadic reputation and make the club more accessible to fans, the Fosse Committee explored the city, searching for a permanent football ground. Local businessman and senior committee member, Joseph Johnson – whose four sons had already played for Fosse – identified a site, negotiated the lease and personally guaranteed the rent; Leicester Fosse had their first permanent home – Filbert Street.

The site of the former Filbert Street ground (bottom left) is just yards away from the King Power stadium.

Leicester Fosse (wearing blue and chocolate half jerseys) in action at Filbert Street during the 1890s.

Filbert Street hosted its first senior game on 7th November 1891 - a 1-1 draw against rivals Nottingham Forest. When Fosse joined the Football League three years later, the higher standard of opposition attracted larger crowds which meant that the club had to develop the ground at a considerable rate – and substantial cost – and by the time the First World War ended, Fosse had severe financial difficulties and the club was wound up and resurrected as Leicester City.

Attendances following the war continued to increase and the new Board of Directors prioritised further ground improvements. The capacity was increased to 45,000 with the erection of the Double Decker at a cost of £31,000 and the Main Stand for just £26,842, both built in the nineteen twenties. The renowned architect, Archibald Leitch, who listed Old Trafford, Anfield, Hillsborough and White Hart Lane as his previous projects, was commissioned to design the Double Decker.

Health and safety didn't apply in 1928 when 47,298 fans watched Leicester City play Tottenham Hotspur at Filbert Street.

During the Second World War the Main Stand was damaged by a German bomb and it also suffered substantial fire damage two years later. But despite being constructed mainly of wood, it survived.

The installation of seating, during the eighties, in most areas of the ground reduced the capacity of Filbert Street to just 18,000 and once the Taylor Report's recommendations had been implemented, there would be a further reduction.

John Sharp, Leicester City director, explains the capacity challenges that the club faced. "Roy Parker and I joined the board on the same day in 1990, and I think it is fair to say that we added some impetus and fresh ideas. We had a programme of replacing the terraces with seats, but that kept reducing the capacity of the Main Stand. The obvious solution was to build a new one.

Alan Bennett, the club's General Secretary and I worked on the specification and a rough sketch of how the offices, commercial and sponsorship areas and dressing rooms needed to be before the Architect, Phillip Dodd, got to work in drawing up the detailed plans."

By 1992, the Main Stand was looking every one of its seventy years and for Leicester City to progress, it needed to be replaced. But it wouldn't be cheap.

The fences and terracing needed to be replaced at Filbert Street.

The Members Stand, Filbert Street
1921 - 1993

Behind the scenes

The Board of Directors created my role, primarily, to raise the money needed to replace the Main Stand. This had been spoken about for decades, but the club had never been able to finance a replacement stand. That was where I came in.

The directors already had plans drawn up and they had received four quotes from several construction companies, so we had a good idea of how much we needed. It was around £5,500,000.

My first thought was, how am I going to raise £5,500,000?

My second thought was, How am I going to raise £5,500,000?

To say it was a huge challenge is an understatement.

Following the devasting Hillsborough tragedy when ninety-six Liverpool fans sadly lost their lives, Lord Justice Taylor conducted an inquiry that concluded with a number of recommendations; one of which was that all football stadia for English teams in the top two tiers would need to be all-seater by the start of the 1994/95 season. The Leicester City Directors wanted to start demolition at the end of the 1992/93 season and open the new stand by December 1993 which would give us an eight-month contingency. We had to build the stand quickly because we would be losing vital revenue while only having three stands and we assessed that we could only afford to be without our Main Stand for four months of the season. This meant that I had just two years to raise the necessary cash!

I first assessed the internal options:

• Did the club have enough financial stability to absorb the cost internally? No. We hadn't recorded a profit for several years and were barely keeping our heads above water.

• Could our directors finance the stand? No. Not all the directors were able to invest money.

• Did we have any assets (i.e. players) that we could sell? Not really, as we didn't want to build a new stand to the detriment of the team. We wanted both.

• Could we increase the ticket prices? No. While this was an easy, quick method of generating funds we needed to keep the games affordable to the average fan and we didn't want to alienate our loyal fanbase or see attendances decline.

• Could we borrow the money from the banks? Some, yes, but we were very loan averse and did not want to compromise the club's long-term financial future. We also had a Restrictive Covenant on the land which restricted the amount that we could borrow. The Covenant meant that we could not use the Filbert Street stadium as security for a loan.

The Board of Directors had helpfully provided me with a list of opportunities that I could explore, but I still had to look externally and find creative methods of fundraising.

I had a morale-boosting early success when I discovered that the government were issuing grants for inner-city employment generative projects. Leicester City Challenge Limited had been set up to regenerate the inner city of Leicester. The area around Filbert Street was very run down and featured very few amenities for the residents. The plans for the new stand included facilities that were not available near the ground at that time, including meeting and function rooms, a restaurant and a gym. The new stand would also create a lot of new jobs. I wanted the club to be more community focussed and I planned to integrate the club within the city; this felt like a perfect opportunity to do both. So, I applied for a City Challenge grant.

Keith Beaumont, Chief Executive of Leicester City Challenge Limited, was responsible for awarding the grants. Keith recalls approving my application for a grant. "We were delighted to able to provide £250,000 towards the building of a new stand for Leicester City. In return, the club offered crucial facilities and match tickets to the residents of Filbert Street and the surrounding areas. This was a key factor in transforming depression into hope and deprivation into opportunity. That sort of change is pivotal in its impact upon the lives of some people. Barrie's drive and humour were key factors within the transformation of the football club. It is a great privilege and joy to know him."

A quarter of a million was just a small windfall but it encouraged me in my quest to raise the rest of the money.

Source	Total raised
City Challenge Grant	£250,000

| Remaining balance | £5,250,000 |

Our next port of call was The Football Trust, a government initiative established to improve the safety aspects of sports stadia in the UK. It received funding from the Pools' companies and donations from Spot the Ball competitions run by Littlewoods and the Football League. We applied to the Trust and we were awarded £1,000,000 – the maximum amount available for a Second Division club.

Source	Total raised
City Challenge Grant	£250,000
The Football Trust	£1,000,000
Remaining balance	**£4,250,000**

With a range of exciting state-of-the-art facilities being created, we needed to find people and businesses with deep pockets who would utilise the new amenities, so we searched for potential corporate clients who hadn't previously been involved in the club. My team created brochures that detailed the services which the new stand would house and the opportunities that were available to local businesses.

I went out to as many businesses as I could to raise awareness and present my vision of Leicester City, what we were doing and where we were going. I delivered presentations to engage them and to ask them where they could fit into our plans. I discovered that a lot of businesses were not interested in the football club and a lot of their staff hadn't ever attended a game. Several businesses told me they that were investing in the Leicester Tigers Rugby Club because they didn't like the hooligan element associated with football. Others told me to come back when something had been built.

As we were not selling out our home matches, I had an idea of offering complimentary tickets to local businesses so that they and their staff could experience for themselves what we were doing at Leicester City Football Club. The idea was that businesses would reward their staff with free tickets to recognise their efforts. The staff didn't know that the tickets hadn't been bought by their employers, so the businesses would gain goodwill from their staff and we would attract new fans, as well as increasing our profile within the business community. It was a win, win. I met with the directors and made a compelling argument and the directors agreed that we could give away some tickets.

I went back out to businesses, this time armed with matchday tickets and more brochures. Many businesses accepted the complimentary tickets to give to their staff and, as predicted, some of those people became City fans. It gave the club visibility to a new audience, increased our merchandise, food and drink sales and we gained some goodwill within the business community; this in turn led to them investing in other ways, such as sponsorship, hospitality or using our facilities for meetings, etc. The other advantage was that bigger gates meant a larger customer base for potential sponsors and investors. I was mindful not to give out too many free tickets, though, because I didn't want to displease our loyal season ticket holders or members.

My approach worked. As our reputation soured, instead of me having to go out to businesses, they were coming to me to speak about match-day hospitality and sponsorship opportunities. I explained that we were creating twenty-eight luxury executive boxes that were priced at an average of £8,000 a year, with the middle boxes costing a bit more. Continuing our innovative thinking, we became one of the first clubs in the UK to allow companies to use the boxes on non-match days too. So, not only were businesses leasing a place to entertain clients, or reward employees on match-days, they were buying an office space to hold meetings, interviews – anything they wanted to use it for. They also had the prestige of being involved with Leicester City.

Alan Marvin, who was the owner and director of a local packaging firm, showed a tremendous amount of faith in me and my team when he said, 'Barrie, I'm so impressed with everything you have said. I have confidence in this club, so I would like to write you a cheque to lease an Executive Box for the next ten years.'

The *Leicester Mercury* were another business who secured an Executive Box. John Aldridge explains why he was so confident that it would be a good investment. "Barrie insisted from the start that the décor, fixtures and fittings in the boxes were to be of the highest standards – more akin to a five-star hotel than the perceived standards hitherto expected in a football stadium. We agreed that the Mercury would sponsor a box for a three-year period. We gladly allowed Barrie to publicise our commitment with a message from the newspaper to express our reasons for making the investment. It certainly turned out to be a good investment for us.

Our decision to take a box was swiftly justified: we sent invitations out to join us for a high quality lunch around a boardroom style table, watch the match in seats outside the box, enjoy warm drinks at half time and to celebrate the result of the match (sometimes!) with a drink after the game. Barrie arranged for each box to have a visit from a past player, who would spend pre-match time talking to our guests about the game and helping them to enjoy this unique experience.

The invitations that we sent out were almost always accepted with alacrity and some of our contacts, when writing afterwards to express their thanks, would add, 'Please invite us again.'

We were also able to offer seats in the box to local charities as a valued prize in competitions which they might be running, fulfilling our ongoing commitment to engage with our community. Sponsorship of the box sometimes included the opportunity to sponsor the match ball, to go out onto the pitch before the match, meet the officials and the team captains and to hand the ball over to the referee. It was all good stuff. The crowds grew, the whole ethos of the football club was changed – much for the better. Barrie found time ahead of each match to visit each of the boxes. It was like a whirlwind arriving, but somehow, he greeted everyone and in those few minutes made everyone feel important; the Chief Executive had taken the trouble to welcome them. The 'feel good' factor abounded!

Our successful partnership with Barrie and the Club continued for the whole time that the new stand was in use until the present state-of-the-art new ground was built. It was an investment that paid off for us as a newspaper, for the club and importantly for the community."

We sold all 28 boxes for a total of £1,100,000 before any building work had started. This surpassed my expectations and was testament to the hard work of my team. As soon as the steel frames started going up, demand for the boxes increased and people started arguing over which box they wanted and offering me more money for their preferred location. It was too late for any changes though as I did not want to break any agreements that I had already made.

The total raised now stood at:

Source	Total raised
City Challenge Grant	£250,000
The Football Trust	£1,000,000
Executive Boxes	£1,100,000

Remaining balance	£3,150,000

Leicestershire was home to some of the wealthiest people in the UK, many of whom I felt might be able to invest in the Club. But these people had not made their vast sums from being profligate, so I really had to incentivise the whole idea and make investing in Leicester City an attractive option.

To reward their support and to ensure that they didn't miss out on this opportunity I began with people who were already involved with the club.

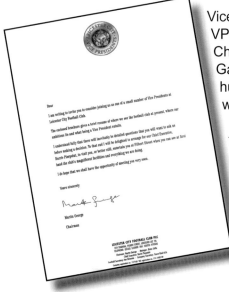

We created positions for twenty Vice Presidents and we targeted potential VPs with a personal letter from our Chairman, Martin George. We named Gary Lineker and Gordon Banks, two huge City legends as honorary VPs which gave the role a high status.

Vice Presidents paid £25,000 up front which covered a five-year period. They received perks, including their own match-day suite where they received a complimentary glass of wine on arrival, a pre-match meal, a club tie, parking spaces, four tickets for each match and an opportunity to meet the manager and players. These packages sold out fast. In fact, we could have sold many more, but we decided to limit them to twenty to retain the significance. The Vice President package brought in £500,000 which meant that, in total, we had raised more than half of the required amount.

Source	Total raised
City Challenge Grant	£250,000
The Football Trust	£1,000,000
Executive Boxes	£1,100,000
Vice Presidents	£500,000

Remaining balance	£2,650,000

We had previously operated a debenture scheme in the old Belvoir Suite and decided to continue this in the new stand, so we offered two hundred and fifty debentures to the public. A debenture was basically a posh season ticket. Supporters paid a one-off fee of £2,500 for an unsecured, non-interest-bearing debenture and in return, they were able to purchase – for an additional £975 a season – two luxury seats in the exclusive debenture holders' area within the new stand. They also gained match-day access to the Belvoir Suite where their names were displayed and they could also purchase match day hospitality, receive discounts on merchandise, advertising and hiring of the facilities, free parking and a complimentary programme. Holders could sell their debenture at any time or the Club could buy it back. The debenture was effectively an interest free loan for the Club and the money raised from ticket sales was profit.

When I had exhausted the list of current investors, I compiled a register of potential high net worth individuals whom I met to try to convince them to part with their hard-earned cash. I had to engage with them and sell the future vision of the club – that we were going places.

I worked tirelessly and contacted many people including David Wilson, Trevor Bennett, Freddie Linnett, Hugh Murphy, George Davies, John Bloor, David Samworth and many others. I met with a number of these potential investors to explain what we were doing at Leicester City. It sounds like fun, wining and dining people, but it was very intense, especially after a hard day's work

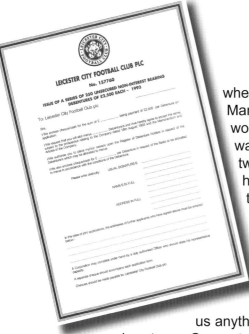

where I was liaising with the Project Manager to ensure that the stand would be built to time and standard. I was seeing up to six people a day for two years and gained a stone and a half in weight. It is a good job that the stand did not take any longer to build!

Some directors felt that people should have given us money because we were their local football club, but I knew that people were unlikely to give us anything without us providing something in return. One potential investor wanted a seat in the boardroom in return for his hundred thousand pounds. I ran this by the directors and was told no. I think that there was some fear that adding another board member would reduce some of the power that the current directors yielded. I suggested that we give him an honorary title as Patron which the investor thought was a great idea and asked if he could attend board meetings, not to contribute but just to listen. Again, I took this to the directors and again I was told no. So off he went – to invest in Newcastle United – and I had to find £100,000 from elsewhere. It was disappointing.

Another frustration was when I schmoozed a local multi-millionaire. I invited him to Filbert Street for lunch and I asked one of the directors to come along too. Over a delicious meal I began to sell the club and our vision, with the aim of making the investor feel special before asking him if he wanted to be a part of making our dream a reality.

'Why am I here, Barrie?' he asked cautiously after the waiter poured the drinks.

'Because we are on the brink of something exciting here. We have an exciting, young manager who has got the team playing fantastic football, we're building one of the best stands in the UK and we want you to be involved. Our directors are keen to meet you too,' I explained, passionately.

He appeared intrigued. But one of the directors ruined any chance of investment. He arrived at the meal late and was too direct. 'So, how much are you giving us?' he asked as soon as he sat down.

'I'm sorry?' replied the potential investor.

'How much money are you giving us?' repeated the director, totally oblivious to the change in atmosphere.

'I haven't agreed to give you any money,' he said, visually put out. Having ruined a potential deal, the director then left five minutes later, leaving me to finish what had become a very awkward lunch.

Jim Mutton, Chief Executive of Loughborough College, was one corporate guest who I invited to lunch to discuss how Leicester City and Loughborough College could work together. "Barrie is something of an epicure – he really does enjoy good food and vino! My first lunch with Barrie was in the Captains' Restaurant back in 1993 while he was trying to raise funds for a new stadium. This was the first of many luncheons I enjoyed with Barrie. I always remember that when asked, 'Would you like your glass topped up, Sir?' or 'Would you like an extra helping of food?' Barrie would always respond, 'I'm a growing lad.' It became his catchphrase and almost always raised a chuckle. Barrie's big personality enlivened the day of staff and guests. Laughter amidst doing things, Barrie's key style and a credit to him."

In total nearly two hundred and fifty businesses were met and entertained by my team and myself and we sold every single debenture.

Source	Total raised
City Challenge Grant	£250,000
The Football Trust	£1,000,000
Executive Boxes	£1,100,000
Vice Presidents	£500,000
Debenture Scheme	£625,000

Remaining balance	£2,025,000

One of the most important deals that I had to make was selling the naming rights to the new stand. Stadium sponsorship was incredibly popular and profitable in the United States, yet in the early nineties, very few football clubs had stadium or stand sponsorship. This was a lucrative avenue that I was determined to exploit.

The deal that we eventually negotiated in 1993 was with the Carling brand. We agreed that Carling would pay us £250,000 for the naming rights to the stand and another £250,000 for the exclusive pouring rights in the stadium. In return, they received a hospitality suite, seats in the Directors' Box, their branding displayed all over the stand and on the front of the programme and an allocation of tickets for their staff. We also renamed the Belvoir Suite as the Carling Belvoir Suite.

I always made sure that we looked after Carling, and our other sponsors, and also made sure that the deals which we agreed were right for both Leicester City and for them. I found out that this was different to how other clubs managed their sponsors.
One evening Wolves were holding a sporting dinner event and I had been invited to attend as Leicester City's representative. It was a strange evening as they had booked the controversial comedian, Bernard Manning, to compere the evening. Crowds of protestors were camped outside Molineux when I arrived and I could still hear them chanting their disapproval when I was inside the stadium.

I sat next to a senior board member of Goodyear, the tyre company who sponsored Wolves. Always keen to check out the opposition, I asked him what they received for their sponsorship package. Their reply astounded me. He told me that they got their name displayed on the team's shirts and that was it! Football now had global appeal which meant that we were competing against other clubs for the most lucrative contracts. I discovered that we were receiving much more money from our deal with Walkers Crisps than Wolves were from Goodyear and it reminded me of the need to foster a good relationship with sponsors.

Martin Glenn, who later became the Chief Executive of the Football Association, was the Chief Executive of PepsiCo, who owned Walkers Crisps. Martin was very supportive and helpful during my time at Leicester and he was a pleasure to do business with.

Carling continued to sponsor the stand until it was

demolished in 2002 and Walkers remained Leicester City's shirt sponsors during my entire time at the Club, so I must have managed the relationships well.

Source	Total raised
City Challenge Grant	£250,000
The Football Trust	£1,000,000
Executive Boxes	£1,100,000
Vice Presidents	£500,000
Debenture Scheme	£625,000
Stand naming rights	£500,000
Remaining balance	**£1,525,000**

The Board of Directors had agreed to take out a loan for the remaining amount. The problem was that the Leicester City Council held a Restrictive Covenant on the land that our Filbert Street ground was built upon. This restricted the freedom for us to develop the stadium which affected the value of the land and limited our borrowing potential. Leicester City's lawyer was Henry Doyle, of the law firm Edge & Ellison.

Henry was a lifelong Leicester supporter and I asked him to work his magic. "I had known Barrie for a few years before I became the lead partner working on the Leicester City account. Barrie's aim was to increase the profile of Leicester City, both nationally and locally, and he brought a new approach to marketing to the club.

Barrie asked me if there was anyway that the Covenant could be modified or, even better, released. Normally, both parties would sit down with surveyors and thrash out a financial deal. There was just one problem; the Club did not have any money to pay the council! Barrie, in his usual creative way, found a solution.

So, rather than Leicester City paying the City Council any money, we negotiated a community and leisure package, whereby the Club would promote the Council's Leisure Pass scheme by advertising in home programmes and making 1000 matchday tickets available at half price for each home game to Leisure Pass members. In addition, we allowed the City Council to sponsor one home match a season free of charge, gave them £20,000 worth of conferencing and banqueting facilities each year to use for various community groups and special council events, and we also promoted Women's football and disability football at both Filbert Street and Belvoir Drive. This solution allowed the City Council to recoup the value of the land in other ways that also had great benefit to the Leicester community. The City Council agreed to release the Covenant."

Peter Soulsby, the current Mayor of Leicester, was, at the time, the leader of Leicester City Council and he was incredibly supportive in allowing us to lift the Covenant. With no restrictions on the land, we were able to take out a small loan of around £1,525,000 to pay the remainder of the balance.

Source	Total raised
City Challenge Grant	£250,000
The Football Trust	£1,000,000
Executive Boxes	£1,100,000
Vice Presidents	£500,000
Debenture Scheme	£625,000
Stand naming rights	£500,000
Loan	£1,525,000
Remaining balance	**£0**

Sir Robert McAlpine, builders of the original Wembley Stadium in 1924, were the contractors that we appointed to turn the architect's drawings into reality and, with the majority of the money in place, our seventy-two year old Main Stand was demolished in May 1993 after our final home league match of the season against Bristol City.

We had made the play-offs again and had a home leg against Portsmouth to stage. With the Main Stand in the process of being demolished, we had to play our first – and to date, only – home match outside Leicester. Our fans didn't have to travel too far, though, as Nottingham Forest allowed us to use their ground, the City Ground. Julian Joachim's wonder goal separated the two sides and for one day only, Leicester City supporters all wanted the home team to win at the City Ground!

While building work was underway, we kept fans informed of the progress. Cliff Ginnetta, Leicester City Supporters' Club Chairman, explains how we kept the fans engaged. "Barrie organised tours for the fans to show us how the stand was developing and explained how it would look. Barrie was his usual charming self and was in his element. It generated a lot of excitement."

Superfan, Ashley Barratt, shared Cliff's excitement for the new stand. "Filbert Street was in a sorry state. The Main Stand was so run down, it looked like it belonged in another era. When I heard that we were building a new stand I was so excited. I couldn't wait to read the regular updates in the *Leicester Mercury* and, during the summer holidays, my brother and I spent many an hour at Filbert Street watching the builders turn our dreams into reality. When it was finished it was magnificent. The only downside was that when it was finished it made the rest of the ground look worse!"

At the beginning of the 1993/94 season, we only had three stands for match days. That meant that we were without most of our facilities including dressing room, boardroom and corporate facilities for a few months. We relocated our hospitality to the Holiday Inn and our offices and Fox Leisure store were situated in the empty Sturgess car showroom opposite the ground. I remember Charles Rayner and his team laying out the shop immaculately, ready for the grand opening. That evening I received a phone call from the police to say that it had been ram raided. When we arrived at the store, we were devastated to find that most of the merchandise had been stolen and there were tyre marks all over the carpet. It was heart breaking, but we were very resilient. Charles and his team worked through the night and we opened to customers in no time.

Whilst it was challenging for us off the pitch, the players' facilities were temporarily downgraded. They actually got changed in a portacabin in the car park! Gary Mills believes that the inferior facilities actually benefitted Leicester. "While the stand was being constructed, we had to get changed in portacabins which was different, but we got used to it. However, other teams found it really tough which helped us and we only lost once at home while using them. The Carling Stand was state of the art at the time and gave us much better facilities than we'd had before. Fans had a better view of the games too."

Colin Hill agrees with Gary. "Away teams hated coming to

Filbert Street while it was being redeveloped. There were some bad grounds around, but the portacabin must have contained the worst dressing rooms in the top four divisions. The hot water ran out after just four showers, so there was always a race after the game to see who could get in there first. It worked out very well for us. It helped us build character and it gave us an advantage."

Brian Little remembers the temporary changing rooms occasionally disrupted his team talks. "The portacabins were a nightmare. I'd be giving instructions at half time and then you'd hear the tannoy messages drowning me out. I remember one match where I was trying to deliver a team talk and someone walked into the dressing room with a briefcase and asked if anyone wanted to buy a watch! We politely asked him to leave and then the players burst into laughter. Things like that helped build team spirit."

A lot of thought had gone into the design of the Carling Stand. It was quite right that the primary purpose of the new stand was to increase our capacity and enhance our fans' match day viewing experience. But that didn't mean that we shouldn't be making best use of the facilities for the rest of the time, so I made some changes.

One thing that I changed was the conference rooms. The original plans were for four rooms next to each other. I felt that we were limiting ourselves to the maximum capacity of each room. I altered the designs so that we created one huge room that included sound-proofed partitions which could be used to split the room into four, giving us the option of hosting one large or four smaller functions. This allowed us to maximise our potential.

My team and I were very hands on with the interior design of the stand. Branding is so important, hence the change in our corporate identity. We decided that the carpet in the Executive Boxes and in the corridors should quite rightly feature the newly designed fox logo. However, we laid a plain carpet in the banqueting suite as we felt that some people wouldn't want a football club logo on the carpet at their wedding reception.

There was also a big issue with the lack of signage around the stadium in the original plans. As we neared completion, my team and I walked around the concourse and corridors to work out what signs were needed and where.

We were able to open the top tier of the stand to spectators in October 1993 for a league game against Notts County. The rest of the stand would be ready for the start of December.

While the building work was taking place, my team had been selling our conference and banqueting facilities and they did an amazing job which meant that we were fully booked for the whole of December – not just in the restaurant, but in the conference rooms too, as Filbert Street was chosen to be the venue for several Christmas parties.

Leicester City Director, Tom Smeaton, was responsible for the project management, and despite a few problems along the way, completion was achieved roughly on schedule. The Carling Stand contained 750 tonnes of steelwork, 1570 steps, 206 foundation piles and 105 toilets. It held 9300 fans over three tiers taking Filbert Street's capacity from 18,000 to 22,517. In addition, it had twenty-eight Executive boxes, an eighty-seater restaurant, conferencing facilities to entertain hundreds of people and various function rooms that could each hold between 10 and 400 people. It was like a five-star hotel without bedrooms. Witnessing the construction of the Carling Stand was so rewarding for me as two years of hard graft came to fruition.

Mike Whitlow was impressed by the new stand. "Throughout my time at Leicester, they always had a big fan base and great supporters. The biggest change I saw was the environment we played in. The more you achieve the more the club developed. I witnessed the feel-good factor around the city that we created as we became a more successful club – on and off the pitch."

Geoff Peters, a regular in the Press Box, was pleased with the new facilities. "Fair to say from the old stand to the new, the facilities were chalk and cheese. Such a massive improvement in every way. Media facilities in the old stand were extremely basic. The Carling Stand made it a much more pleasurable experience for us press guys."

The Carling stand was built inside a year for just over £5,500,000 and finally gave us the potential to generate a seven day per week income. The next challenge for my team was to identify methods to achieve this. We made a good start when, due to the top facilities in the Carling Stand, the FA asked us to host an England v Portugal Under 21 international game in 1994. What was great was that Leicester's own Julian Joachim lined up for England alongside Robbie Fowler, Jamie Redknapp and Sol Campbell. We charged just £10 for adults, kids were free and we used the occasion to support the various Children's Homes in Leicester.

In his book *Starting a Wave* Brian Little wrote, "I believe the football club has made a major step forward with the building of the Carling Stand. Just going out on the pitch tells the players and the public and me that we are involved in a football club which is genuinely trying to go in the right direction.

Without this complex we would have stayed still, for sure. This gives us a chance to compete at the top level. Players can see the club means business. There's nothing greater from a manager's point of view than talking to prospective signings and telling them of the work which is going on. It fills them with enthusiasm. It shows them the club is going in the right direction. We could well be signing bigger name players and breaking transfer records in the near future. Those things will happen. This building enhances those chances of that happening and the work behind the scenes improves the manager's chances of telling all sorts of people all over the country that Leicester City is going in the right direction and persuading them to become a part of the success story."

Brian's words proved true. The club's commercial turnover eventually rose from £736,000 to £8,000,000, a huge increase of which the profits were ploughed into the playing side. When I joined in 1991 the record signing was Mike Newell who had joined for £350,000 in 1987. We broke that record five times during my time at Filbert Street; Mark Blake (£360,000), Mark Draper (£1,250,000), Matt Elliot (£1,600,000), Frank Sinclair (£2,000,000) and Darren Eadie (£3,000,000). We would not have been able to do this without the revenue which the Carling stand generated and the teams' performance on the pitch.

The stunning view from the newly built Carling Stand.

Chapter six - Family night football: second string, but first class

On the pitch - season 1993/94

After back-to-back play-off final defeats, automatic promotion was the goal for City as Brian Little aimed to finally achieve the elusive goal of bringing top-flight football back to Filbert Street.

If anyone had any concerns over how the players would react following a second successive Wembley heartbreak, they need not have worried as Lee Philpott explains. "We just had to reset. We knew that we were a good team and that we had a chance of going up. We just had to roll our sleeves up and go again."

Gary Mills believes that Leicester's team spirit was different to other sides and this helped them to overcome adversity. "It took great character to bounce back the way we did. Most teams would have crumbled, but our dressing room was so strong that we were able to come back from two tough defeats."

After another long, gruelling season, Colin Hill was expecting a gentle pre-season. "Brian had this soft, gentle persona, but people who know him, realise that he is a tough cookie. We knew that we could pick ourselves up; we had already done it once, so why couldn't we do it again? The play-offs extended the season so we only had a short rest and we thought that we would not have much of a pre-season, but we were wrong. Brian, Allan and John worked us hard. They were determined for us to finally win promotion."

Once again, Little dipped into the transfer market, though no one could have imagined one of his signings would be the villain of 1992 – David Speedie. Speedie had a good pedigree, having played for Liverpool and Chelsea, amongst others, and he had an impressive promotion record; helping both Blackburn and West Ham achieve Premier League status. He was a controversial signing.

The City captain, Steve Walsh, was stunned. "I remember Brian calling me into his office to tell me that he was signing Speedie. My initial reaction was, 'Are you joking?' But Brian explained his plans and I said, "He's a good player and I'd rather have him on my team than play against him. It was a strange one for me, but we clicked upfront and formed a good partnership."

Ian Ormondroyd was also surprised. "Brian told us that Speedie was coming to Leicester and we were shocked. Walshy was one of the best players I ever played with and he was unhappy with the signing at first, though eventually things were resolved and the two got on."

Joining Speedie was £250,000 Manchester United defender, Brian Carey, and Cardiff City goalkeeper, Gavin Ward, who signed for £175,000. Ward's arrival signalled the end for Leicester-born 'keeper, Carl Muggleton, who remembers that he was sad to leave. "There was a lot of competition for the number one jersey during my time at Leicester. When Gavin Ward came in, it was time for me to go. I was gutted because I am a City fan, but my football head kicked in and I knew that leaving was the best thing for my career. I went on loan to Stoke City and then Sheffield United before I was signed by Celtic at the end of the season."

The Main Stand had been knocked down during the summer, so City kicked off their season surrounded by only three sides and no away fans.

Leicester – determined to avoid the play-offs – got off to a great start and after seven games they were sitting in third place. Thanks, in part, to David Speedie whose four goals had won over most of the City faithful. But then disaster . . . An away trip to Middlesbrough ended in defeat, but more devastating was an injury to the previous season's top scorer, Steve Walsh, that ruled him out for most of the campaign.

By the end of November, Leicester had slipped to sixth place in the league, so Little signed Huddersfield's prolific striker, Iwan Roberts, who immediately began repaying the £300,000 transfer fee by scoring a brace on his debut against Wolves.

The signing of Roberts helped to rejuvenate City and, as March began, they had risen to second. Little's combined spending for the season surpassed the million-pound mark when he splashed out £360,000 – a club record transfer fee – to bring in midfielder, Mark Blake, from Portsmouth. It was satisfying to see some of the profits from the club's commercial ventures being ploughed back into the playing side.

One of the surprising regulars in the side was Gary Coatsworth, who had endured a difficult start to life at Filbert Street. "I only made four appearances in my first season as I snapped my cruciate ligament which was really hard. Football was what I lived for, so to go from playing to sitting on the side-lines was tough. I probably came back too soon and only managed ten games in the 1992/93 season. I was a spectator for the play-off final defeats to Blackburn and Swindon and it wasn't easy watching the lads from the stands.

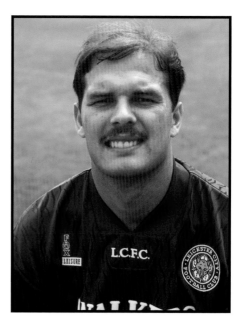

Gary Coatsworth established himself in the side during the 1993/94 season.

I managed to fight my way back into the first team towards the end of the 1993/94 season which was great and I scored the best goal of my career against Luton. The ball was headed back to me and I just hit it. It was one of those shots where you connect perfectly and the ball flew into the net."

In March, the Foxes took on the Lions at the New Den, in an ill-tempered match that saw three players sent off. Well, four actually as Brian Little explains. "Millwall, like us, were chasing promotion and you always knew that you were in for a battle when you faced them. In the first half they had Terry Hurlock and Pat Van Den Hauwe sent off. A few minutes later David Oldfield and Neil Lewis simultaneously fouled their opponents. The referee gave a free kick and held the red card aloft. Oldfield and Lewis both departed down the tunnel to the dressing room. Oldfield's red card was justifiable, but Lewis's was never a red. We were shouting at the linesman asking why Neil had been sent off. After a few minutes the ref came over and explained that he'd only sent off Oldfield! We had to run back to the dressing room and tell Neil to get back on the pitch!"

City finished the season with a nine-match unbeaten run, though they only won two of those games which meant that they had to settle for fourth position. It would be the dreaded play-offs again.

Tranmere Rovers stood in front of Leicester and a place at Wembley. A goal-less draw at Prenton Park in the first leg meant that it was evenly poised for the return leg at Filbert Street.

In the second leg, David Speedie went from hero to villain as he scored and was then sent off in the dying minutes as the Foxes beat Tranmere 2-1 to set up another trip to the Twin Towers where they would face Arthur Cox's big-spending Derby County.

The Rams had spent more on two of their players – Craig Short and Tommy Johnson – than the Foxes had spent on their entire squad, so the odds were stacked against the blues, especially considering their injury list.

Richard Smith was one of the many players out injured. "I'd struggled with injuries for most of the season, so I had to watch the final from the bench. We weren't the favourites so that took the pressure off us and we also had the experience of the occasion which Derby didn't."

Walsh had been stripped of the captain's armband earlier in the season and been replaced by Gary Mills, but Mills had suffered an injury which meant that he would miss the final. He was devastated. "I was out with a hamstring injury which was a real blow as this was a game that I was desperate to play in. On the day of the match, Brian told me that he wanted me to lead the players out onto the pitch which was the next best thing to playing. It meant so much to me that the manager wanted to do that for me. I will never forget what Brian did. After he told me, I went back to my room and shed a few tears."

With Speedie suspended Little needed someone to lead the line. Steve Walsh had not completed ninety minutes since September and had suffered a recurrence of his injury when attempting a comeback in March. Most players in that situation wouldn't have been able to play. But we are not talking about any mere mortal; this was Wembley and this was Steve Walsh – Mr Leicester City himself. There was no way that he was going to miss this.

More than a few eyebrows were raised when Little named the line up. Gavin Ward in goal, Mike Whitlow and Simon Grayson as fullbacks with Brian Carey, Jimmy Willis and Gary Coatsworth – three big, burly centre halves – completing the defence. Mark Blake and Colin Gibson were picked in midfield and Ian Ormondroyd, Steve Walsh and Iwan Roberts – up front. Surprisingly, there was no room for teenage sensation, Julian Joachim, in the starting line-up.

For Brian Little, it was a huge gamble that could have cost him his job. "We'd been to Wembley twice, and I honestly believe that if we'd lost the Derby final, I'd have got the sack. Derby were a great team; a real footballing side and I was a huge admirer of their players. In fact, I later signed Tommy Johnson and Gary Charles, and I also tried to sign Mark Pemberton. I knew that if we went toe-to-toe with them and tried to play them at their own game that they would have beaten us.

I often got labelled as a long ball manager, but there are lots of ways to win a football match and I picked the team that I thought could beat them. Nobody expected the line-up that I chose. I've spoken to Gibbo many times since them and he still asks me why I picked him, but he was a little terrier in midfield. Before the match, I reminded the lads that we'd lost twice and we needed to go out and do whatever it took to win."

After twenty-seven minutes Tommy Johnson gave Derby the lead and Leicester fans got a familiar feeling. The players, however, drew inspiration from the previous year's come back against Swindon Town and levelled just before the break. Gary Coatsworth recalls the moment. "Walking out at Wembley was the proudest moment of my career. Before the game, people were telling me to take in as much as I could. When we walked out the tunnel the noise from the fans was deafening and I was in awe of the situation. I can't remember much of the game, but I do recall setting up the equaliser.

I was just inside the Derby half when the ball came to me on the right-hand side. We had Iwan Roberts, Ian Ormondroyd and Steve Walsh up front, so I just lifted the ball into the box knowing that one of them would likely get their head to it. Walshy leapt above the Derby 'keeper, Martin Taylor, and nodded the ball into the goal."

The second half was dominated by the Rams, who struggled to find a way through the brick wall that was Gary Coatsworth, Brian Carey and Man of the Match, Jimmy Willis.

There were just six minutes on the clock when history was made. Simon Grayson picks up the story. "I remember Julian Joachim played the ball out to the right hand side for me to run onto. I crossed it first time to Ian Ormondroyd in the penalty area. Derby's 'keeper, Martin Taylor, parried

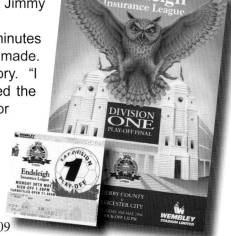

Steve Walsh celebrates his winning goal in the 1994 play-off final - "Leicester City are in dreamland now!"

Ormondroyd's header and the ball fell into the path of Steve Walsh who prodded it into the empty net. He made a fortune off the photo of that goal!"

City had ended their Wembley jinx and as commentator Alan Parry declared, "Leicester City are in dreamland now." After three years of heartache, the Foxes had finally made it to the Premier League.

With Mills out injured, the captain's armband had been given to Simon Grayson. Simon describes the moment when he became the first City captain to lift a trophy at Wembley. "It was a huge honour and a proud moment for me and my family. I remember walking up those famous steps to lift the cup surrounded by happy City fans. After heartbreak in the previous two seasons, it was an incredible achievement. My only regret is that someone put a stupid beanie hat on my head and I am wearing it in all the photos!"

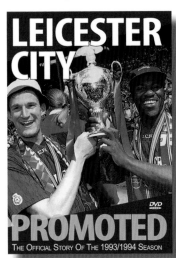

Simon Grayson (with *that* beanie hat) and Mark Blake featured on the cover of the commemerative video that we released.

110

Geoff Peters remembers the sheer joy that he experienced watching from the gantry at Wembley. "After two near misses we finally did it. I was lucky enough to be commentating for Radio Leicester and that was an incredible moment for me as a 21-year-old. I never thought anything would top that amazing day against Derby and then 2016 came along…"

The hero of the day was Steve Walsh who had put his body on the line to play in the final for Leicester. "I owe Brian a lot, he bought out the best in me. I wasn't 100% fit, but I couldn't miss the final. I enjoyed some fantastic moments as a footballer, but those two goals against Derby at Wembley were the best. I tore something in my knee, though, and it cost me later in my career."

Three years after leaving Derby, Ian Ormondroyd was delighted to defeat his former employers. "Derby should have won that game. My favourite moment from my time at Leicester was assisting Walshy for the winner. I felt so much emotion during the celebrations, it was wonderful. After the game, the celebrations continued at the Sketchley Grange hotel in Hinckley where we had a great party."

The Blue Army were ecstatic when Simon Grayson became the first City captain to lift a trophy at Wembley.

Jimmy Willis, David Lowe, Ian Ormondroyd and Steve Agnew proudly show off the play-off trophy to Foxes fans during their open top bus parade.

Mike Whitlow believes that Leicester were just too strong, physically, for the Rams. "Derby had so many good players, but we won that match by beating them up."

After the disappointment of the two previous finals, Ian Stringer was ecstatic. "I remember my dad driving me down to Wembley for the Derby match. As we travelled through Narborough Road, the street was lined with people, flags and scarves and there was excitement in the air. When Tommy Johnson gave Derby the lead, my dad ran from his seat because he was fuming. He came back, though, and so did Leicester. When Walshy scored the winner, I leapt at my dad and he caught me. I will never forget the look in his eyes. It was so emotional, that love of football that we shared. After two defeats, that victory was so sweet."

Ian Ormondroyd's winners medal.

Jersey Budd still remembers the feeling of euphoria, "I was in the stands with my dad and sister. We were crying at the end of the game as 'We are the Champions' was playing over the Wembley speakers. We felt like kings, after three attempts, we'd cracked it and we were now a Premier League team.'

Behind the scenes

We now had a shiny new stand that increased our total capacity to 21,500 and the next target for my team and myself was to boost attendances and to fully utilise the world-class facilities that we now possessed. We couldn't just sit back and expect people to come and watch us – we had to go out and create new fans by marketing the club and introducing Leicester City to a whole new audience. The on-pitch performances were important, obviously, but we also needed to create an exciting overall experience to entice supporters.

One day in 1993, my colleague, Richard Hughes, attended a second-string match on a cold, wet autumnal evening. Reserve games in the early nineties were weekday affairs where both teams typically fielded a combination of youngsters and experienced players returning from injury or not currently in the first team. The crowd consisted of a handful of die-hard fans who parted with their hard-earned cash to sit and enjoy a steaming hot cup of tea.

Richard was one of just thirty people inside Filbert Street that night. He noted that there were some fantastic, established players on display, as well as some talented youngsters and it was a shame that they didn't have an atmosphere to motivate them. Richard sensed an opportunity to create a new product that would appeal to a different type of supporter and also help to improve our standing within the community. With the primary focus of putting more bums on seats, we sat down to discuss his idea and conceived Family Night Football (FNF).

We wouldn't change anything on the football side without Brian Little's approval, so we pitched the idea to him. Brian explains that he thought it was great. "I embraced it. I didn't want any changes made to the first team matches, but this concept was ideal for reserve games. I had a few people asking why I was letting Barrie and Richard change the reserve matches, but I loved that they were trying to do something different. It was great for kids."

We had developed a close relationship with the local community and understood that some families could not afford tickets to first-team games, while others were put off by the large crowds and heavy traffic. The concept of FNF was to provide a good quality, live, football experience for fans who would not usually attend first-team matches.

Richard had previously attended a college football game in Florida that combined live sport and off-field entertainment such as a 200-strong marching band, cheerleaders and cartoon characters. The safe, fun environment attracted 90,000 people. We didn't have anything like this in England, so we decided to give it a go – but Leicester style.

A key driver was to provide value for money, so we priced tickets at just £2 for adults and a quid for kids (or free if they were Fox Club members) and we provided affordable catering from our Fox Fast Food kiosk for families to purchase.

Football was appealing to a broader spectrum of society and our supporter demographics were changing. In the eighties and early nineties live football was watched by a predominantly white male audience. Towards the mid-nineties there was increased interest from women, black and Asian supporters. We wanted Leicester to be an inclusive club, so we worked with local African-Caribbean and Asian football clubs and communities within the city to create anti-racist initiatives for Family Night Football, providing a safe environment for those wishing to watch a live game. In 1994 the national average for Asian spectators attending Premier League football games was just 1%. At Leicester City's FNF games ethnic minority fans regularly accounted for 25% of the crowd.

While City's first team competed in the Second Division, the second string played in the reserve Premier League alongside famous teams like Manchester United and Liverpool and this became a handy promotional tool as they always brought a few big names with them.

We promoted the games in schools, advertised in the newspapers and on the radio and, as always, we put the fans first. By making FNF a night out for the whole family, we saw an increase in female supporters and the benefits of this initiative were realised over a number of years. In 1999/00, the season that I left Leicester, we had one of the highest ratios of female season ticket holders in the Premier League at sixteen percent.

We again teamed up with the *Leicester Mercury* who helped us to promote the games as John Aldridge explains. "Readers could apply for free tickets to Family Night Football matches through the newspaper. It was a win, win situation – fans bought the paper, initially for the coupons, the club increased its fan base and its crowds and its support began to grow. The project was so successful that it won the Mercury a national award, presented to them by the Newspaper Society (the employers body of the Regional Press)."

Leicester Sound radio station hosted the evenings. We added some razzamatazz to a previously uneventful low-profile occasion. To gain ideas, we visited other sporting events, like Sheffield Steelers Ice Hockey team. Before the games we had a Samba or calypso band outside the stadium and inside there was face painting and cartoon characters greeting fans inside. In our shop Charles developed a new range of branded Filbert Fox, Vicki Vixen, Cousin Dennis and other FNF merchandise which was hugely popular with children.

We introduced cheerleaders, initially at reserve games and then to the first team matches as their popularity grew. We called them the Foxy Ladies (FXL). Caroline Scott became our Community Development Manager and spearheaded our team. By 1997 FXL reached double bronze in the UK Cheerleading Association Finals and double silver in the more prestigious International Cheerleading Finals – European Division. This meant FXL went on to represent the United Kingdom.

The award-winning Foxy Ladies cheered on City at Wembley.

the FXL files

Name: Natasha Awan
Squad: Junior FXL
Age: 15
Home: Oadby
Brothers and Sisters: One sister, Rosie and one brother, Danyal
School or Job: Beauchamp College
Hobbies: Boy hunting! Also bugging my brother and shopping.
Music: I like most pop music. At the moment, I especially like Spice Girls, Fugees and Backstreet Boys.
Food: Sunday roast
When you were a child what was your favourite toy? A purple puppet of a bird with a really long neck. It's name was Purple. (Why? Ed.)
Ambition: To be famous!
Favourite Colour: Red
Favourite Players: Scott Taylor, Trevor Sinclair, Jamie Redknapp
What do you like best about FXL? All the girls and having fun!

What was your most embarrassing moment? Almost falling down the stairs whilst doing a fashion show.
Who is your favourite FXL Cheerleader and why? Jo Williams because she's such a laugh!

FXL Galaxy
x x x

15

Everything we did was professional and we wanted to be the best, both on and off the pitch. Steve Welch, our groundsman, had so much passion for his job and, even for reserve games, that he wanted our pitch to look like Wembley. It's no surprise that he later became the groundsman at the National stadium.

Before the match Geoff Peters, Radio Leicester's sports presenter, was the man responsible for warming up the crowd, though he doesn't remember how effective this was. "I was working for Radio Leicester at the time, covering the club, and got asked by Barrie or one of his team if I'd fancy getting on the microphone to try to whip up the crowd. I was probably a complete embarrassment in hindsight, but I was about 21 or 22 and didn't know any better. That's my excuse and I'm sticking to it!"

As players entered the pitch, they kicked signed footballs into the stands, or handed out fixture cards, team sheets and photos to the fans. We gave the fans an opportunity to experience something that they couldn't get at first team matches.

During the game, when the ball went out of play the DJ played some music such as Queen's 'We Will Rock You' for the kids to sing along, clap and dance to. We kept it fresh by introducing new things at each game and the fans had a great time. Filbert Fox entertained the youngsters whenever there was a break in play and the Foxy Ladies captivated the crowd (especially the dads) to provide a carnival atmosphere.

At half time, Alan Birchenall took to the pitch, microphone in hand. "Family Night Football was incredible, what a great idea that was. Big Baz encouraged me to do stuff on the pitch that I couldn't get away with these days. I'd do pre-match and half time at first team matches too and he allowed me a lot of scope. I wouldn't last five minutes today. 'What did you say on Saturday?' he'd ask me.

'I might have had a pop at the ref.' I'd reply.

'You'll get into trouble,' he'd laugh."

Also, during the interval, Nev Hamilton and his team showcased some soccer skills and we ran competitions with great prizes that we had persuaded businesses to donate. Pontins were the sponsors of the reserve league and Richard arranged for us to meet with one of their directors at a hotel in Manchester the night before an FA Cup tie against Manchester City. The first team were having their pre-match meal at the same hotel and Brian Little, who was always so supportive, came over to say hello to the Pontins' director. We explained our plan for FNF and negotiated for Pontins to donate a free family holiday for four people at every FNF match. Pontins didn't even sponsor Leicester City, yet here we were persuading them to give us a prize – it was a great achievement.

FNF gave some glitz to the game and created a non-hostile, affordable, family-friendly environment for anyone with an interest in football to come and sample a live, professional game. If fans enjoyed FNF they would likely attend a first team fixture which was our ultimate aim.

Our first FNF match was held on 17th January 1994 against the previous year's FA Cup finalists, Sheffield Wednesday and was played out in front of a record 2156 spectators. Our average attendance for reserve games shot up to 6000, which was amazing, but it was a game in February 1994 against Manchester United reserves – our third FNF fixture – when we converted the doubters and we realised just how successful it had become.

We had expected a decent crowd as United's first team were the reigning Premier League Champions, but what we experienced was unprecedented. Demand was so high that crowds were snaking around the stadium and the kick off had to be delayed so that we could open up additional areas and get everyone inside safely. The official attendance was an incredible 14,419 fans – higher than our first team match against Tranmere Rovers that same month!

Almost 15,000 watched Leicester City beat Manchester United in the Pontins reserve league in 1994.

Emile Heskey remembers that match well. "I was in the youth team at the time and it was my job to fetch the balls during the game. I remember watching in disbelief as more and more fans entered the ground. By the time the match kicked off, the ground looked as full as it usually was for first team games.

Family Night Football was a great initiative that made reserve matches more family oriented and playing in those games definitely helped me in my development."

When the game eventually kicked off the fans were in for a treat. The Red Devils lined up with a mix of household names and future superstars, including Gary Walsh, Brian McClair, Dion Dublin, Gary Neville, Nicky Butt, Paul Scholes, David Beckham and future Fox Keith Gillespie.

In the stands that day was young Jersey Budd. "Some of my mates at school were Man United fans, so they went to watch United while the rest of us went to support Leicester. Most of my school attended that match. There were some parents there with us, but it felt like we were on our own and it gave us our first real taste of watching a game without supervision and without feeling intimidated by the hardcore fans. It was a great idea and I loved watching those FNF games."

Sam McMahon was in the Leicester side that faced United and retains strong memories of that match. "As a second year YTS, I made the step up to the reserves in the 1993/94 season. It was a huge jump in terms of both quality and experience. I went from playing against players my own age to facing 30-year old internationals. My first few games weren't too exciting; I remember an away match against Blackpool when we played on a field with just two men and a dog in attendance! For some games we included John Gregory and Allan Evans – both already retired and nearing their forties – in our team to make up the numbers.

As players, we didn't really concern ourselves with off field activities at the club as it didn't really affect us, but the introduction of Family Night Football was different. FNF transformed reserve games into big occasions that drew large crowds; the biggest turnout was for the visit of Manchester United.

I remember the game vividly. It was the eve of my eighteenth birthday and I was trying to impress the manager and earn my first professional contract. My family and friends were there to cheer us on, as were my mates from the youth team. As we lined up in the tunnel, I could hear the noise emanating from the stands and I felt a surge of excitement.

I felt energised and the whole team got a real lift from the vocal home supporters. It was unlike a typical reserve match - the atmosphere was more akin to a first team game – and I think United were a bit surprised. We completely dominated the first half.

I got my name on the scoresheet and Ian Ormondroyd scored two which gave us a deserved 3-0 lead after just thirty minutes. Dion Dublin pulled a goal back for United on the stroke of half time. During the second half, the visitors brought on David Beckham for Paul Scholes, but even the future England Captain couldn't prevent us from running out 3-1 winners. As I came off the pitch I felt for the first time that I might be able to do this. That match still ranks as one of the highlights of my career and I turned pro at the end of the season."

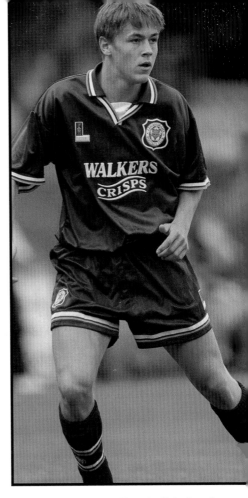

Family Night Football helped Sam McMahon in his development.

Not all of our opponents were as glamorous as Manchester United, so for some games we brought in celebrity guests such as Wolf from Gladiators or cartoon characters like Bart Simpson, and that first season we averaged crowds of nearly six thousand.

Stefan Oakes was another youngster who felt FNF helped to prepare him for the first team. "Family Night Football was a big thing for me as a young player. I had been playing well for the youth team against players my own age at the training ground with few fans. When I made the step up to the reserves, I was suddenly playing in front of thousands of people for the first time which made it feel like a proper game and it inspired me. The big teams brought their famous players and it gave me an opportunity to impress the manager. Martin O'Neill watched me in some of those FNF matches and my performances proved I could handle it against experienced players and large crowds."

As Sam and Stefan have highlighted, the FNF matches benefited the young players, but the more experienced enjoyed playing in them too.

Colin Hill: "I played in a couple of Family Night Football games when I was coming back from injury. The new concept made the matches more competitive. I was coming up against young kids who wanted to make a name for themselves by making a fool of me in front of a big audience."

Lee Philpott: "As a senior pro, you don't really want to be playing reserve football, especially as some matches were played out in front of a handful of people. The fans who came to watch FNF made the games more enjoyable for me and I'm sure they helped the youngsters in their development."

Ian Ormondroyd: "FNF helped senior players too. It made the games more of an occasion and the additional fans gave you more exposure, especially when you were in the shop window."

Pontus Kamark who joined in November 1995: "I thought Family Night Football was brilliant. We got bigger crowds for our reserves than a lot of teams did who were playing in the Swedish First Division. It was a great idea and I enjoyed playing in them when I was building match fitness after my injury."

Jamie Lawrence who joined in January 1996: "FNF was unbelievable. There was such a good atmosphere. Bear in mind that I'd joined from Doncaster and we were only getting 2000-3000 for our home games and I played in front of double that for the City reserves."

We kept Family Night Football fresh and were not afraid to try new things, although our ideas weren't all successful as Geoff Peters recalls. "I missed one Family Night Football game because of a car accident (nothing serious, thankfully, the car was more damaged than me) and at the next one, they had me wheeled in on a stretcher which I think was being pushed by Filbert Fox. It sounds like a bad dream, doesn't it?"

We later evolved FNF to include affordable hospitality and sponsorship opportunities to local businesses. Businesses who didn't have the budget to sponsor a first-team game were able to enjoy the intimacy of seats in hospitality areas, meet the players and advertise their services to a wide family audience. These businesses also brought their staff, customers and their children to the matches. The demographics for FNF meant that we attracted different companies to first team games, further raising the club's profile.

FNF improved our bank balance too, as our approach created an additional twelve trading match days per season where we made around £60,000 a season through ticket sales, sponsorship, Fox Leisure merchandise, Fox Fast Food and covers at the Fosse restaurant. We also introduced a package for children's birthday parties on an FNF match day which gave kids a truly unique experience.

We, as a club, really looked after our fans. One FNF game was played in the middle of winter and the snow meant that we used an orange ball. By half time, the players couldn't even see the ball, so the referee abandoned the match. There were two hundred brownies and girl guides stranded at the stadium due to the torrential snowstorm outside, so we put them in one of our conference rooms, fed and provided hot drinks for them until their parents could collect them.

Ashley Barratt was in attendance for most of the FNF games. "Family Night Football was groundbreaking and it became a rite of passage for all young Foxes. I remember that the club gave away thousands of tickets to local schools and junior football clubs, so it was a lot more accessible than a first team game. It was a different experience too and it gave me an opportunity to attend a match without a parent for the first time – my friends and I felt so grown up! FNF introduced a whole new generation to City, fans who probably wouldn't have become Leicester supporters otherwise."

Our creation was the envy of other clubs, many of whom tried to replicate our model including Everton, Manchester City and Bristol City. In fact, we received so many enquiries from other clubs that we decided to charge clubs £500 to attend a seminar where Richard explained how they could create and run their own Family Night Football events. Manchester United, Liverpool and Blackburn were just some of the clubs who attended. Norwich spent a whole day with us to learn more about what we did and they even offered Richard a job!

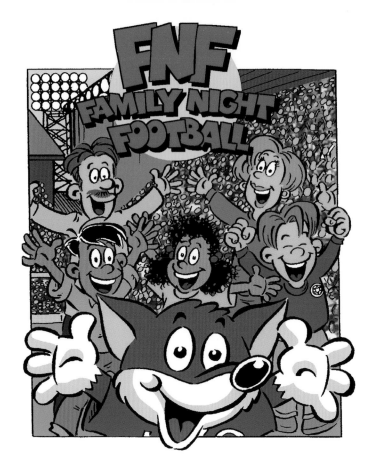

I really appreciated the support that the first team managers gave to FNF. We were grateful to Brian for giving Richard and I the freedom to try Family Night Football and to Mark McGhee for allowing us to continue improving the experience of reserve team football.

Mark recalls attending some matches as a fan. "A lot of managers would have objected to it, but I thought that it was fantastic and only someone like Barrie could have pulled it off. I took my sons along to one game and they loved it so much that they kept asking me to take them again. I had to take them out of school for the afternoon to get to Filbert Street in time for kick-off, but I had a good relationship with their headmaster. It helped that I brought his son with us too."

Whilst bringing in money was important, what I'm most proud of is the positive impact that FNF had within the community. We made football affordable and accessible which attracted a bunch of new fans. Our aim was to introduce people to the club at a young age, give them a good experience so that they would be fans and customers for life.

Watching those early FNF games was Matt Heath, a young Leicester-born supporter with aspirations of one day playing for his beloved City. "My dad introduced me to Leicester City in the late eighties and my earliest memories are watching Ali Mauchlan, Paul Ramsay and Gary McAllister. We missed the famous 'Great Escape' game as we had to go to a wedding, but my dad managed to sneak a transistor radio into the church, so he kept me updated on the score!

When Brian Little arrived, I was hooked. Filbert Street became my second home and I had made my mind up – I wanted to be a footballer. I was playing for Ratby and Groby Juniors who, along with Beaumont Town, were the best teams in the county. Leicester sent some scouts to watch and I, and most of the team, were invited to a trial. We were a good team because we had the best players. Beaumont were good because they had Matt Piper. I played well in my audition and was invited to join the School of Excellence.

Although I was training, playing and watching the first team with my dad, I couldn't get enough of football, so when FNF was introduced, I had another way of getting my football fix. The fact that they were so family friendly meant that I was allowed to attend with my mates for the first time. We'd get dropped off and picked up, but we could watch the matches on our own. I thought FNF was a great concept, the games were great fun and we watched some good football. As a teenager I probably spent more time watching the cheerleaders than the match, though!

Seeing some of the YTS lads, who were only a few years older than me, playing FNF football against big teams and top players, in front of large crowds – and the cheerleaders – further enhanced my desire to play for City.

As a thirteen or fourteen-year-old you are so far away from making it. I kept receiving praise from my coaches, but I never counted on it or thought it was possible – I never stopped dreaming, though.

When I was fifteen, I got my first taste of the big time. I was doing my GCSEs and I was asked to train with the youth team ahead of their FA Youth Cup clash against Liverpool. I couldn't believe it when I was told I'd be playing that night. The game was played in front of a decent crowd and although we lost 3-2, the other players were great towards me - I thought I really want this.

Shortly after that match I was offered a three-year YTS contract and joined a very talented youth team. The club had a real community feel to it and the senior pros were great. I cleaned the boots of Matt Elliott and Neil Lennon and they looked after me and protected me from some of the mickey taking that took place in those days. Matt, a fellow defender, was constantly giving me advice and tips and he really helped my game.

I was gradually exposed to the squad with players like Steve Guppy who would regularly stay behind to work on his crossing with us youth teamers. I remember the first time I was invited behind the scenes of a first team match. At half time I was sitting in the boot room and I could hear Martin O'Neill giving the team a right bollocking; we were thinking, wow, this is what it's like for the pros.

In my second year as a YTS I made it to the reserves and started really mixing with the first teamers. Players like Arnar Gunnlaugsson and Graham Fenton were regulars in the team and we often fielded others in need of match fitness or coming back from an injury. Playing in the FNF games was an amazing experience. I got such a rush and just wanted to do well. All I wanted was a professional contract and this was my chance to impress.

It was a step up because I was playing with, and against, older and more experienced players, but it wasn't too intense because there wasn't much on the line. It helped that as a defender the game was playing out in front of me and playing alongside better players made it easier; they got into better positions to receive the ball and coached me throughout the match.

The opponents were unbelievable too. During one match against Chelsea I found myself marking Champions League winner, Gianluca Vialli, with former Barcelona defender, Winston Bogarde, another big name in their line-up.

The FNF games were fun to play in and helped my development, though nothing can prepare you for the Premier League. I made my first team debut in 2001 and enjoyed four good years at Leicester before moving on to Coventry. I also played for Stockport County, Leeds, Colchester, Brighton, Southend and Northampton before moving into non-league football.

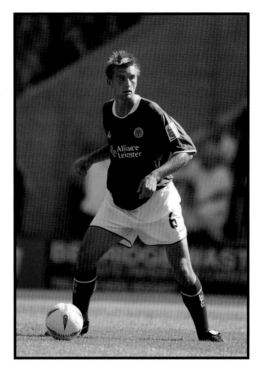

Matt Heath went from City fan to first team player - via FNF.

Looking back on those early days I realise how fortunate I was. As a schoolboy I joined Leicester at a time where we were undergoing a period of positive change off the pitch and achieving success on it. It was a real family club and a central part of the community.

For me, to play for my hometown club after all those years of following the Foxes was incredible. I had grown up around Filbert Street and to have a chance to play there in the Premier League and be part of the history of the club was indescribable. I am privileged to have lived my dream."

Ian Stringer, now BBC Radio Leicester's football commentator, was another young fan who enjoyed the Family Night Football experience. "The first Leicester game I attended was against Sunderland one winter and all I can remember is sitting in the Double Decker eating the hottest pie ever. In the coming years I stood on the Kop, or depending on which steward was on, I would jump on top of the groundsman's lawnmower shed and watch the game from there.

I became a fully-fledged member of the Junior Foxes and enjoyed the various perks that brought, like training on the AstroTurf with Jack Curtis and leading Leicester City out at Molineux as the team's mascot.

Family Night Football was great fun. At the time, I was playing football for Syston who were managed by my friend Mark Warren's dad, Tony. A couple of hours before kick-off, we'd meet at Mark's house and then climb into Tony's Ford Cortina estate and head to Filbert Street. There must have been five or six kids in the back! FNF gave us a rare opportunity to sit in the posh Carling Stand. I enjoyed watching the young players coming through the ranks and when they eventually progressed to the first team, I knew all about them which gave me kudos with the older fans.

My visits to Filbert Street created a love of the sport that made me want to get involved in football in a professional capacity. I wasn't good enough to become a professional but covering the matches for Radio Leicester is the next best thing."

Almost twenty years later, Cliff Ginnetta retains fond memories of FNF. "People still talk about Family Night Football today and, although reserve football has changed considerably, I think most fans would have FNF back in an instant. I think the players would welcome it too."

Family Night Football's legacy lives on. A report published in 1998 stated that Leicester fans were twice as likely to be family members than average clubs and many of City's current fans fell in love with Leicester City through FNF.

The Carling Stand was sold out for most reserve matches during the nineties.

Chapter seven - Rubbing shoulders with the rich and famous

On the pitch - season 1994/95

The summer of 1994 was full of excitement for Foxes' fans as they counted down the days to the start of the new season. It had been seven years since Leicester's last top-flight game and a lot had changed.

Inspired by American sports, Premier League players were allocated a squad number and displayed their names on the back of their shirts, in contrast to the traditional one to eleven that City fans had been used to. The half time interval was increased from ten minutes to fifteen and teams were allowed to name a goalkeeper as a third substitute. The biggest change was that, for one season only, four teams would be relegated instead of the usual three as the Premier League looked to reduce the number of top-flight teams from twenty-two to twenty.

The enormity of the challenge was clear to all. You only had to look at how the previous seasons play-off winners had fared. Swindon Town had narrowly pipped City to promotion in 1993, but struggled in their solitary Premier League season. It took them sixteen matches to record their first win and they conceded five or more goals in six matches, including a 7-1 defeat away at Newcastle. It was no surprise that Swindon finished bottom of the table, conceding 100 goals in the process which is still a record today.

Brian Little had been prolific in the transfer market during his first three seasons, but added just two players to the first team roster during pre-season. Brian provides the rationale for this decision. "I always worked to budgets which were connected to the commercial profits. I never pushed to have more than was offered. At the start of each season, I'd speak to the Chairman and ask, 'How much do I have and what do you expect me to do?' The three Wembley trips, promotion and the money that Barrie brought in, meant that I had a bit more to spend in the Premier League. I felt we had a good squad with enough quality to stay up and I only really wanted players who would add more quality."

First came Nicky Mohan, a central defender, who joined from Middlesbrough for £300,000. Little's second signing, Mark

Draper, had the distinction of becoming Leicester's first million-pound man when he joined from Midlands' rivals, Notts County, for a club record of £1,250,000, dwarfing the £360,000 City had paid for Mark Blake the previous season.

Draper had been on Leicester's radar for a while as Little explains. "During my first season at the club, we played Notts County – who were then a First Division side – at Meadow Lane, in the Northern Semi-Final of the Zenith Data Systems Cup. I remember the match was played out in torrential rain and I could see our supporters standing in the open terraces getting absolutely drenched,. To show solidarity with our fans, I moved our benches out of the dugout so the subs, coaching staff and I could sit in the wet too – I wasn't very popular for that decision as you can imagine!

Anyway, we won the game 2-1 thanks to an extra-time winner by Paul Fitzpatrick, so it was worth getting soaked. Mark Draper was playing for County and he was fantastic. I knew that I would sign him one day, so I approached him after the game to shake his hand and say, 'Well played.' Nothing else, just that. But my aim was to plant a seed in his mind that I admired him as a player."

Draper recalls that moment and says that Little was a key factor in his decision to join City. "I'd experienced top-flight football with Notts County and was keen to push myself to get back there. When Leicester secured promotion, they, along with a few other clubs, made an offer. County wanted to keep me and while it was hard to leave – I'd been there since I was nine years old – I wanted to play Premier League football. As soon as I spoke to Brian, I knew that Leicester was the place for me. They were a real family club.

I remember Barrie welcoming me on my first day and he was friendly and helpful throughout my time at Filbert Street. Alan Birchenall was another character I got on well with.

Mark Draper became City's firs million pound signing in 1994

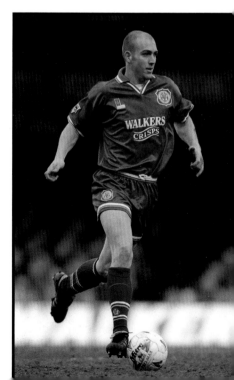

I met the lads at training and wanted to show them what I could do. I was a playmaker rather than tackler, but I knew that Leicester were a good, physical team, so I wanted to prove myself to them. During a practice match, Richard Smith had the ball and I went in over the top, absolutely smashing him. There was a gasp from my teammates, and when I looked up, I saw the shock on their faces. I found out that Rich was hard as nails when he got his own back the following day! They were a great bunch and I felt part of the group immediately.

Before the season began, I was asked to model the new Fox Leisure kit which was a bit of a laugh as I hadn't done any modelling before!

The tribunal set my fee at over a million pounds, so I did feel a bit of pressure, even more so when I missed a penalty on my debut against Newcastle United, live on Sky Sports!"

City's maiden Premier League campaign kicked off on a Sunday in front of millions of viewers around the world. Sporting a new Fox Leisure kit, Julian Joachim scored Leicester's first Premier League goal, but it was merely a consolation as Newcastle ran out 3-1 winners.

Richard Smith noticed the step up in class immediately. "Andy Cole and Peter Beardsley (who both scored that day) were the best players that I ever played against. In that first match, we played three centre backs and still couldn't get near Beardsley. It was a real baptism of fire."

In the following game, a 3-0 defeat to eventual champions, Blackburn, Steve Walsh suffered a knee injury that required surgery and restricted him to just five appearances for the season.

Gary Coatsworth was also out injured but remembers the good team spirit around Filbert Street. "We did a lot of team building activities and they were great fun and really brought us all together. I remember one round of golf where Gary Mills hit his shot, it took a ricochet off a tree, came back and whacked Millsy!

Mark Draper was a character. Mark had a car that auto locked, but he forgot once when he ran into a shop. The car locked and he'd left his keys inside so had to call someone to unlock it for him!"

Leicester picked up their first point in a 1-1 draw at home to QPR at the end of August. Gary Mills' cross was headed home by Phil Gee. It was the final game that Mills played for the club as, after five and a half years as a Fox, he returned to former club Notts County. "I'd been the club captain for the past two seasons and thought that I would be leading the team out in the Premier League, but Steve Walsh was given the armband before one pre-season game. I was disappointed because nothing was said to me. I played in the QPR game but then I was told that I wasn't travelling to Wimbledon for the next match. I'm an honest bloke and felt that I'd done well at Leicester, so I approached Brian. He told me that I wasn't in his plans and, as I needed and wanted to play, I asked to leave. Looking back now, I still had a lot to offer the club, even if I wasn't playing, so I should have told him that I was sticking around. I didn't really want to leave, it was heart-breaking."

City recorded their first win with a 3-1 victory over a strong Spurs side featuring World Cup winner, Jurgen Klinsmann. Joachim bagged a brace, but these were the last goals that he scored that season as he succumbed to a foot injury that ruled him out for the bulk of the campaign. With both the captain and star striker sharing the treatment table, fans didn't think it could get much worse for the Foxes – but it did.

On 10th November 1994, Aston Villa lost 4-3 to Wimbledon and their manager, Ron Atkinson, was dismissed. Speculation was rife that the Villa Chairman, Doug Ellis, had made Brian Little his number one target. Two weeks later Little became the new manager of Aston Villa.

Mark McGhee was appointed Leicester City manager in December 1994.

It didn't take long for Leicester to appoint his replacement. Mark McGhee became Alex Ferguson's first signing at Aberdeen in 1979 before enjoying a successful playing career with Celtic, Newcastle and Hamburg. He then took the plunge into management with Reading. McGhee led them to the Second Division (third tier) Championship in the 1993/94 season and had taken them to second place in the First Division (second tier) by the time that Leicester came calling.

Despite the lure of the Premier League, it wasn't an easy decision for him to make as Mark explains. "I felt huge loyalty towards Reading and had a great relationship with their Chairman, John Madejski. Leicester City made a formal approach and John gave me permission to speak to them. My contract at Reading was minimal as it hadn't been reviewed since I became manager. I was hardly paid anything and, as I had done well at Elm Park, I was due a new contract. John warned me that Reading couldn't compete financially with Leicester, but my decision wasn't about money. I was torn between the excitement of the Premier League and the challenge of finishing my task of winning promotion with Reading.

However, after I met Martin George, I knew there and then that I wanted to join Leicester. When I told John that I wanted to leave he offered me a new deal, but I wanted to compete at the highest level. It was sad to leave Reading, but I still stand by my decision.

I had a firm belief that I could keep Leicester up, but I was aware that it was a monumental challenge. Before taking the job, I spoke to some of my confidantes – football people who I respect – and they were telling me it was an impossible task. Sir Alex Ferguson was concerned that relegation would affect my reputation, but my thinking was that if we went down, we would come straight back up with a stronger team and I would then have my own system and players in place.

I had played for some huge clubs and was used to working in top environments. I hadn't worked at a big club though and the facilities at Reading were very different to what I was used to. Elm Park was the one of the worst grounds in the country; we had scaffolding holding up the stand and the dressing rooms were like something from the Victorian era. We didn't even have a training ground – someone had to lend us a place to train.

It was completely different at Leicester. On the day that I signed, Colin Lee (my assistant) and Mike Hickman (my coach) were sitting in the Fosse restaurant saying, 'What a difference this is. This is the kind of place we want to be.'

The Board of Directors were incredibly supportive. I already had a great deal of respect for Martin George and knew that he would back me in the transfer market. Barrie was a brilliant ally and gave me so much support. Nothing was too much trouble for him. When I first met him, he told me that his job was to give the manager everything they needed to be a success.

When I arrived at Belvoir Drive the following day and took in the facilities, they made my mouth water. I met the players, but it was clear that there was a sinking mentality. With some key

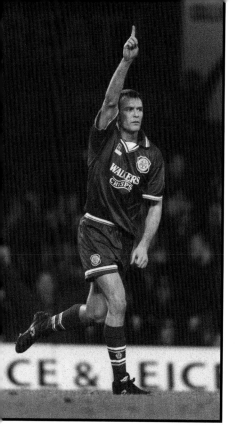

Mike Whitlow's goal gave City a point at Old Trafford.

players out injured, I don't think the overall quality was there. I liked my teams to play a fluid passing game, but some of the players couldn't play that way. I knew that some players would adapt and others couldn't. David Lowe is an example of one who did change. He had been swamped with the energy and power of the Premier League, but when we became a passing team, Lowe became a footballer."

City gained a valuable point in McGhee's first game in charge, away at Blackburn. A narrow defeat to Liverpool followed before a tough match at Old Trafford against the reigning Champions, Manchester United.

It was this game that gave Mike Whitlow his career highlight. "I'm proud of the career that I had. All I wanted to do was to put my kit on and play football. I won the League title with Leeds in 1992, won the League Cup with Leicester in 1997, played at Wembley several times and was voted – by Jay-Jay Okocha, Youri Djorkaeff and Ivan Campo, amongst others – as the Player's Player of the Year at Bolton. But the best moment of my career was undoubtedly scoring at the Stretford End, where I used to stand and watch United with my pals.

We were losing 1-0 when we won a corner. The cross came in, Gary Walsh made a hash of it and the ball fell kindly for me to stab home from all of three yards. Hardly a classic, but what a feeling. My mates were sitting behind the goal, supporting United and they weren't happy with me – especially as my goal meant that the game finished 1-1 and cost them a valuable two points. You won't be able to print what my friends said to me after the match!"

In January, City dipped into the transfer market to sign Jamie Lawrence and Mark Robins, with Mike Galloway and Garry Parker joining them in February. McGhee felt that these players could fit into his system.

For Lawrence it was a dream move. "I'd only been out of prison a few months when I signed for Sunderland who were managed by Terry Butcher. I played a few games and then Terry was sacked and replaced by Mick Buxton. Buxton sold me to Doncaster in League Two and it was a great move. I played regularly and loved it there. I'd been there for ten months and had heard rumours that other clubs were watching me. I was visiting friends and family in London when my agent rang and told me that Leicester wanted me. McGhee felt that I could bring the team some pace and power and I jumped at the chance. I'm so grateful to Leicester for taking a chance on me.

Jamie Lawrence made the unlikely journey from prison to the Premier League.

I thought Fox Leisure was a great idea. The quality of the kit was good and it didn't bother me that it wasn't a famous brand, afterall, I had been used to playing in prison stripes!

I made my debut at Selhurst Park in a defeat to Crystal Palace and we played Manchester City at Maine Road in my next game where I set up Mark Robins for the only goal of the game. People often ask me if I found the Premier League a big step up, but I didn't really. I don't fear the unknown and I take everything in my stride. I'd been through much worse, this was just football. I never cared who I played against; opponents are just opponents."

Leicester had been eliminated in the second round of the League Cup, but a favourable draw against non-league Enfield gave fans excitement of an FA Cup run. David Oldfield and Iwan Roberts bagged the goals in a comfortable 2-0 victory.

Colin Hill played in that match and recalls a story from after the game. "The Enfield game is a great example of Barrie's generosity. After the game, it was customary for the players to have a drink in the player's lounge. When I arrived, I saw the Enfield lads standing outside because they didn't have the right tickets and hadn't been let in. I went to see Barrie and explained the situation. He found a room for them and looked after them for the rest of the night. They were in there for hours, enjoying free hospitality. That really sums Barrie up. Bob Dowie, brother of my Northern Ireland teammate Iain, was at Enfield at the time and he still recalls that whenever Leicester comes up in conversation."

While there were some encouraging performances, results were not good enough and by March, relegation was on the horizon, so McGhee decided to hand a debut to a seventeen-year-old by the name of Emile Heskey.

McGhee had no doubt that Heskey would become a star. "From the first moment I saw Emile kick a ball I knew he would become a great player. He was an incredible athlete; his attitude was first-class and he had a strong family network supporting him. In our youth team, he did everything – corners, free kicks and penalties. I enjoyed watching his career flourish."

Gary Coatsworth remembers that Heskey made an impression on him when he was still a youth team player. "I remember Heskey training with the first team when he was just fifteen. You could tell he was going places. He had confidence in his ability, but was also so strong, even at that age he was able to hold off grown men."

"I had been around the first team squad for a while and was expecting to eventually make my debut, although I didn't think it would be so soon," recalls Heskey. "I travelled with the squad to QPR and some players fell ill the night before the match. I was the only fit striker and I got an opportunity to play. The game didn't go too well for us – we lost 2-0 – but I did ok.

The players were great and helped to put me at ease. I felt like I belonged at this level, it was just a case of becoming more comfortable in the first team environment."

Sam McMahon also made his debut under McGhee. Sam remembers it vividly. "While the FNF games gave me the experience of playing in front of a big crowd with, and against, some top players, nothing can prepare you for playing in the Premier League. My debut against Wimbledon was a nothing game really as we had already been relegated, but I still felt incredibly nervous when I came on for the last half an hour. I did ok and remained a part of the squad for the next four seasons."

Mark Draper had been outstanding for Leicester all season and his performances hadn't gone unnoticed by England manager, Terry Venables, who named him in the England setup for a three-day get-together in April 1995. This was the first of several England call-ups for City's record signing. He didn't play but he still learnt a lot from the experience. "It was a huge honour when Venables brought me into the three lions' squad and a great opportunity to train alongside some of the best players in the country. Competition was fierce as I had the likes of Gazza, David Platt, Paul Ince, and Matt Le Tissier ahead of me. After Terry had been replaced by Glenn Hoddle, I remained in the squad, but by this time Paul Scholes and David Beckham had emerged. I was a substitute when Beckham made his debut against Moldova but, unfortunately, I didn't get on. I'm still proud of the achievement."

Relegation was confirmed in April. Leicester City would be playing second tier football again. The players had learnt some valuable lessons as Lee Philpott explains. "As a young player, I wanted to play at the highest level and I achieved that. That Premier League season was an amazing experience. The quality of opposition was far superior to what we were used to. We probably needed one or two players with top-flight experience.

In some ways I found it easier because the opponents showed more respect and gave me more time on the ball, but we were defending a lot, so my role became a defensive job, which didn't really suit me as my strengths were attacking."

Colin Hill was blunt with his assessment of the season. "The biggest difference is that Premier League players will punish you. In the Championship, if you can restrict your opponents to three chances, you'll probably keep a clean sheet. If you give the top strikers – Alan Shearer, Andy Cole, Robbie Fowler and others – three chances, they will likely score two. Sadly, we lacked in both areas of the pitch."

Record signing, Mark Draper, was disappointed that the season ended in relegation. "It was devastating to be relegated. I truly believe that we would have survived had Joachim and Walsh stayed fit. Squads weren't as big in those days so any club would have found it tough losing two of their best players. I would have stayed if City had stayed up, but I felt I belonged in the Premier League. I was on the cusp of the England squad and knew that I needed to remain a top flight player. When Brian came back for me, I had no hesitation in joining him at Aston Villa. It was sad to leave Filbert Street, but the £3,250,000 that Villa paid for me meant that Leicester made a decent profit. I've returned to Leicester as a guest several times and I am always treated well by the fans and staff. It's still a real family club."

The loss of Draper was a blow, but the City faithful were confident that there was enough quality in the squad to mount another successful promotion bid.

Behind the scenes

Premier League football gave fans the opportunity to see the most famous players live at Filbert Street. As a board member, I was fortunate to make the acquaintance of a number of famous celebrities over the years.

In 1991 we celebrated 100 years at Filbert Street. While we were laying the foundations for an exciting future, it was important to remember our roots and pay homage to our rich heritage, so I helped put together a variety of events that would be the envy of even the most active socialite.

The first event was a grand gala ball that we held at the Grand Hotel in Leicester in November 1991. This was a fundraising event and an opportunity for us to introduce Leicester City to a new audience. I wanted everything that my team and I did to be top quality and this event was no exception. In attendance were the first team squad and a who's who of Leicester City legends, including Gary Lineker, Arthur Rowley, Frank Worthington, Alan Birchenall, Davie Gibson, Gary McAllister and Charlie Adam.

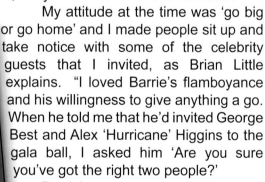

My attitude at the time was 'go big or go home' and I made people sit up and take notice with some of the celebrity guests that I invited, as Brian Little explains. "I loved Barrie's flamboyance and his willingness to give anything a go. When he told me that he'd invited George Best and Alex 'Hurricane' Higgins to the gala ball, I asked him 'Are you sure you've got the right two people?'

Barrie's response was, 'Let's just try it.' I loved his innocence in that respect because he wasn't inhibited by anyone and I liked that he was a risk taker like me. I was personally delighted that George Best attended because he was my hero when I was starting out in my playing career."

Alex Higgins had courted controversy during his successful snooker career, but he was a big draw for us. He was friendly and well behaved during the ball before getting himself arrested at 2:45 for fighting a fellow hotel guest!

That aside, the event was a huge success, raising money and the club's profile and a good time was had by all. I certainly wasn't the only one adding signatures to autograph collections!

The climax to our centenary celebrations was a Festival of Football day held at Filbert Street at the end of the 1991/92 season.

Not quite the headline that we wanted!

We wanted the festival to be inclusive, so we included events for all. We commenced the festivities with our youth team taking on a group of supporters in a penalty shootout, before we hosted the first Leicester City ladies match held at Filbert Street when they competed against TNT of Quorn.

Next up was Brian Little's first team v Frank Worthington's International X1, including Paul Gascoigne, Gary Lineker, Mark Hughes, Glenn Hoddle and Ally McCoist. Gazza was the hottest property in world football at that time.

As if that wasn't enough, the main event and a real treat for Foxes' fans, Alan Birchenall's 1970's All Stars, featuring Keith Weller, Mike Stringfellow, David Nish and Lenny Glover took on Nottingham Forest's 1979 European Cup Winners including Peter Shilton, Viv Anderson and future Leicester coach John Robertson. The 'Birch' summed it up in his programme notes when he wrote, "You will never get another chance to see as many stars on display at the same time in the same place again."

And the following week, we hosted Stuart Hall's 'It's a Knockout' where local businesses competed against each other. It was great fun and brought in a further £16,000. The event had been arranged months in advance and at the time, we didn't know that we'd make the play-off final. So, while hundreds of people were competing in all kinds of wacky team games inside the stadium, outside we had thousands queueing for tickets for Wembley!

My staff were an integral part of the club, but they didn't enjoy the celebrity status that the fans bestowed upon the players. This didn't mean that the supporters only chanted for players and managers, though, as Charles Rayner found out at one match. "Shortly after the 1992 play-off final defeat, the Chairman told me that we would be increasing season ticket prices by twenty percent. I argued that this would not be well received as we had lost, but I was told that fans would accept it as they could see that the club were progressing. The Chairman then asked me to announce the increase in my programme notes which I did. At the next home match, I was sitting in the Director's Box with my partner when she pointed to the kop and said, 'They are singing.'

I replied, "They sing at every game."

"But have you heard what they are singing?"

I then realised what they were singing, "Charles Rayner, what a wanker, what a wanker." On the plus side, at least it showed that they read my column in the programme!"

Another popular event we held was 'Little in the Middle' – an Executive Buffet that included a question and answer session with our manager, Brian Little. Customers really enjoyed it, so we started bringing in other icons of the sporting world to speak about their careers and lives. We attracted the biggest names too – Martin Peters, George Cohen, Bob Wilson and Will Carling were just some of the speakers.

These were typically great nights that were well attended and each event brought in around £4000 profit. One of our earliest dinners was hosted by the legendary George Best and his former Manchester United teammate, Denis Law. Best was still a big draw, despite finishing his career several years earlier. Both were on top form and the crowd loved it. I asked Richard Hughes to drive them to their hotel.

"I was incredibly nervous," recalls Richard. "Although I was too young to have seen them play, I knew that I was in the presence of football royalty. I felt a little nervous and was making small talk, while constantly keeping an eye on my speedometer to ensure that I was driving within the limits. The last thing I wanted was to have an accident with this pair in the car. As we approached the Holiday Inn in the centre of Leicester, Denis, in his distinctive Scottish accent, asked me, 'Does everyone in Leicester drive through red lights?' I had been so focussed on my speed and my celebrity passengers that I had failed to notice the traffic lights! Luckily, I delivered them to their hotel in one piece!"

A few years later we welcomed Best back to Filbert Street (in a taxi this time!) along with his long-term friend, and fellow former footballer, Rodney Marsh. However, this event was a disaster as the clearly intoxicated pair kept falling asleep – in front of 500 paying customers! On the rare occasions when they were awake, they were so incoherent that I had to ask them to leave. This left me with a dilemma as people had paid for entertainment.

I will always be grateful to our manager at the time, Mark McGhee, who stepped up to avert a disaster by taking to the stage and giving the audience a fascinating insight into his successful playing career with stories of Alex Ferguson, league titles and cup finals against teams like Real Madrid. We were paying Best and Marsh £1,000 each and their representative even had the audacity to phone me the following day to check that they were still getting their fees. Guess what – No!

Gary Lineker was coming to the end of his playing career when I joined Leicester and, although I don't think he knows, I helped him to become the face of Walkers Crisps. During a discussion with Martin Glenn, Chief Executive of PepsiCo who owned Walkers Crisps, he mentioned that he wanted a local angle to promote the Leicester-based crisp brand. I mentioned Gary and explained how his clean-cut image would be ideal for Walkers. Martin liked the idea, so I put him in touch with Gary's agent.

Gary helped us to launch one of our new Fox Leisure kits and he was later given the Freedom of the City in a lavish ceremony at the Town Hall. I was incredibly fortunate to be invited to the ceremony by the Lord Mayor of Leicester and we arranged to hold a black-tie reception for Gary at Filbert Street.

Leicester City's Promotions Manager, Trevor Dempsey – known as Jack by everyone at the club due to his surname – explains how he helped to organise the event. "It was customary for a former freeman to join the ceremony. Richard Attenborough attended and we made a donation to his charity. Willie Thorne and Gordon Banks were two other high-profile guests, along with Brian Little and the first team squad. In addition to the celebrities, there were around one hundred and fifty other guests and we knew that they would be expecting to hear some amusing anecdotes from our famous guests, so we invited the co-founder of satirical magazine Private Eye, Willie Rushton, knowing that he'd have a tale or two. Rushton was an actor and also a talented cartoonist, so I asked him to draw a portrait for Gary. Well, when a man has several Golden Boots and an FA Cup winners medal, it's difficult to find a suitable gift. Willie drew a picture of Gary in the various kits he wore during his playing career and included a packet of Walkers Crisps in a dubbing flavour!"

Lineker was one of two City legends who had suites named after them. The other was Gordon Banks who was a lovely, accommodating man and a real gentleman.

Trevor recalls filming a promotional video with Gordon. "Filming is an incredibly slow process. Everything has to follow a detailed storyboard. This particular TV director had an idea that Gordon would catch a football with the Leicester City logo facing the camera. Not as easy as it sounds. My job was to throw him the ball. After the fifth take I had a moment of realisation – I was throwing a football to one of the greatest goalkeepers that the world has ever seen! It took about ten takes but we got it right eventually."

Jack Charlton was another member of England's World Cup winning side who visited Filbert Street. Trevor was responsible for organising the event and looked after Charlton on the day. "Jack was a lovely man and he impressed me with his ability to multi-task. He was at Filbert Street to speak at a dinner. When he had finished his piece, I was thanking him for coming and, while he was listening to me, he was signing autographs for guests and also smiling for the photographers. It was incredible because we all felt like we had his full attention."

Jack's brother, Bobby – another World Cup winner – opened the Belvoir Suite in 1994 as Trevor explains. "The Belvoir Suite was the centre piece of our new Carling Stand and I was asked to find a legend to perform the opening ceremony. Bobby Charlton was one of the biggest stars about and I was delighted when he agreed to officially open the suite. It was a challenge to find a key date as he was heavily involved in Manchester's bid for the 2000 Summer Olympics, but he had a slot in his calendar and he agreed to come to Leicester.

I booked him a room at the Holiday Inn and, when I met him, I thanked him for his time. Bobby surprised me when he explained that he had fond memories of Leicester. 'When I was a young footballer, I remember coming to Leicester to play in youth matches. I used to catch the train from Manchester and then caught a double decker bus from the station to Filbert Street. I always enjoyed my trips to Leicester,' Bobby told me. He was a great guy and didn't even charge us a fee."

Kevin Keegan was really friendly when he visited Filbert Street for a Sportsman's Dinner.

Bobby was, of course, a legend of Manchester United who were managed by Sir Alex Ferguson at the time. I sat next to Sir Alex at the premiere of Batman Forever, which was screened at the newly opened cinema on the Meridian Leisure Park. He was friendly, but we didn't talk much as we were too engrossed in the movie.

One manager I did speak to a lot was Kevin Keegan. He hosted a Sportsman's Dinner when he was at the peak of his powers as Newcastle manager. He was very different to what I expected. He was really friendly and showed a lot of interest in what we were doing at the club. Considering that he was a high-profile manager, he was so relaxed and had time for everyone.

Sir Stanley Matthews was another gentleman whom we were fortunate enough to meet and Trevor remembers the respectful footballing legend. "He was a very humble man who was a big draw. We had queues of older fans waiting to meet the great man and all Stan kept saying to me was, 'Please look after my driver.' I treated him to some fish and chips."

Directors and chairmen of clubs frequently mixed together during the season. There were the matches, obviously, but also lots of events and meetings where our paths would cross. These could often produce comical moments.

I remember travelling to a Premier League meeting with the chairman and a fellow director. We were all standing on the platform at Leicester railway station when the chairman put his hand in his pocket, brought out his mobile phone, pressed a few buttons and held it up to his ear. When he didn't hear a dial tone, he looked at the phone and realised that it wasn't a phone at all. He'd picked up his television remote controller instead! 'Oh dear,' he said. 'I seem to have picked up my TV remote!'

One of the perks of the job was watching the matches from the director's seating areas at some of Europe's biggest clubs. Leicester City always laid on a good meal for visiting directors, but it wasn't always reciprocated. Hospitality at Manchester United and Chelsea was very poor in comparison to ours and other clubs, although I had a lot of time for the Chelsea owner, Ken Bates, who was funny and could be slightly sarcastic.

In contrast, Newcastle United looked after us very well and I enjoyed my chats with their Chairman, Sir John Hall and CEO, Freddy Shepard. Jack Walker, the owner of Blackburn, was great; very friendly, told everyone, 'Call me Jack,' and he was very easy to get along with.

I am sometimes asked how directors get on with each other, especially considering transfer and managerial disputes. For us it was just business and there were never any conflicts in the directors' seating area during match days. In fact, Doug Ellis (Aston Villa) and Sir Jack Haywood (Chairman of Wolves) were always incredibly friendly and welcoming – despite them pinching two of our managers between them!

There were also the regular Premier League meetings where I got to know the other club's owners, Chairmen and Chief Executives. Alan Sugar, Tottenham's Chairman, was very down to earth and always told it like it was. I liked him immediately. I remember him telling me how he sometimes felt that running a football club was like pouring money into a bottomless pit!

Lord Sugar, Martin Edwards (Chairman of Manchester United), Ken Bates (Owner of Chelsea) and David Dein (Vice Chairman of Arsenal) were the four main stalwarts of the Premier League meetings. They were the ones who did the bulk of the talking and there was always some good banter between them.

Lord Sugar now fronts the BBC's *The Apprentice* TV programme and takes advice from Karren Brady. Karren became the youngest Managing Director of a football club when she joined Birmingham City in 1993 and I invited her to Filbert Street to give an overview of what we were doing at Leicester City and how innovative we were being. I explained how we had successfully launched Fox Leisure and how Family Night Football had revolutionised reserve football. Karren was very feisty, professional and full of confidence. She had the full backing of the owners which gave her a free reign to transform Birmingham. I think she did a great job and, given her drive and contacts, I am not surprised by the success that she's had.

**I introduced Rustie to City fans before
some of our home games.**

Speaking of TV stars, Rustie Lee was a regular visitor to Filbert Street during the nineties. I used to watch her cookery show in the mornings. She was always giggling and so happy that it made me feel positive and put me in a good mood. When she attended one of our events, I got to meet her and realised that she was just the same in real life. So, I invited her back to the club to spread her infectious positivity to our customers, staff and players.

Rustie takes up the story. "I knew Emlyn Hughes (the former England Captain) through my television work and one day we were both invited to an event at Filbert Street. Barrie greeted us and I took to him immediately. He was welcoming and made me feel so comfortable that we became firm friends. He is such a lovely, kind-hearted man.

Barrie offered me a job, entertaining clients in the Belvoir Suite on matchdays. I loved it and had so much fun. My role was to tell jokes and make people laugh. I was also responsible for announcing the team line ups to the guests, although I did get it wrong once!

I remember the first time that I watched Leicester play. My partner and I took our seats in the Director's Box and I told him not to shout and cheer too much. However, when the game began, I found that it was me whooping and cheering for Leicester City. The Leicester supporters were so passionate and created a fantastic atmosphere. It got me into it and I became a City fan. Barrie was so hardworking and he did so much for Leicester City

Everything he did was to benefit the people of Leicester – the supporters, staff and players. Mind you, he knew how to have a laugh too. I remember us in the Boardroom at the end of one match. We had a few drinks and were dancing on the tables!"

Even the players loved Rustie as former captain, Gary Mills explains. "I'm not sure how it all came about but Rustie was really big at the time. She was a bubbly person and brought a lot of fun and energy to the club. It all helped to galvanise team spirit and make Filbert Street a happy place."

In the mid-nineties Beckham-mania was just beginning, but it was actually David Beckham's soon-to-be wife, Victoria, who was the most famous half of the couple when Manchester United visited Filbert Street for a game in 1996. After the game, a club official approached me. 'Excuse me. Is there a private room we could borrow please?' he asked.

'I'm sorry but all our rooms are fully occupied.' I explained. There was never an empty seat when United were in town.

'Is there anywhere? We'd like somewhere private where David and Victoria can meet,' he continued.

'OK,' I relented. 'My office is empty, so I'll open that.'

'Thank you,' replied the official who collected David and Victoria and followed me to my office. I unlocked the door and gave David the key.

'Please come and find me later to return the key,' I asked.

They entered my office, locked the door, shut the blinds and didn't appear again for a good forty minutes.

When they had finished using the room, they found me and returned the keys. Both shook my hand and thanked me for my help. They were a lovely, friendly and down to earth couple.

When I was tasked with raising the club's profile, I could never have dreamt that I would rub shoulders with royalty. But that's exactly what I did on several occasions, starting with Prince Charles's visit in 1991. I also met the Queen at Buckingham Palace, Princess Diana and Princess Anne at various functions while I was representing Leicester City.

In 1999 our community team were helping the city's Asian and Ugandan population and we invited the King and Queen of Buganda – a subnational kingdom within Uganda – to a tour of Filbert Street followed by Christmas Lunch in the Fosse restaurant. It is a good job that our conference, banqueting and catering operation was 'fit for a King' by then because it certainly wasn't when I first joined Leicester City!

Chapter eight - Maximising the stadium's facilities

On the pitch - season 1995/96 (part one)

The disappointment of relegation soon evaporated as Mark McGhee outlined his vision for the club with the catchy slogan 'The Future's Marked Out.' With a talented young manager and, arguably a stronger squad than two years previous, most fans were optimistic about the clubs' promotion chances. Even the bookies were backing City for an instant return.

As expected, there was quite a bit of transfer activity in the summer of 1995. Brian Little returned to Filbert Street to purchase Mark Draper for £3,250,000. Gavin Ward, Nicky Mohan, Ian Ormondroyd, David Oldfield and Steve Agnew also departed as McGhee made space in the squad for his own signings. Reading's Scott Taylor was reunited with his former boss when the midfielder became Leicester's first signing of the season. Australian duo, Steve Corica and Zeljko Kalac, were next in and they were joined by French defender Franck Rolling who was signed from Ayr.

Despite relegation, it wasn't hard to attract players or sponsorship as Director, John Sharp, explains. "We had been relegated from the Premiership back to the First Division and I remember Mark addressing a meeting of sponsors. He said that we had a team currently in the First Division, but we had a club of Premiership standard – paying tribute to Barrie Pierpoint and his work at developing an off-field performance equal to the best."

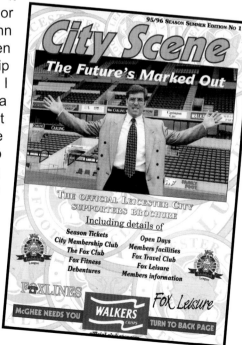

The campaign began with a 2-1 win away at eventual champions, Sunderland. A debut goal from Corica gave the Foxes the lead before Mark Robins wrapped up the points.

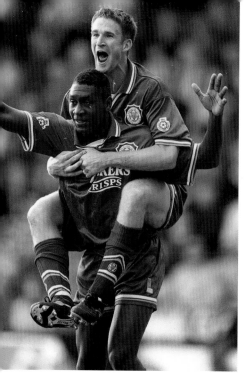

Emile Heskey celebrates his first senior goal with Simon Grayson.

After six games, fit again Julian Joachim scored the only goal of the game away at Derby which took City to the top of the table.

Leicester fans were enjoying the newly adopted passing style which was in complete contrast to the more direct style they had witnessed under Little. McGhee was also keen to give youth a chance. In September midfielder Sam McMahon scored the opening goal in a 2-0 win over Port Vale in only his second appearance and later that month, seventeen-year old Emile Heskey came off the bench to score his first senior career goal, which gave City a 1-0 win over Norwich.

In November 1995, Mark McGhee received a telephone call from Norwegian agent, Rune Hague, regarding the availability of his client, Pontus Kamark, a vastly experienced Swedish defender.

McGhee explains that Pontus was a player that he had admired for a while. "I'd seen Pontus Kamark play on TV and had always thought that he was a good player, so when I found out he was available, I asked Martin George if he wanted to jet out to Sweden to watch him play for IFK Goteborg. I didn't tell the Chairman who the agent was, though. Martin arranged for his driver to pick me up on the day of the game. We got halfway to Heathrow when I realised that I'd forgotten my passport, so we had to go back to my home collect it! Fortunately, we managed to arrive at the airport on time.

We arrived at the stadium and took our seats ready for the kick off. In those days, a lot of English teams would begin the game by knocking it back to the defender who would usually hump it forward. Goteborg kicked off and passed the ball back to the centre half who played it to Kamark who was playing a bit wider. Pontus played a first time pass round his opponent straight to the winger's feet. It had quality written all over it and after that one pass I turned to Mr George and said, 'Let's go. I've seen all I need.'

When we got back to England, we arranged to meet his agent in London to complete the deal. When Hague walked in Martin George's face hit the ground and he punched me in the shoulder!

Kamark was a tremendous signing for us. His preparation was second to none. As soon as training finished on a Friday, he was already preparing for the match. He was a true professional and had a positive impact on the youngsters like Emile Heskey."

Pontus Kamark remembers that he was delighted to join City. "I was ready for a new challenge in the 1995/96 season. I was part of the Sweden side that finished third at the 1994 World Cup, Goteborg were Champions of Sweden and I'd even scored in a 3-1 victory over Manchester United in the Champions League, so I felt that I had achieved all I could with Goteborg. I had offers from Leicester City and Sporting CP, but I wanted to come to England. Leicester was a fresh, friendly club and I enjoyed the style of play.

I almost came to the East Midlands a few years earlier following a trial with Nottingham Forest in 1989. Brian Clough wanted me to join but I chose Goteborg instead.
English football had a completely different culture to Sweden.

Two weeks after I joined, we were due to have a team night out. It was fancy dress, so I got myself a Viking costume because of my Scandinavian origin. The day before the event, I was told that we were meeting at eleven o'clock. 'Eleven?' I asked. 'Isn't that a bit late to be going out?'

The lads burst out laughing and replied, 'No, eleven in the morning!'

I'd never been on a night out that began in the morning before! It was good fun and at the end of the evening I knew everyone and felt a real part of the team."

Kamark made his debut in the televised match against West Bromwich Albion at The Hawthorns at the beginning of November. Also making his bow was goalkeeper, Zeljko Kalac. The Australian had cost Leicester £760,000 – at the time it was a record fee for an Australian – in the summer, but he'd had a long wait for his debut due to lengthy registration and work permit issues.

While fans instantly recognised Kamark's class, Kalac had a debut to forget. A brace from Scott Taylor and one from

David Lowe had given City a pretty comfortable lead before West Brom pulled two goals back and Leicester's new number one looked nervous.

The worst was yet to come, though, when Kalac made his home debut three days later in the League Cup third round reply against Bolton. City conceded the first goal. Kalac clumsily gifted the Wanderers a corner, which he then flapped at and John McGinley hooked into the open net.

Mark Robins equalised, finishing a fantastic, quick passing move that even Pep Guardiola would have been proud of. Bolton restored their lead when Kalac let a speculative twenty-yard effort by Richard Sneekes slip under his body.

Leicester fought back and levelled the score again thanks to a trademark Iwan Roberts' header. It was fully deserved and, if anything, City deserved to be in front. The deciding goal game from another corner, and another mistake from Kalac. The giant Aussie came out to claim the corner, missed the ball and Sasa Curcic smashed home. Leicester were out of the Cup but there was much worse news after the game as Pontus Kamark had damaged his cruciate ligament and would be out for a year. To be fair to Kalac, he took responsibility for all three goals, but it was no surprise when Kevin Poole retained his place in the first team for the next match. Poole remained the number one for the rest of the season and Kalac never touched the ball for Leicester again, though he did go into City folklore later in the season, but more on that later.

Kalac eventually won the Champions League while playing for Italian giants, Milan. It was a shock to Foxes fans, but not McGhee. "It didn't surprise me that Kalac hit those heights later on in his career. What really surprised me was that he didn't make it at Leicester. I had brought a young Shaka Hislop to England from Trinidad while I was at Reading. After an uncertain start, he became an incredible 'keeper and went on to play in the World Cup. I thought that I could do the same with Zeljko. The problem was that he struggled with confidence. If I had stayed at Leicester for longer, he'd have had more opportunities and I'm sure he'd have come good."

As December began, the Foxes occupied second place and it appeared that nothing could derail City's promotion train. But then on 13th December 1995, Mark McGhee dropped a huge bombshell when he resigned as Leicester manager after just twelve months in charge to replace Graham Taylor at Division

One foes Wolverhampton Wanderers. City fans were devastated; for the second successive year, their manager had walked out to join a rival.

McGhee explains why he decided to leave the Foxes. "The brand of football that I created at Leicester is a great memory and something I am proud of. It was the style of football that my teams played that had attracted Wolves. When I was at Reading, we went to Molineux and totally dominated them. After the match I was in a lift and Sir Jack Hayward, the Wolves Chairman, walked in. He asked me if my teams always played like that and I replied that they did. That stuck with him, so when he needed a manager, he made an approach for me.

I wanted to speak to Wolves, and when I did, they told me that they would build a new training ground and they asked me who I wanted to sign. I replied, 'Paul Ince, but he'd cost around £8,000,000.' They said, 'No problem,' which was music to my ears. That sort of money wasn't available to me at Leicester.

I spoke to Sir Alex Ferguson and he felt that Wolves were a bigger club than Leicester and that they would be a good stepping stone to where I wanted to get to. There were lots of things going for Wolves and once I had decided to go, there was nothing that anyone at Leicester could have done to persuade me to stay.

I enjoyed my time at Wolves and don't regret the decision as far as the football is concerned, but it doesn't sit well with me that I walked out on Leicester in the way that I did. The Directors, Martin George and Barrie had given me so much support and were desperately trying to keep me. To be honest, once I had told them that I was going, they should have booted me out of the door, but they didn't. It really wasn't fair on Martin George as my departure meant that he had lost two managers and it didn't reflect well on him with the supporters.

When you leave a football club, you become ostracised and it is difficult to keep in touch with the people that you have worked with. But I have often told people along the way about Barrie; what a brilliant ally he was to me and how much support he had given me. He kept away from the football side, but where he had a huge impact was in creating, and maintaining, a great atmosphere around the football club. He inspired positivity, always had a smile on his face and he had so much energy. Whenever my friends came to watch us play, they would always remark on what a friendly club Leicester were. Barrie went out of his way to help people and to make them feel welcome.

There are two stories that really sum up Barrie's generosity. I once asked him if he could get me a kit for a friend of mine in Glasgow. 'Of course, what age do you need?' He replied.

'Eleven please.'

'Leave it with me,' he said.

Three days later I walked into my office and there was a complete set of kits: sixteen shirts, sixteen shorts and sixteen pairs of socks. I rang Barrie. 'Barrie, what's all this kit? I only needed one for my friend's son.'

'Oh, I thought you needed a kit for a whole team,' replied Barrie. 'You might as well keep it and give it to a team,' he added. I gave it to a youth team in East Kilbride who were delighted.

Another example was just before I left Leicester. England had been drawn against Scotland in Euro 96 and I had been asked to play a senior's match at Wembley before the main event. Even though the game was months away, I was inundated with phone calls from people who wanted me to get them tickets, including my former teammates, Gordon Strachan, Alex McLeish, as well as other friends and family. I told Barrie that I was trying to get 52 tickets. Not a problem, I was told, and he got me all the tickets I needed. I paid for them, obviously. Nothing was ever too much trouble for him."

I had a good relationship with Mark. He had saved the day at the infamous Best/Marsh sporting dinner and I was saddened when I heard that he was leaving us. I was enjoying a winter break in Majorca at the time when I received a phone call from McGhee who told me he wanted to join Wolves. I ended my holiday early, flew back to the chilly East Midlands to help negotiate his exit. While I didn't want him to go, when someone has made their mind up to leave you just need to move on. We agreed a deal that was fair to all parties and then we turned our focus to filling the vacant manager's post.

Up next for Leicester, in just four days, was the visit of Norwich in a match that had been selected for television.

**The lure of Molineux
proved too strong
for McGhee.**

Behind the scenes

On match days Filbert Street came alive as thousands of Foxes flocked to see the boys in blue. The streets bustled with excitement, merchandise was flying off the shelves in the club shop and hungry fans were feasting on the delicious food served in the concourse kiosks. Inside the stadium the boisterous Blue Army cheered on their heroes. There was no better place to be.

The rest of the week, though, the ground was a like ghost town – and ghosts don't spend money!

My team and I had been working tirelessly and had produced some fantastic results; a beautiful new stand, a new brand, twelve additional match days thanks to Family Night Football and we were also enjoying a better standing in the community. Our off-field revenues meant that we could reciprocate our fan's loyalty by giving them something back.

I recommended to the Board of Directors not to increase the price of season tickets following relegation. With two additional home games this was in real-terms a reduction of 7% which meant Season Ticket holders were forking out just £10 a game. To further support our loyal fans, we also negotiated some special offers for them including free mobile phones, discounted holidays and various money saving vouchers.

Even with a healthier bank balance we couldn't afford to rest on our laurels. The Carling Stand would be a colossal waste of money if we didn't exploit and fully utilise the world-class facilities within it.

Like most football clubs during the nineties, the majority of Leicester's turnover was generated on match days and, even accounting for cup runs, we only had around twenty of those each season. So, after three years of convincing people to open our stadium all week, I turned my attention to diversifying the club's off-field activities so that Leicester City could finally become a seven day a week profitable business.

I decided to focus on our conference and banqueting operation which was very much still in the Dark Ages. Before the Carling Stand, we were a football club with a restaurant, but in order to grow, we had to sell the restaurant on its own merits and appeal to non-football fans too. Our match day catering had been outsourced for years, with Leicester City receiving an annual fee of £20,000. We didn't have control over the quality of the food or staff and this was evident with the quality of our match day catering offering around the stadium.

The exception was the main restaurant, the Captain's Table, which was renowned for the quality and quantity of food. The idea was to serve decent comfort food and pile it high. The menu included favourites like steak and kidney pie or sausage and mash, followed by stodgy desserts such as bread and butter pudding and jam roly poly. I ate there a lot, entertaining potential new sponsors and investors, while raising money for the Carling Stand and the portions were so big that I didn't need any dinner most nights!

When I arrived in 1991, the food served in our hospitality areas was pretty basic and the service was poor. It was buffet-style food with curled up, stale sandwiches and a great big cauldron of gruel that was slopped on to plates. It wasn't a very relaxed atmosphere and people weren't encouraged to stay and have a few drinks; staff were cleaning up while customers were still eating – it was like we were trying to get rid of them!

Richard Hughes came from a hospitality and catering background and he brought in some immediate changes; simple things like using tablecloths and producing more appealing, fresher food. We needed to completely transform our operation and become more appealing for customers and we needed to take total control, so we replicated the Fox Leisure model and brought all our catering in house.

There was talent in the ranks in Alex Irving who I promoted to be the new Conference and Banqueting Manager and his first task was to recruit our own catering staff. This led to the creation of jobs in the city as he increased the number of both full and part time staff.

To ensure our conference and banqueting team were the best in the trade, we delivered high quality training and we ensured that everyone knew their role. We worked with Loughborough and Leicester Colleges to provide work experience for their catering students. We recruited some very enthusiastic chefs who gained hands-on experience of working in a busy kitchen. We produced training manuals to assist them and to ensure consistency and we won food hygiene and safety awards. Some students even joined us full time when they graduated. Alex and I completely overhauled our food and beverage offering and set our sights on becoming one of the best catering operations in the Midlands.

Alex retains fond memories of his time at Filbert Street.

"Barrie would call me into his office, tell me what he wanted me to achieve and then cut me loose like setting a dog off its leash. He gave me so much freedom because he trusted me. I earned a new nickname 'Sorted' from Barrie....he would give me direction or set me a project and that was always my response.

Barrie encouraged me and always demanded more and, as a result, I became the first Chairman of the Football Catering Association. In fact, he was the most inspirational boss, and friend, that I have ever had the pleasure of working for. He taught me so much about business and I would not be where I am today had it not been for him. It wasn't all plain sailing though.

I remember we hosted a boxing event one evening in the Belvoir Suite. The sales guys had done their jobs and the room was packed. The drinks were flowing, and everyone was having a great time, but then the fights began – and, no, I don't mean in the ring!

Two rival double-glazing firms got into a huge brawl; chairs were being thrown, things were being knocked over – it was mayhem. It didn't take long for the police to arrive. I remember one officer in khakis who was dragging people out of the suite and chucking them down to the officers outside who put them into the police vans and carted them away. While this was going on, we pulled the shutters down on the bar and kept the staff – and glassware – away from the action.

We always put the staff first and treated them well. We were like a family really. I am still in touch with dozens of former colleagues, many of whom wish we could do it all over again."

Alex was supported by a fantastic team and while there isn't space to name all the hundreds of people who worked in our catering, conference and banqueting department, I would like to mention some of the key players.

Amanda Williamson who had a hotel sales background and was involved with developing new business in the operation.

Margaret Marshall was the Hospitality Supervisor. On a matchday, Margaret and her teams looked after our customers in the Executive Boxes and, during the week, she supported our corporate clients ensuring all their rooms and catering was ready and served on time.

Suzanne Preston was the Conference and Banqueting Coordinator, she was responsible for the administrative side and ensured that all bookings ran like clockwork with the appropriate staffing.

Two young rising stars, off the field, were promoted from within the Club; Neil McGowan became the manager of Fox Fast Foods and Mark Humphries managed all the bars within Filbert Street and they successfully ran busy operations.

Another member of our team was a French Maitre d', Yann Floch, he was very good at his job, but we did have one very amusing complaint. One afternoon Michelle Newman, my PA, took a call from a disgruntled customer who wanted to speak to the Chief Executive. I received lots of phone calls and letters and one of Michelle's primary duties was filtering through the correspondence, so that I only received what was appropriate to me. She was very good at this so when she told me that I needed to take this call I had no hesitation.

'Is that the Chief Executive?' the customer asked.

'Yes, Barrie Pierpoint here. How can I help you?'

'I wish to make a formal complaint about the staff in your restaurant. I phoned to make a reservation and was told that I couldn't because there had been a F' up. I want an apology from you and from the member of staff,' the customer demanded.

'I apologise. Please leave it with me. I will look into it and get back to you,' I replied, making a note of their phone number. I couldn't believe that our Maitre d' would swear at a customer, but I had to investigate.

'Hello Yann. A customer has complained that you swore at them. Do you know what happened?' I asked when I tracked him down.

'I didn't swear, Mr Pierpont,' Yann explained. 'A customer phoned to book a table for Wednesday evening, but I told them it is not possible because of the FA Cup,' he said, though with his French accent it sounded like, 'It is not possible because of zee fack up!'

We rebranded the food kiosks in the stands and named them 'Fox Fast Food' and, again, bought the operation in-house.

Alex recalls another terrifying moment. "We had our own branding on our packaging from bags to burger boxes – it really was something to be proud of. Then Barrie had us buy our own mobile catering trailers so that we could enhance our external fast food offering. It was visionary and they were highly successful.

However, I did receive a visit from one of the local 'Burger Boys' in the mobile market to warn me of the consequences of stepping on the wrong patch. He showed me his photos of burnt out trailers! It was quite scary to be honest."

Our new head chef, Barrie Roberts, revamped the menu in the Fosse Restaurant.

The biggest change was in the Fosse Restaurant, which had replaced the Captain's Table within the building of the Carling Stand. We brought in a proven, top-class chef, Barrie Roberts, who was a fantastic and passionate culinary wizard. He headed up all the food preparation team areas and was responsible for creating up to a thousand meals each matchday. People loved his food. He increased the opening times and provided a fine dining experience for the corporate fans who wanted to enhance their match-day experience and for people who just wanted to enjoy a mouth-watering meal.

The players enjoyed Barrie Roberts' culinary creations as Colin Hill recalls. "Barrie was very pro the players. When the Fosse restaurant was built, he often invited the players to dine there and enjoy a spectacular meal. He ran Leicester City as a business, but also respected what happened on the pitch. Happy players and happy club was his goal."

We catered to local businesses during the week at breakfast and lunchtime and couples and families in the evenings and weekends. In our off-peak periods we ran two-for-one promotions which ensured that the eighty-seater restaurant was almost always fully booked during the typically quieter months of July and August. On Sundays Filbert Fox made an appearance in the restaurant to say 'Hi' to the kids and we hosted the Sunday lunch club in the Belvoir Suite which was for members of the Filbert Fox club and families.

There were facilities to house up to four hundred people,

people, so we established a conferencing department to cater for corporate clients who wanted somewhere to host meetings or training events during the week. The same rooms were altered for the weekend where we held parties and wedding receptions. My innovative staff came up with the idea of providing the full wedding service, so that we evolved from merely providing a venue for the happy couple and their guests, to offering a full service, including wedding planning, hosting the ceremony and taking photos of the newly-weds on the pitch.

We were especially popular at Christmas time as local companies booked us to celebrate their festive parties. While we always maintained a five-star service, our customers occasionally displayed one-star behaviour . . .

It was a novelty for fans to be inside the football ground and many fans took the opportunity to explore. One evening the Chairman had forgotten to lock the door to his office. The security staff should have checked, but they didn't. The following Monday morning, I was sitting in my office preparing for the busy week ahead when I received a phone call from the Chairman who yelled, 'Pierpoint, get up here now.' I walked into his office and he beckoned me over to his desk and opened his draw.

'What do you call this?' he asked, starring at a long, brown, sausage-like shape sitting on top of his papers.

Our Filbert Street wedding package was very popular.

'It looks like shit to me, Mr Chairman,' I replied straight faced.
'How did it get in here?'

'I'm not sure, Mr Chairman. We had a Christmas party here on Saturday night. Did you lock your door?' I replied and I also noticed that someone had drawn a moustache and horns on his photo on the wall.

'Get it out of here,' I was instructed. 'And what have they done to my face?' he asked, finally noticing the vandalism to his portrait.

I arranged for the excrement to be cleared up and thereafter ensured the Chairman's door was always kept locked.

Most of our customers were well behaved though and in time, we created one of the best banqueting and conference set ups in England. On match days we were able to cater for a thousand corporate customers, providing three course meals with food of the highest quality – our customers told us that it was the best in UK football.

Saturdays remained our busiest day, but we mastered the art of a quick turnaround so that we could entertain the corporate match-day clients during the day and by 18:30 the suites would be cleaned, reset and ready to go for other functions, such as business events and wedding receptions. We operated seven days a week from 06:30 am until 02:00 the following morning, hosting breakfast meetings, networking, functions and corporate events. We sweated our assets to maximise profitability.

Our innovative thinking created an opportunity to introduce our weekday clients to a live match experience. There were often one to two hundred people attending a conference during the day. I recognised that many conferences were a hard slog, so on match days, we put on a continuation package which included an evening meal and tickets to the match. So, instead of attendees returning home at 17:00 after the conference, they would stay and enjoy a game. It was a big hit and resulted in a number of our corporate clients becoming Leicester City fans.

As word of mouth spread, we found huge multi-nationals were taking advantage of our wonderful facilities. Companies such as BP, Barclays Bank and PepsiCo enjoyed our hospitality and then enquired about sponsorship deals. It proved very lucrative.

The Fosse Restaurant offered stunning views of Filbert Street. Mind you, there was one occasion where the customers would have preferred not to have chosen a table with a view of the pitch.

The problem with football stadiums is that they are open which means that birds can nest in the alcoves at the top of the stands. We had a problem with pigeons who were dropping their white mess on to the seats and into the concourse. This represented a huge health and safety risk to the public who attended matches, so we were granted a license to employ an authorised person to cull the pigeons. We were practically a 24-hour a day operation – especially in our restaurant – so we explicitly told pest control to be discreet. 'No problem,' we were told.

So, one Sunday evening, we were hosting a family celebration in the Fosse restaurant, while a marksman was ridding the stadium of our pest problem. Apart from a bang every now and then, you wouldn't have known he was there – until one pigeon decided not to go quietly. There was a loud boom, but instead of it dropping to the floor, the pigeon flew out of the Double Decker, bounced onto the pitch and continued its death roll until it smacked against the restaurant window, smearing blood on the glass as it slid onto the ground beside the pitch. Needless to say, we gave that poor family a free meal by way of apology.

That incident aside, we became so successful that I had some very unhappy hotel managers calling me as their customers had defected to us. Our clients had a unique experience when dining with us; tremendous views of the lush, green, hallowed turf, a chance of bumping into one of the players and when you factor in the fact that we were charging slightly less than hotels, but providing better quality food and facilities, it's no wonder that we became the number one hospitality, conference and banqueting venue in Leicestershire.

The Fosse Restaurant gave diners spectacular views of the hallowed Filbert Street pitch.

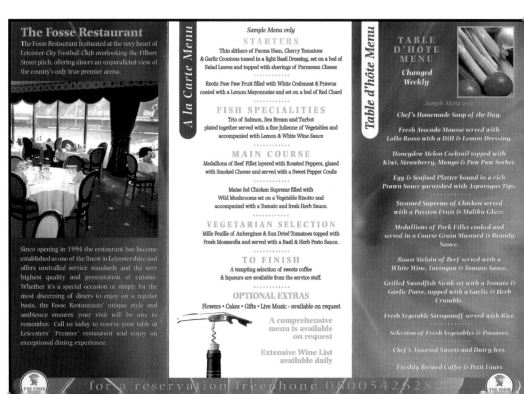

The Fosse Restaurant

The Fosse Restaurant is situated at the very heart of Leicester City Football Club overlooking the Filbert Street pitch, offering diners an unparalleled view of the county's only true premier arena.

Since opening in 1994 the restaurant has become established as one of the finest in Leicestershire and offers unrivalled service standards and the very highest quality and presentation of cuisine. Whether it's a special occasion or simply for the most discerning of diners to enjoy on a regular basis, the Fosse Restaurants' unique style and ambience ensures your visit will be one to remember. Call us today to reserve your table at Leicesters' 'Premier' restaurant and enjoy an exceptional dining experience.

A la Carte Menu

Sample Menu only

STARTERS

Thin slithers of Parma Ham, Cherry Tomatoes & Garlic Croutons tossed in a light Basil Dressing, set on a bed of Salad Leaves and topped with shavings of Parmesan Cheese

Exotic Paw Paw Fruit filled with White Crabmeat & Prawns coated with a Lemon Mayonnaise and set on a bed of Red Chard

FISH SPECIALITIES

Trio of Salmon, Sea Bream and Turbot plated together served with a fine Julienne of Vegetables and accompanied with Lemon & White Wine Sauce

MAIN COURSE

Medallions of Beef Fillet layered with Roasted Peppers, glazed with Smoked Cheese and served with a Sweet Pepper Coulis

Maize fed Chicken Supreme filled with Wild Mushrooms set on a Vegetable Risotto and accompanied with a Tomato and fresh Herb Sauce.

VEGETARIAN SELECTION

Mille Feuille of Aubergines & Sun Dried Tomatoes topped with Fresh Mozzarella and served with a Basil & Herb Pesto Sauce.

TO FINISH

A tempting selection of sweets coffee & liqueurs are available from the service staff.

OPTIONAL EXTRAS

Flowers • Cakes • Gifts • Live Music - available on request

A comprehensive menu is available on request

Extensive Wine List available daily

Table d'hôte Menu

TABLE D'HOTE MENU

Changed Weekly

Sample Menu only

Chef's Homemade Soup of the Day.

Fresh Avocado Mousse served with Lollo Rosso with a Dill & Lemon Dressing.

Honeydew Melon Cocktail topped with Kiwi, Strawberry, Mango & Paw Paw Sorbet.

Egg & Seafood Platter bound in a rich Prawn Sauce garnished with Asparagus Tips.

Steamed Supreme of Chicken served with a Passion Fruit & Malibu Glaze.

Medallions of Pork Fillet cooked and served in a Course Grain Mustard & Brandy Sauce.

Roast Sirloin of Beef served with a White Wine, Tarragon & Tomato Sauce.

Grilled Swordfish Steak set with a Tomato & Garlic Puree, topped with a Garlic & Herb Crumble.

Fresh Vegetable Stroganoff served with Rice.

Selection of Fresh Vegetables & Potatoes.

Chef's Assorted Sweets and Dairy Ices.

Freshly Brewed Coffee & Petit Fours

THE FOSSE RESTAURANT   for a reservation freephone 08005426282   THE FOSSE RESTAURANT

Chapter nine - Diversifying Leicester City's business operation

On the pitch - season 1995/96 (part two)

Leicester were without a win in five at the time of Mark McGhee's departure and the Directors knew that they had to act fast to appoint a new manager who was capable of getting City's promotion bid back on track. Former Everton and Norwich manager, Mike Walker, was identified as the number one target and he was in advanced talks with Leicester by the time Norwich City came to town on 17th December 1995. Walker was attending the match as a television pundit and was widely expected to be named as the Foxes' new manager.

You just couldn't make up what happened next! Norwich's manager, Martin O'Neill, resigned just hours before the Canaries' game against Leicester after a rumoured falling out with the Canaries' Chairman, Robert Chase. Martin George had been a long-time admirer of O'Neill and he made an approach to Norwich and suddenly Martin O'Neill was Leicester's new manager.

Cliff Ginnetta was one of the many fans left surprised that it was not going to be Mike Walker's name written on the door to the manager's office. "Before the game against Norwich we were hosting a children's birthday party in the Supporters' Club when in walked one of our Directors alongside Mike Walker. Walker was introduced to us as our next manager but, at the last minute, Martin George changed his mind and appointed Martin O'Neill instead! It proved to be an excellent decision, but it also highlights how conflicted things were in the boardroom at that time."

The Norwich game is also remembered as the day that Emile Heskey came of age. He was outstanding in a 3-2 victory and deservedly bagged the winner.

O'Neill's football philosophy was the polar opposite to his predecessor and it took the players some time to adjust to a third manager in just over one year.

Colin Hill describes the fickle nature of football. "Football is a very strange game and things change very quickly. Having been a regular for two seasons, I found myself out of the side after the second game of the 1994/95 season. Then Mark McGhee came in and I was not only back in the team, but I was made captain! I loved it. I was playing as the spare centre back and getting lots of the ball which really suited me. Then Martin came in and he wanted bigger centre halves. He told me I'd be in until he could replace me. So, in twelve months I'd gone from reserve to captain to sub. I was still playing internationally at that stage too."

While the team were adapting to their new manager, there was the small matter of the annual Christmas party. The players kitted themselves out in fancy dress and the club's official photographer saw it as a good photo opportunity. It didn't turn out as well as he thought it would though, as Jamie Lawrence explains. "We were all posing for the photo and desperate for it to be taken so that we would go out. The lads were egging me on to do something funny, so I adjusted my costume and got my knob out. The photographer didn't notice at the time, so they just took the photo, thanked us and left us to it. We had a great night out – as usual – and I didn't think anymore of it, until I saw the photo, including my manhood, published in an official Leicester City magazine! That image still does the rounds today"

It took O'Neill two months to get his first win which was a satisfying 3-2 victory over McGhee's Wolves with Heskey in scintillating form again. By this time, Corica had decamped to Wolves and fan's favourite, Julian Joachim, had joined Aston Villa for £1,500,000. Mark Blake, Phil Gee and Richard Smith had also moved on to pastures new and City's squad was looking a bit light.

Richard Smith, a boyhood Leicester fan, was sad to leave Leicester. "Martin told me that I could stay and fight for my place, but I was twenty-six and wanted to play first team football. Brian Laws was building a decent team at Grimsby and I'd enjoyed a loan spell there, so I decided to make the move permanent. It was tough to leave Leicester after so many years, but I had a good few seasons at Grimsby – we were even top of the Championship at one stage – before injury ended my career."

Lee Philpott was another player who moved on. "I knew my time was up when we changed to three at the back. I wasn't a wing back, so knew I wouldn't be getting into the team regularly. I was gutted to leave. I enjoyed the city, the fans and my teammates, who were a great group of lads, but I wanted to play football, so I joined Blackpool."

Fans who were expecting big names or expensive replacements were left disappointed. Neil Lennon and Steve Claridge were signed in February with Julian Watts and Muzzy Izzet joining them in March. Household names now but they were all relative unknowns in 1996.

Julian Watts had experience of the Premier League, but was looking forward to more regular game time with City. "I began my career with Rotherham before earning a move to Sheffield Wednesday. They had a very talented side with the likes of Chris Waddle, David Hirst and Nigel Pearson and I found it hard to get into the side regularly, so I jumped at the chance to join Leicester on transfer deadline day."

Julian Watts was one of four new signings in 1996.

Martin endured a tough start to his tenure at Leicester City, while the players adjusted to his changing style of play results went against Leicester and the fans became restless. At the end of March, Leicester lost 2-0 at home to Sheffield United and they slid down to ninth in the table – three places below the play-off berths. With City's hopes of promotion seemingly in tatters, a section of support turned on the team and the manager. This proved to be the turning point.

Julian Watts recalls his debut. "My first game for Leicester was against Sheffield United and, if I'm honest, I didn't have a great game. I had the away fans on my back because of my Wednesday connections and the home fans weren't too impressed with me either! Muzzy Izzet also made his debut in that game, coming on as a substitute. Like most inside the ground, I didn't know too much about Muzzy, but what a player he became – a real Leicester legend.

We lost the game and some fans were protesting after the game. I learnt a lot about the gaffer's character that day when he went outside and invited a couple of supporters into his office so that they could have a chat. That took a lot of bottle from Martin. After that game things changed, and we went on a fantastic run."

Mike Whitlow also played in that match and explains that the players were always behind the manager. "The Sheffield United game sticks in my mind. We played poorly but the reaction after the game was disappointing. It was tough in the dressing room as we were aware that there was a section of supporters outside the ground trying to hound Martin out. The problem is that people were expecting too much. It takes time for a team to gel, but people wanted success straight away. We knew what Martin was trying to do and we knew that he'd get it right."

I didn't think it was right that the supporters were getting on Martin's back and I felt that we needed to give him more time.

As the tension mounted after the Sheffield United game, I and a couple of fellow Directors went outside to remonstrate with the fans and to plead with them. The problem was that Brian had completely reversed the club's fortunes and the fans were expecting too much, too soon. I told the supporters that it was in everyone's best interest to support the manager and be patient.

The fans eventually dispersed. One disgruntled fan rang the Radio Leicester phone in to give his view and Martin never forgot that. During those dark, early days I was one of the few people who publicly supported him. Ironic, really considering the lack of support I received when the fans later turned on me.

Sure enough, results improved. City recorded back-to-back wins for the first time since November with 1-0 victories over Charlton Athletic and Crystal Palace and lost just once more before the end of the season. Four wins in the final four games catapulted Leicester into the play-offs.

One player who wouldn't be participating in the play-offs was Jamie Lawrence. "We had a great social life at Leicester which helped us to bond as a team. You got to know your teammates and learnt what made them tick and that helped you out during a match. The gaffer encouraged us to socialise and often took us away on trips, purely to socialise. The only thing he would say is not to let it affect your football. That was my mistake.

I'd missed out on a football education because I didn't come through a club's youth academy, so I didn't know how to be a footballer. I'd gone from prison to the Premier League and all of a sudden, I had a bit of money and time on my hands. I liked to party and overdid it a bit and the gaffer wasn't impressed. He told me to take the rest of the season off to sort myself out. To be fair to him, he told me that I would have a chance to prove myself during pre-season. That was a wakeup call for me and I turned my career around."

Stoke were the opponents in the two-legged play-off semi-final. After a drab 0-0 draw at Filbert Street, City produced a heroic display in the return leg at the Victoria Ground with Garry Parker scoring the only goal of the game in front of the travelling fans who were watching from the cage-like pen behind the goal.

The referee's whistle sparked bizarre scenes as Julian Watts recalls. "What a match that was. At the end, we went to applaud the City fans and got stuck at the away end with mounted police holding back the Stoke fans who were on the pitch baying for our blood. A few players threw their shirts into the crowd and Neil Lennon came back to the dressing room with no kit on!"

So, Wembley again. Many of the Leicester players were Wembley veterans by now, though for some it was a new experience.

Julian Watts was one. "I remember driving up Wembley Way and feeling incredibly nervous. A lot of the lads had been there before and I remember Walshy cracking jokes about it being tense, but for me it really was. Once I took to the field, the nerves became adrenaline and that carried me through the game."

**The Blue Army returned to Wembley for
the fifth time in six seasons.**

Emile Heskey had been to Wembley several times before, but this was different. "I was a ball boy for the 1993 play-off final against Swindon and was in the stands the following year. But to play on the hallowed Wembley turf for Leicester City – a club that I had been at since I was nine – was amazing and a huge honour."

Crystal Palace were all that was standing between Leicester City and an immediate return to the Premier League. The two sides were evenly matched, with one win each in the two league games between the clubs.

The game, as expected, was a tight affair. Andy Roberts gave Palace the lead after fourteen minutes and Garry Parker equalised, through a penalty, with fourteen to go to take the game into extra-time.

During an evenly contested extra-time, neither team looked able to take the lead and the game appeared to be heading to a penalty shootout. With just one minute on the clock Leicester were awarded a free kick just inside their own half. O'Neill used the break in play to send on substitute keeper, Zeljko Kalac, expecting the giant Aussie to be better equipped at saving penalties than the diminutive Kevin Poole.

While the substitution surprised the fans, the players were expecting it as Colin Hill recalls. "I came on for Steve Walsh in the second half of extra time and I, like most people, was expecting the game to go to penalties. We knew that Kalac would come on for the penalty shootout, but the Palace boys weren't expecting it and I think that it unnerved them."

Julian Watts describes what happened next. "The Wembley pitch saps your energy and towards the end of extra time I think both teams were finding it tough.

When 'Spider' Kalac came on, I remember feeling quite sorry for Kevin Poole because he'd had a really good game and had been fantastic in the run up to the final. I could understand why Martin brought him on though as Zeljko was great at saving penalties because of his large frame.

The substitution definitely rattled Palace. Their players weren't set up properly at the free kick and they were wondering what was going on. When the free kick was chipped in, I won the ball in the air and headed it down to Steve Claridge, who had loads of space on the edge of the area and he hit it into the top corner. To assist the winning goal in the last minute at Wembley was the best moment of my career."

Leicester City won the game 2-1 and secured their return to the Premier League. The Blue Army were ecstatic in the stands as they celebrated a successful end to what had been a turbulent season.

City's heroes celebrated their play-off victory at Wembley.

Mike Whitlow believes it was the collective team, rather than any particular individuals, that were responsible for the victory. "It was credit to the strong characters that we had at the Club. There were no egos, no one was better than anyone else and everyone worked for each other. That's one of the reasons the young players like Joachim and Heskey adapted so well to first team football. Martin was great to me; he was off his rocker, but he loved every minute of every game and just loved football."

A jubilant captain, Steve Walsh, lifted the play-off trophy. "A lot of people didn't think we'd get to the play-offs, let alone win, but we had that never-say-die-attitude and loved proving people wrong."

City fans flocked to Filbert to applaud the players on open top bus parade.

Julian Watts' shirt and medal from the 1996 play-off final.

Behind the scenes

With a successful conference and banqueting operation joining Family Night Football and Fox Leisure as profitable ventures, by 1996 the commercial operation had grown to the extent that it accounted for just under half the club's total revenue. An achievement, yes, but I wasn't satisfied yet.

There was still more to do and I challenged myself and my team to go out and find additional revenue streams. One of the biggest challenges that I faced was that people often struggled to recognise that a successful commercial operation would ultimately lead to greater investment in the football side. Not everyone bought into the ambition that I had. I didn't want to focus on football. That was for the Chairman and the manager. My job was to look at how we could fulfil our potential by turning us into a thriving business off the field.

Leicester City had a completely different model to most clubs. We were, primarily, a football club, yet we were also a profitable company making money from multiple non-football ventures. This was essential to assist with the funding of the playing side. There is a misconception that football is dripping with money. The reality is that football does not make money, it costs a lot of money. It is commercial activities that make the money. There just wasn't enough cash coming in from TV revenue and ticket sales. In the days before billionaire owners, we had to diversify and make money from non-football related ventures, whilst also staying true to our purpose which was to become a successful football team. While Martin's rivals were Wolves, Derby and Portsmouth, off the pitch I was competing with hotels, conference centres, bowling centres, cinemas and other leisure facilities.

Director Roy Parker was delighted with the impact that my team and I had made. "In marketing terms, Barrie's appointment was the best thing to happen to Leicester City. He is one of the best marketeers I have ever worked with. You could suggest something to Barrie and off he'd go and do it. He was one of a kind and I have never found anyone comparable to him. He sometimes worked 18-hour days and I would say to him that he wore his job like an overcoat! His hard work paid off and we were one of the best run football clubs in the country."

With a strong leadership team working in positive surroundings, I needed to recruit more employees to allow us to take ideas and turn them into hard cash. We increased the number of full-time employees from twenty to over one hundred. It wasn't just a case of increasing headcount, we brought in highly sought after and talented people. The fact that people were leaving companies such as the Waldorf Astoria, Ernst & Young and the QE2 was testament to our growing reputation within the business world. We spent £25,000 on the very best training available and we won the coveted Investors in People award. We became the biggest marketing operation in British football. The managers created profit centres and our staff all became a cog in our money-making machine.

My principles were encouraging my team to work in a creative environment, nurturing them to identify opportunities and giving them the freedom to try things without worrying that they might fail. In my teams there was no failure – we either succeeded or we kept trying until we found something that worked.

Sometimes, however, the staff were working too well together . . .

On one occasion I was walking down the corridor where the Executive Suites were located when I heard a noise coming from one of the cupboards. I stopped and listened and there it was again, thump, thump, thump on the door. I thought it could be a trapped animal, so I tentatively opened the door and was shocked to see a naked woman fall out of the cupboard! Still inside was one of the bar supervisors quickly trying to grab his clothes and cover himself. After a pause, I asked, 'What's going on here?'

'Erm, erm,' the girl – a member of the bar staff – stuttered before replying, 'We were just doing a stocktake.'

'A stocktake?' I replied. 'More like a cock take. I want to see you both in my office in five minutes,' I added. When they arrived, I gave them both a stern telling off and warned them that if it happened again, they would be dismissed. The Carling Stand was often described as a five-star hotel without bedrooms – maybe I should have included some in the design!

Our PR team drip fed details of our off-field exploits to the local press and we received greater media coverage than ever before. Geoff Peters covered Leicester City for BBC Radio Leicester and we developed a good relationship as Geoff explains. "I always got on well with Barrie. He didn't seem to have loads of football nous but commercially he was top drawer, very smart. It helped that the club was on a positive curve on the pitch, thanks to the work started by Brian Little and continued by Martin O'Neill. He transformed the business operation, especially on non matchdays. He was shrewd enough to open up non-football revenue streams. I used to DJ in the corporate areas of the Carling Stand but had to lug all my mobile equipment in and out which wasn't great fun. I suggested to Barrie about getting some permanent stuff in there – decks, lights, speakers, etc. – and he invested heavily on that side. They had loads more events so it quickly paid for itself.

Barrie overhauled so many things and should get plenty of credit, even if he didn't always endear himself to those on the football side."

As our profile grew so did our customer base as people began to realise that we were more than just a football team. This increased the club's profits which led to more investment in the playing side.

Our commercial operation was the envy of several other clubs, many of whom were sending their executives to Filbert Street to learn from us. In 1996 Peter Varney, the new Managing Director at Charlton Athletic, spent some time with me to see what he could learn. Peter said that Leicester, on and off the pitch, was a club that they would like to emulate.

The club's medium-term strategy was to create sufficient income streams to ensure that we were not overly reliant on performance-related income such as gate receipts, shirts sales and TV revenue. My aim was to create a long-term sustainable model so that the club would be financially stable even if television money disappeared or if the club were relegated.

The nineties saw the rise of quality leisure facilities in the country, including multi-plex cinemas, laser quest and bowling centres, while Sky Television gave viewers access to more television shows, movies and football games than ever before. Competition for people's custom and money was fierce, so we had to entice people to visit us. Before I joined, Leicester City were passively hoping that supporters would come to Filbert Street. We had to reverse that and make the club go out to the public and bring in new fans and customers.

We did this by promoting the health and fitness club, a sport and leisure superstore, hospitality suites and conference centre, all of which were housed in the Carling Stand. I was aware of the history that was attached to the club and I wanted us to retain and be proud of our heritage; thus I used legends' names (Lineker and Banks) for the suites and we brought in many former players and legends of the sporting world, including Barry McGuigan, Will Carling and Jimmy Greaves, to speak at after dinner functions in our 400-seater conference and banqueting centre.

We knew that our greatest assets (in terms of marketability) were the players. Not only were they responsible for the results on the pitch, but they had prestige and people wanted to meet them. As a way for businesses to get closer to the players, we arranged for player sponsorship. A business could sponsor a player and in return, they got to meet the player, they received a signed shirt and were invited to the end of season player sponsorship awards.

I was very aware that our core support were not businesses or corporate fans and I did not want them to miss out so, in agreement with the team manager, we arranged for signing sessions in our club shop, made our players available to charities and to local sports teams, so that everyone had an opportunity to meet them.

Mike Whitlow loved the family feel of the club. "Barrie was a happy chappy and loved a chat. He always had time for the players and we didn't mind helping out with the various corporate and commercial activities the club arranged. I did a lot of stuff with schools and in the community. Leicester had – and still has – a culture of looking after their own, be it fans, players or staff. They were always keen to bring young, local players through the ranks and the support they gave to us players was fantastic. When my daughter contracted meningitis, Barrie and the club were great; so supportive and they couldn't have done anymore for me. It was a real family, on and off the pitch."

A lot of players return to their former clubs as a manager or in a coaching capacity. Colin Hill re-joined us to work in the hospitality team. "When I was captain Barrie asked me if I wanted to work at the club, but I couldn't as I was still playing. I left Leicester in 1997 but I kept in contact with Barrie and he kept telling me that that he'd help me out when I finished playing. A couple of years later, I called him to say that I was retiring and, true to his word, he offered me a job at Leicester working on the new stadium project and as a club ambassador in the hospitality areas. I'd only been there a few weeks when he asked me if I could take over the hospitality team! I came into the office one morning and he said, 'Colin, come in here. What do you know about hospitality? You're running it now.'

'What?' I replied.

'Don't worry, Charles Rayner and Richard Hughes will help you. Here is your hospitality team. The match sponsorship needs doing for the next game, off you go.' He said. I'm really grateful to Barrie for giving me that opportunity."

I was accused, from within the club, of focussing on our corporate clients, rather than our fans in the stands. The reason I did this was because if we made sufficient money from our supporters in the hospitality suites and Executive Boxes, we could pass on savings to fans by freezing season ticket prices and running free events, such as the open days and signing sessions.

To bring in new businesses, we relentlessly campaigned to businesses with marketing material and pitched it along the lines of, 'Ask not what you can do for Leicester City, ask what Leicester City can do for you?'

On match days the Chairman and Directors entertained the opposing club or their own clients. My job was to entertain, welcome and look after new businesses to the Club, so that they could understand what matchdays were all about. It is not just 'stuffing your face and drinking' – it was the whole experience. While they enjoyed four course meals, plenty of wine and an opportunity to sit in the best seats in the house to watch the game, I would VIP them to death and constantly looked for opportunities

171

to tell them about sponsorship, Executive Boxes and everything else that we could offer them. It was important to me that the customer experience was exceptional and I am delighted that some of our old corporate clients have provided feedback for this book.

Martin Page, owner and director of Walker's Tyres had an Executive Box at Filbert Street for decades. "I remember Barrie was very flamboyant with his bright coloured glasses and ties, but it was obvious from the moment he joined Leicester City that he was very driven and determined to take the Club to the next level.

My brother, Roger, and I were box holders for over forty years. We found Barrie to be very accessible. He could be contacted any time of the day or night and was always happy to answer questions and resolve any problems. He introduced luncheons for corporate clients to get to know each other. The lunches were great fun and not many made it back to work in the afternoon! Barrie made being a supporter a much more enjoyable experience."

Our legal partners, Edge & Ellison, also leased an Executive Box which was great news for City fan Henry Doyle. "We would generally use the Executive Box to entertain clients. Barrie and some of the players would also pop in and say, 'Hello.' I had season tickets with my wife, Karen, and our children, Suzanne and Kieran, but when we had a guest drop out, I had to do my duty and take a seat in the Executive Suite to host our guests over drinks and a nice meal instead!"

It was one thing to bring businesses, sponsors and individuals into the Club, it was another thing keeping them. As soon as we brought new customers onboard, we made sure that they were well looked after. We wanted to cultivate our associations with the aim of retaining their support for years to come. Yes, we wanted money, but I did not want it to be cold transactions. It is easy to bring people in, take their money and ignore them. I did not want that. I negotiated, built and maintained relationships and used leverage, rather than exploitation. The Club gained and the business benefited too. We always looked to see what we could give back. Biffa are a good example. They paid us for our waste so that they could recycle it. In return, we gave them the contract to put their skips up outside the ground and we used their logo in adverts too. Win, win.

We continued to improve the experience for our customers. For our Executive Box holders and Belvoir Suite guests we brought in an A La Carte service where we sold a number of experiences and gifts on matchdays, all of which would be delivered to their seat. We sold gift packs consisting of a tie or scarf, programme and magazine for just £7.95, a signed football for just £15 and for £6.50, you could meet one of the players who would pose for a photo.

Continuing the momentum, I introduced a bi-monthly Chief Executive's luncheon, always held on a Friday. I invited four of our current sponsors and Executive Box holders, four businesses I was courting and they were joined by three senior members of Leicester City and myself. It was a high brow affair. We had our own room and arranged the seating plan to mix everyone up. The idea was to thank our existing clients and to allow prospective businesses to hear what our current customers were saying about us. We enjoyed a lovely three course dinner with fine wines, brandy and lots of jokes and storytelling. The format really worked, and I received feedback from attendees who said that they felt privileged to have been invited. There was an investment from the Club as these events were not cheap, but sometimes you must speculate to accumulate. These were highly successful and people were phoning me to get an invite.

Over the years we introduced a lot of new businesses to the Club who went on to become sponsors. I also know that some clients did some business together as a result of us introducing them at our luncheon events.

During one particular luncheon, one of our corporate clients kept refilling my glass and I didn't realise how much I had drunk and I ended up completely pissed. I did not act drunk, but I could certainly feel it! When our guests had left I felt woozy. I stood against the wall and lit a cigar. Just then, a young lad who was a porter came in to clear the room and he noticed that I was a bit wobbly, so he asked, 'Are you alright, Mr Pierpoint?'

'What do you think?' I replied, slurring my words.

'You don't look very well, Mr Pierpoint,' the porter said. At that moment I slid down the wall and ended up on the floor! The porter was shocked and ran out of the room calling for help. The poor lad thought that I'd had a heart attack, it was so embarrassing!

Leicester City had a big boost with the support and investment of local businessman, Gilbert Kinch in 1996. "My association with Leicester City began in 1973 when I, through my company G K Kinch Coaches, supplied coaches for the Leicester City Supporters Club. I actually drove one of the coaches, which meant that I got to travel to all our away games.

I later received a phone call from Alan Bennett, the Leicester City Club Secretary, who invited me to Filbert Street to show my coaches to the members of the board. They were extremely impressed and awarded me an exclusive contract to provide the team coach for the first team and reserves.

In 1996 I was invited, by Charles Rayner, to lunch in the Fosse Restaurant where we discussed how I could help the Club to raise revenue. The team manager, Martin O'Neill, was hungry for success and wanted funds to strengthen the playing squad and establish Leicester City in the Premier League. The rapid growth of the football club meant that they were looking for big investors to complement the work Barrie and his team were doing. As a City fan, I was delighted to be involved.

I happily discovered that Barrie had several ideas to continue to build the Club off the pitch (which he later did, working tirelessly) and I had no hesitation in investing a substantial amount of my own money in Leicester City.

I quickly learnt that the some of the Directors were not business people – they were glorified football fans who lacked commercial business focus. They let their footballing hearts rule their heads.

I headed up the President's Club and I had a dream of attracting wealthy investors in a bid to raise £5,000,000 for Leicester City. The idea was that each investor would invest £250,000 for three years. We would pay 4% interest and they would become a Club President and receive numerous perks.
I personally put in £250,000 which demonstrated my belief in the President's Club to potential investors."

Gilbert was working hard to bring additional money into the Club, but not all Directors possessed the necessary skills needed to keep our existing sponsors and investors happy. During the half time interval of one game, I was standing in the men's toilets using the facilities with a Director on my left and the Vice President (VP) of one of our major sponsors on my right. The Director looked over to him and asked, 'Are you enjoying the match?'

'Yes, thank you,' replied the VP.
'Have you been here before?'
'Pardon?' replied a confused Vice President.
'Do you come here often?'
'Erm, yes. Every game.'

'I haven't seen you before. Should I know you?' the Director continued.

'I'm the Vice President of one of your major sponsors. We've sponsored you for the last ten years.'

'Oh yes, of course you are,' replied the Director, before taking out a handkerchief and using it to dry 'himself'. He didn't even wash his hands before leaving the facilities! When he left, a confused Vice President asked me, 'What was that about?'

We helped our core support by introducing a membership scheme to reward their loyalty. Members received a 5% discount in the club shop, season ticket holders 10% and we added their names to our growing marketing database. We were among the first group of clubs to introduce a database. This allowed Leicester City to communicate with our various customers from junior members and season ticket holders, to our conference and banqueting clients. We produced tailor-made newsletters for each customer group to keep them informed of our many events, new products and information about the team and players. This approach generated income because of the highly targeted approach and repeat customer base. We were also able to invite businesses to sponsor the flyers, membership cards and other promotional correspondence. The customers liked it, too, because they didn't ever miss out on events, offers or news that was of interest to them.

We used the database to provide lots of offers, news and competitions to our junior fans as we understood the need to engage them and make them feel part of the Club from a young age. When supporters have fewer responsibilities, they spend money on the things that they want to, football being a big priority for youngsters. Once people get married and have children, for most, football moves lower down in their list of priorities.

Another initiative that we introduced was the 'beamback'. Away matches were always in high demand due to the low number of tickets that we were allocated. So, we projected a selection of our away matches onto a giant screen that we positioned on the Filbert Street pitch which allowed fans to come and watch the game live. It was the next best thing to travelling to the match. Supporters enjoyed the game from the comfort of the Carling Stand, surrounded by fellow Foxes fans. It created a bit of an atmosphere. We had a good response and it generated additional revenue for the Club as we created packages for tickets, food and drink and we sold merchandise on the day too.

In the nineties, we created more sponsorship opportunities than ever before.

Under Brian, Mark and now Martin, Leicester City were experiencing unprecedented success on the pitch and it was crucial for my team to exploit this by taking advantage of the interest that businesses were generating. We created sponsorship opportunities for all budgets to appeal to different sized businesses. We created several packages for businesses to deliver their message; match-day magazine, electronic scoreboard, advertising boards surrounding the pitch, public announcements, match sponsorship, match ball sponsorship, fixture card sponsorship, waste bins . . . you get the point – for a price, we let people advertise anywhere and everywhere.

Our match-day programme was restyled and relaunched as a match-day magazine due to its popular content, news and stories. This was well liked by fans and we used a local business to design and print it for us. Following the success of Fox Leisure, we decided to create our own in-house publishing operation, Fox Design to Print, to write, edit and prepare our magazines for print. Producing our own publications helped us to develop talented individuals within the Club and we won all four major programme awards within three seasons. Programme Monthly, Shoot and Football Programmes Directory all voted our magazine the best in the country which was a fantastic achievement. We also benefitted financially by selling advertising (of course) and we reduced costs by not having to pay a third party for our graphic design, content, pagination and page layout needs. As usual, we passed on the savings to our supporters by having one of the most competitively priced match-day magazines in the UK.

With full time writers and graphic designers in our employ we were able to really develop the brand and use it as another vehicle to engage our fans and create advertising and sponsorship opportunities. We produced:

• Goal Post – a monthly newspaper with a 20,000-print run. Our in-house team produced it with the lowest advertising rates of any monthly publication in Leicestershire. As it was paid for by advertising, we gave it to season ticket holders for free.

• Foxes Mag – a bi-monthly, forty-eight-page glossy magazine.

• Family Night Football match-day magazines – aimed at a younger audience and again, as advertising paid for the programme, we issued it to all our reserve game attendees free of charge.

• Our own Fox Leisure and Leicester City merchandise catalogues.

• Blue Army News – the official Leicester City newspaper sold in local newsagents for just £1.

• The Pitch – a monthly newsletter for all our junior Foxes.

• Books including Brian Little's 'Starting a Wave.'

Our communication with supporters was second to none and we strived to provide them with as much content as our fans could digest.

Our printing and publishing arm grew to the extent that it became an independent operation that, not only produced all of Leicester City's marketing material and printed literature, but it also serviced the design and printing needs of the Leicestershire Chamber of Commerce, Leicestershire Grammar school and other local businesses. We also produced the match-day magazine for Kettering Town Football Club.

Building upon these foundations we decided to bring everything in-house to achieve our ambition of not becoming overly reliant on any one income stream and to ensure Leicester City's financial security. Most clubs outsourced catering, travel, retail, cleaning, security, publishing and kit production. We were pioneers and did it all ourselves which created jobs for local people, gave us greater control over the quality of our products and services and we could reduce costs by introducing multi-tasking where possible and increase profits. We operated a similar model to Virgin; Richard Branson's company evolved from a Virgin record shop to a huge company that is formed of several subsidiaries, such as Virgin Atlantic, Virgin Mobile, Virgin Holidays and even Virgin Galactic.

By 1999 we had created the following subsidiary brands:
- Fox Leisure
- Fox Executive Catering
- Fox Design to Print
- Fox Fast Foods
- Fox Travel

Our revenue soared, but it wasn't the new stand that brought in the money. The stand gave us the opportunities, but it was just bricks, mortar and plastic. It was the innovative thinking from my team that was the real game changer. In January 1996, Champions (UK) plc, reported in one of their prestigious magazines that, "The Carling Stand has become the springboard for one of the most rapid turnarounds in commercial marketing activities of any British based sports organisation."

We also ran a couple of successful lottery schemes and scratch cards and gave a portion of our profits to local children's hospitals. When the National Lottery was launched in 1994 we knew that our sales would be affected. We were a very forward-

thinking and proactive team, so we were able to adapt to the times – we created the City Cashline which was a membership scheme where people paid a pound a week which gave them ten numbers and a chance to win £1500 each week. The membership also gave them discounts with a number of local businesses and we got newsagents to help us to sell memberships.

Another example of us finding unique opportunities was bringing in a separate sponsor for our youth team. In the nineties, Ainleys Music and Video, was the place to go for CDs, VHS and DVDs. As a popular haunt for teenagers, it made them the ideal sponsors for our youth team. They paid us £10,000 a season to have their names blazoned over the front of the youth team shirts.

My philosophy was to create enough revenue that meant that we did not need to borrow huge sums of money and didn't need to go over budget. There were lots of clubs who were setting their budgets based on finishing in ambitious league position or planning a cup run. This was ridiculous and got a lot of football clubs into financial trouble. It was the poker equivalent of going all in. Great if it works, but disastrous if not. I did not want to risk the long-term stability of Leicester City and I was proved right by the events that unfolded after I had left.

Having already planned three visits to the Twin Towers we were well organised behind the scenes. One aspect where I thought we could improve was making things easier for our supporters. They are the most important part of a football club; they pay our wages and will be part of the club for life.

High demand for our past three Wembley matches led to supporters queuing through the night, so that they could purchase their tickets as soon as the ticket office opened. I expected the same for this momentous occasion and decided that I didn't want fans having to queue throughout the night. So, I thought, why don't we just open the ticket office all night so supporters can collect their tickets and get home to bed? I offered the ticket office staff overtime and they agreed to work additional hours.

I never asked anyone to do anything that I wasn't prepared to do myself, so I was there too. Fans were queuing all-round the stadium and I went out to speak to them, handed out hot drinks and thanked them for their support. The result was that the tickets were sold fast and fans managed to get home and sleep in their beds. The good teamwork and spirit of the Leicester City staff did us proud.

Chapter ten - Playing the stock market

On the pitch - season 1996/97

During a season of turbulence, Leicester had displayed remarkable resilience to bounce back and regain their Premier League status at the first attempt. Before the start of the 1996/97 season, Martin O'Neill told Foxes' fans that he felt confident that City could achieve the forty-two points he felt was needed to guarantee survival in the top flight. The bookmakers, however, disagreed and installed Leicester as relegation favourites.

There were three new arrivals during the summer. The first signing was Spencer Prior, a tall defender who had just been named Norwich's Player of the Season and had prior (sorry!) Premier League experience. The other newcomer was USA international goalkeeper, Kasey Keller, who joined from Millwall. Perhaps the most important signing was Muzzy Izzet, who made his loan move permanent.

The Foxes began their campaign in the same place as they had the previous season, Roker Park and a goal-less draw with Sunderland gave them the first point on the board. City sent out a message to their detractors in their first home match of the season when a brace from Emile Heskey gave Leicester a 2-1 victory over Southampton for their first win of the season. At the end of the month, Ian Marshall was signed for £800,000 from Ipswich to add depth and experience upfront.

On 15th September, a Patrick Berger-inspired Liverpool beat the Foxes 3-0 which left them in sixteenth place in the league, just two places away from the relegation zone. Amazingly, this was the lowest position that Leicester would occupy for the next two years.

Two days later, City had a break from league football. Muzzy Izzet and Jamie Lawrence scored in a 2-0 League Cup win over Scarborough. A week later in the second leg, another goal from Lawrence and a Garry Parker penalty sent the Foxes through to the third round. No one knew at the time, but this tie was the launching pad for something incredibly special.

Lawrence was pleased to be back in the team. "The gaffer had told me that I had to prove myself to him during the pre-season. I trained with the first team, reserves, and the youth team, built my fitness up and I won Martin over. He gave me my first start of the season against Scarborough and I made my mark.

I set up Muzzy Izzet's opener in the first half and headed in our second after the interval. I started in the second leg too and got my name on the scoresheet again – apparently!

Neil Lewis whipped in a great cross and my diving header flew past the keeper to give us a 1-0 lead. Well, that is what I am told as I knocked myself out in the process. I got stretchered off and didn't even know that I'd scored until the gaffer came over and said, 'Well done.'"

York City were brushed aside 2-0 in the third round to set up a mouth-watering home match against Manchester United – the Premier League Champions – in the next round. The Red Devils featured a so-called weakened team, that still contained the likes of Roy Keane, Paul Scholes, David May and Jordi Cruyff, but the Foxes were too strong. Goals from Steve Claridge and Heskey put Leicester City into the draw for the quarter final which the furthest that they had been in the League Cup since 1969.

Steve Claridge opened the scoring in a 2-0 win over Newcastle in October 1996. Leicester's Premier League form was surprising everyone.

Away from the Cup, Leicester's league form was surprising everyone outside of the city, with victories over Spurs, Leeds, Aston Villa and a well fought draw with Liverpool at Anfield, leaving the Foxes in an extremely healthy twelfth place at the turn of the year.

Steve Walsh recalls the positive feeling around Filbert Street at the time. "Things were starting to change and we were getting big results. We were not afraid of anyone. People were starting to take notice and began to recognise us as a good team."

Defender, Julian Watts agrees that the team spirit played an important part. "The fight and togetherness that we had was incredible. I have never been part of a team that worked so hard for each other. A lot of that goes back to all the socialising that we did. We were a tight knit group who spent a lot of time together. The gaffer encouraged us to socialise and often gave us a couple of days off after a good result."

In January 1997, Matt Elliott became the club's £1,600,000 record buy when the strong defender joined from Oxford United. Shortly after, Rob Ullathorne – a left-sided defender who had worked with O'Neill at Norwich – was signed for £650,000. Steve Guppy, a left winger, was the final transfer of the season with Leicester playing Port Vale £850,000 for his services. The £5,350,000 combined transfer spend was the most that the club had ever spent in a single season. The Board of Directors were clearly backing the manager financially.

With the new signings in place, City travelled to Ipswich for the quarter final of the League Cup. Mark Robins' twenty-yard strike was the only goal of the game and Leicester City were through to the semi-final where they would face Wimbledon. It was not going to be an easy tie. Wimbledon were a strong, physical side; their line up featured the likes of Vinnie Jones, Ben Thatcher, Dean Holdsworth and Mick Harford. The Dons were enjoying one of their best ever seasons – they eventually finished eighth in the Premier League and reached the semi-final of both the League and FA Cups.

Leicester were also a strong, physical side and they certainly were not going to be intimidated by anyone. In fact, the Foxes relished this type of game. The two sides played out a 0-0 draw in the first leg at Filbert Street.

In the second leg, Wimbledon started the strongest. Kasey Keller made a good save in the first minute and shortly after, Steve Walsh cleared an Efan Ekoku shot off the line. City then suffered a huge blow when Rob Ullathorne broke his leg just eleven minutes into his debut.

Wimbledon, through Marcus Gayle, broke the deadlock after twenty-four minutes. The goal was the wake-up call the Foxes needed and they began to take the game to the Dons. With away goals counting double, Leicester just needed one goal to go through.

Just after half time, Simon Grayson headed home from a Garry Parker free kick to level the tie. Grayson considers it the most important goal of his career. "I was playing in the left back position and I usually didn't go up for free kicks or corners. I think that I had been on a run and hadn't got back in time so thought that I might as well stay up. Parker took the free kick and I remember the ball floated above everyone. I timed my run, shut my eyes and headed it into the top corner. It took me a few seconds to realise that I'd scored.

Later on, Steve Claridge came over to me and said, 'You need this to stay 1-1 so that you get all the credit. If someone else scores, they'll get the glory.' This was while the game was still being played and it gave me an insight into the mind of a striker!" The match finished 1-1 and City progressed to the final on away goals. Unbelievable at the start of the season, but Leicester were on their way to Wembley for the fifth time in six years.

For Mike Whitlow, playing on the Wembley turf was always special, regardless of the number of times he did so. "Wembley was so magical and never lost its spell. I played there five times for Leicester and then twice more when I was at Bolton. I loved it, though it did cost me a fortune in tickets!"

Three weeks before the Cup Final, Middlesbrough – City's Wembley opponents – came to Filbert Street for a league tie. Leicester lined up in their usual 5-3-2 formation, but Middlesbrough's little Brazilian, Juninho, was in devastating form and led his side to a 3-1 victory. The management team analysed the match and by the day of the final, they had formulated a game plan. Pontus Kamark was asked to follow Juninho around and stop him from playing.

Pontus explains that it was a role that he had fulfilled before. "One against one was a key strength of mine, so a man marking role suited me. I had faced the Brazilian striker, Romario, during the 1994 World Cup and marked him very closely and I had also done a similar job against Steve McManaman earlier in the 1996/97 season, so I knew that I could do it. It was a great tactical move."

To fit Kamark into the side, the manager had to change the team's formation and unfortunately, that meant that Julian Watts and Jamie Lawrence missed the final.

Jamie Lawrence was disappointed to be left out. "I'd been involved in every round leading up to the final and I had scored a couple of goals too, so I expected to be included. Just before the match I found out that I had been dropped and had not even made the bench. It really pissed me off, but my attitude is, you get knocked down today, you get back up again tomorrow and that's what I did."

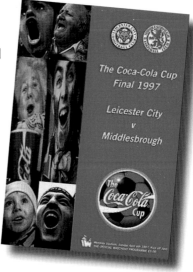

On 6th April, 76,757 Leicester and Middlesbrough supporters packed into Wembley Stadium to watch the first major final of the season. Up for grabs was the famous trophy and a place in the UEFA Cup. Bryan Robson had built a talented squad containing former Inter defender Gianluca Festa, Brazilians' Emerson and Juninho, Champions League winner, Fabrizio Ravenelli and they were captained by a certain Nigel Pearson. Leicester were the underdogs going into the match, but that was how they liked it.

Kamark was outstanding. He played his role to perfection and frustrated the little Brazilian who barely had a kick. "My job was to follow Juninho everywhere he went, even to the dressing room if needed. From the kick off through to the final whistle, I gained the upper hand and had him under control. He was a great player, but I could tell that he was disturbed and he started to get bored. He was a creative player who wanted to have fun on the pitch. He had to do a lot of running to try and find space, but I would not give him any. At one point, I won a duel and saw his frustration, so I said, 'I'm really sorry, but this is the job I've been given.' People might find it strange that I apologised to him, but he was a nice guy, this was a big game and an opportunity for him to shine and I was stifling him."

The game was a very tense affair and neither side was able to find a breakthrough, so the game went into extra time. After just five minutes, Ravenelli smashed the opening goal past

Pontus Kamark did an outstanding job man marking the dangerous Juninho during the 1997 League Cup Final.

Kasey Keller. Middlesbrough had one hand on the trophy, but this resilient Leicester side did not know when they were beaten. With just three minutes left on the clock, Emile Heskey scrambled the ball into the back of the net, following a brilliant cross from Mark Robins. It was Heskey's tenth goal of the season and was enough to force a replay which took place at Hillsborough ten days later.

When the ball landed at Heskey's feet, the young striker calmly hit the ball home. "It was amazing to score for Leicester in a Cup Final, but the enormity of the situation didn't enter my mind. Yes, you get nerves before the game, but during the match they go and I was just focussed on doing my best for the team and getting us back into the game."

Two hours at Wembley had taken their toll on the City players and with two league games to play before the replay, O'Neill decided to rest some of his regular starters to keep them fresh. This decision was beneficial for Jamie Lawrence who played his way back into the Cup Final squad. "The final league match before the replay was at Highbury against Arsenal. I had a good game and the gaffer told me that I would be on the bench at Hillsborough. I was delighted."

Pontus Kamark's performance at Wembley meant that he retained his place and Julian Watts again missed out. Watts explains his disappointment. "I'd played in every round of the League Cup but, sadly, missed out on the final. We usually played three at the back, but the gaffer decided to switch to a flat back four and, unfortunately, I was the man to give way. It was really tough for me to miss the final and the subsequent reply at Hillsborough in my hometown of Sheffield. It was disappointing, but that's football and we won the Cup, so you can't fault Martin's decision."

There was nothing to separate the two teams in a nerve-wracking replay and, once again, the match went into extra time. With just ten minutes to go, Garry Parker lofted a free kick into the penalty area, Steve Walsh headed the ball across the box and Steve Claridge volleyed past Ben Roberts into the Middlesbrough net. City were ahead.

With Kamark again containing Juninho and Walsh putting in a solid defensive display, there was no coming back for Middlesbrough. The referees whistle signalled the end of the match and Leicester City had won the League Cup – their first major trophy since 1964.

Steve Walsh won the Man of the Match award and was delighted to become the first City skipper since Colin Appleton to lift a major trophy. "It was always an ambition of mine to win something at Leicester. I wanted to be a good captain and we had bounced back from some tough moments to enjoy the success we deserved."

It was a sweet moment for Kamark who had fought back from two serious injuries. "Those two performances really put me on the map in English football. After being injured for so long, it was wonderful to win a cup. My whole time at Leicester was a lot of fun. We didn't have the same skill as everyone else, but we had heart and we were a good team on and off the pitch."

The cup victory was the moment Jamie Lawrence realised just how far he had come in such a short space of time. "Just five years earlier I had been in prison and now I was playing in a major cup final. What an amazing feeling. After the game we all had a few drinks to celebrate. Most of the lads were seasoned drinkers, but I remember Emile Heskey wasn't and his dad had to take him home!"

Steve Walsh won the Man of the Match award, while Steve Claridge scored the winning goal in a final for the second successive season.

While City's cup win may have shocked the bookies, Simon Grayson explains that the players were not surprised by their achievement. "We had more talent than people gave us credit for. We were almost always the underdogs, but we knew that we always had a chance. We had so many great players at the club and our team spirit was unbelievable. We always stuck together, whether it was in the tunnel, on the pitch when we needed to dig deep or socialising as a team between games.

There was less pressure for the League Cup than there had been for the play-offs. The play-offs are the culmination of a year's worth of hard work and there is so much at stake. I could enjoy the occasion of the League Cup final more than I had the play-off finals."

It was not just the players who were overcome with emotion. Current BBC Radio Presenter, Ian Stringer, describes the whole feel-good-factor that surrounded the entire city. "The success that Leicester City were enjoying on the pitch brought everyone together. I remember experiencing the ecstasy of victory at Hillsborough and the joy it brought to everyone. As my dad and I were walking back to our car, a fellow Leicester fan – a stranger – asked if we could give them a lift back to Leicester and my dad said, 'No problem.' It was such a special night."

Buoyed by the totally unexpected cup win, the Foxes ended their season with a draw at home to a full-strength Manchester United, followed by victories over Sheffield Wednesday and Blackburn Rovers and finished in ninth place, their highest league finish for twenty years.

Emile Heskey capped a tremendous season by finishing runner-up to David Beckham as the PFA Young Player of the Year. Heskey recalls that season. "Martin inspired the players and gave us belief. We knew that we had been considered as relegation favourites at the start of the season, so for us to achieve what we did was incredible.

We didn't overthink it. I don't know about the senior pros, and maybe it was just naivety on my part, but I didn't ever consider the possibility that we might go down or even be in a relegation battle. I just went into each game thinking, 'lets see what we can do.'

Martin encouraged me. 'Run at the defenders, Emile,' he'd say. 'Don't worry if you lose it, take them on again next time.' As a young player, given freedom to play to my strengths was incredible."

City fans were in for another treat as captain, Steve Walsh, was awarded a testimonial at the end of the season.

Julian Watts' League Cup Final medal.

A Leicester City XI – featuring Paul Gascoigne and radio presenter, Chris Evans – took on a Brian Little select XI. It was an entertaining evening; Chris Evans got on the scoresheet and Gazza played for both teams.

1997 was a good time to be a sports fan living in Leicester. Leicestershire County Cricket Club won the Britannic Assurance County Championship, Leicester City won the League Cup and Leicester Tigers won the Pilkington Cup. To celebrate this outstanding local achievement, The *Leicester Mercury* and Leicester City Council commissioned a statue, which still sits proudly in Gallowtree Gate.

Gazza and Chris Evans celebrate Evans' goal during Steve Walsh's testimonial match.

Sports fans in Leicester had much to celebrate in 1997.

Behind the scenes

When we had our first – albeit brief – taste of Premier League football in 1994/95 we learnt a lot; mainly that we needed a bigger squad with better quality players if we wanted to compete with the best in the land. The gulf in class between Premier League and Championship teams was huge and we needed a serious cash injection to bridge that gap.

With the advent of the Premier League and the revamped Champions League, player wages, transfer fees and payments to agents had grown exponentially. Television revenue and our own commercial activities had also increased but our Filbert Street ground was holding us back and preventing us from making more money.

The prospect of top-flight football meant that supporters were turning up in their droves and most of our games were sold out. We were unable to satisfy the demand of our fans who wanted to watch us live, or the businesses who wanted to use our facilities, so in effect, Filbert Street was costing us money. It was clear that we would either need to redevelop our ground or build a new stadium in a different location. If we could replicate the facilities housed in the Carling Stand in the other three stands, we could possibly quadruple our conference, banqueting and hospitality income.

During the mid-nineties, many football clubs were joining the Stock Exchange as a way of generating funds relatively quickly and those clubs who got in early made a lot of money. Leicester City had been keeping a keen eye on proceedings.

The Directors had several meetings before they agreed that floating the club on the London Stock Exchange was the most expedient way to raise significant capital. This would involve Leicester City selling a percentage of the Club in the form of shares which would then be traded on the Stock Market.

Floating a company is not an easy thing to do, though, so to see if this was a feasible option, the Board of Directors agreed to engage KPMG – one of the largest accountants and business advisory firms in the world. They concluded that Leicester City were a well-run football club and that our profitable commercial activities meant that we were less reliant on on-field success to generate profit than other football clubs. As such, KPMG considered Leicester City a sound, viable business, suitable for flotation.

I was particularly pleased with the following extract from the report. "Leicester City realised that commercial activities are imperative in order to achieve long term survival and to build a squad that is capable of performing in the Premier League. It became and remains one of the leading UK football clubs in relation to the development and exploitation of non-football revenue streams.

Barrie Pierpoint has been a tremendously positive influence on the club. He has been largely responsible for the development of the club's commercial activities."

The work my team and I had performed off the pitch was (excuse the pun) paying dividends.

Turning Leicester City into a public entity was a huge step in the development of our club. Since its formation in 1884, Leicester Fosse (later City) had always been a privately owned company, with very few shareholders which gave the Directors the power to run the football club in the way that they felt fit. Anyone wishing to join the Board of Directors had to be co-opted by the current Directors and shares were not easy to obtain. Floating on the stock market would allow anyone to purchase shares and would mean that the club would come under the ownership of a wide variety of investors – many of whom were likely to be fans. When we made our intentions public, this essentially signalled that Leicester City intended to expand its operations and improve its facilities and for this, we needed to borrow from the stock market.

The London Stock Exchange is one of the largest exchanges in the world and is split into two parts; the Main Market which is solely for large, established companies and the Alternative Investment Market (AIM) which was created for smaller companies that are seeking capital but do not meet the stringent requirements of the Main Market.

The Directors felt that the Alternative Investment Market was the best route for us, especially considering KMPG's initial estimate of Leicester City Football Club was £24,000,000. Filbert Street was valued at £7,500,000, but only because Henry Doyle and I had previously arranged with the Leicester City Council to remove the covenant.

John Sharp, a City Director at the time of the flotation, explains the board's thinking. "In principle, floating the club on the AIM Stock Market was the right thing to do. The purpose was to democratise the club, changing it from a company controlled by six families in varying degrees to one with ownership shared by

**Our legal expert, Henry Doyle, with his wife, Karen,
Steve Walsh and the League Cup.**

a wide-cross-section – and hopefully thousands of local people included. This was much on the lines of many foreign clubs. I remember reading a book about the history of Real Madrid, who at one period pre-war were struggling and about to go out of existence for lack of finance. Santiago Bernabeu, after whom the Bernabeu Stadium was later named, took over, offered shares to the people of Madrid – and the rest is glorious history."

The traditional method of floating a company is by offering shares to the public via an Initial Public Offering. This usually takes six to twelve months and involves significant fees, as there is usually a need to hire an investment bank to underwrite the shares. We were advised to float by performing a reverse takeover which is considerably quicker – anywhere from just a few weeks to four months – and substantially cheaper.

A reverse takeover is where a private company takes control of a shell corporation – so called because they are a dormant company who rarely have any assets or net worth. The crucial aspect is that shell corporations have already gone through an Initial Public Offering and are an existing public company. In our case, Leicester City were approached by a Manchester-based shell company, Soccer Investments PLC. We merged the two companies and renamed the new corporation Leicester City PLC. The Directors of Soccer Investments became shareholders of Leicester City PLC, one of whom was former Liverpool defender, Alan Hansen who was, at the time, working alongside Gary Lineker on Match of the Day.

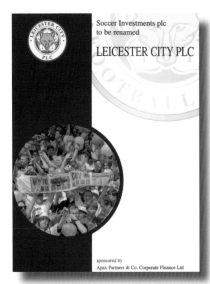

In October 1997 we floated on the Stock Market and raised £12,000,000. We used the money to purchase some new players and put an amount aside for further ground redevelopment or moving to a new stadium, which was looking increasingly likely. We also invested £1,000,000 into the youth academy

Matt Heath was a product of the Leicester City youth academy who benefitted by this investment. "I played under some fantastic coaches – Terry Whitehead, Kevin McDonald, Jon Rudkin, Chris Tucker, David Nish, Nev Hamilton and Steve Beaglehole – who all helped me develop from schoolboy to professional.

It is credit to them, and the first team managers, that so many youngsters were given an opportunity during the era I

Steve Kind (Finance Director), Tom Smeaton (Chairman) and myself at the London Stock Exchange.

played; Jon Stevenson, Matt Piper, Jon Ashton, Martin Reeves, Tommy Wright, Chris O'Grady, Richard Stearman and Jordan Stewart, all progressed from the youth to the first team."

Some of the players that Matt has mentioned were later sold for a combined fee of over £4,000,000, meaning that our investment in the academy was one of the best million pounds that we ever spent.

The *Leicester Mercury*'s front page when I became Leicester City's PLC Group Chief Executive.

Once the takeover was complete and Leicester City had become a public company, we had to make changes to the structure of the club, the way in which we operated and our governance process, so that we could meet the stringent requirements of the London Stock Exchange.

After we floated, one of the first tasks was to create a new Board of Directors with some additional roles. The biggest changes were that we created a PLC Chief Executive role that I later occupied and we had two boards instead of one – a Football Board and a PLC Board.

Over a six-month period, I had to attend many training sessions aimed at Directors and Chief Executives of public companies. The training covered corporate governance and was in place to ensure that I was capable and had the right level of skills to do the job – basically, how to run a public limited company.

Gilbert Kinch bought shares in the new company and we invited him to join the board because of his enthusiasm and efforts to raise money for the club. With a whole host of new shareholders – many of whom were our loyal supporters – we became more accountable for our actions and finances and it was essential that we were transparent in all of our PLC business dealings.

The Board of Directors set out clear demarcations in responsibilities. For example, the football board could only spend a certain amount per transfer without seeking approval from the PLC board. This was not to add unnecessary bureaucracy or because any Directors wanted to control the football team because that was the manager's job. It was because we were now answerable to our shareholders and had to adhere to the various regulations. We had to ensure that all transfers or contract renewals were financially viable and would not risk our shareholder's investments or the long-term future of the club. Any major decisions we made had to be made public to the stock market.

On reflection, John Sharp considers the flotation was a missed opportunity. "It was mishandled. The monies raised were intended to develop the club and company in order to further its longer-term prospects of creating sustainable income streams. Unfortunately, the newly constituted boards allowed the benefits to be frittered away on wasteful overhead expenditure and buying sub-standard players."

Roy Parker, another Leicester City Director, says, "One of the biggest challenges that we faced was that some Directors did not understand that you could not run the Football Club in the same way. Some Directors were making decisions as if it was their own company. I had to keep reminding them that you cannot run a public company that way. It was infuriating."

With the flotation now complete, the Club turned its attention to the stadium.

Chapter eleven - The stadium that never was

On the pitch - season 1997/98

The 1996/97 season was Leicester's best season for over thirty years. It was important that the Club did not rest on their laurels, so Martin O'Neill spent the summer of 1997 buying and selling in a bid to strengthen and improve the squad. Fans bade a fond farewell to several crowd favourites; Neil Lewis, Jamie Lawrence, Simon Grayson, Kevin Poole and Mike Whitlow all departed for pastures new and Mark Robins and Steve Claridge followed them out of the exit door as the season progressed.

Simon Grayson explains why he decided to leave Leicester. "My contract was up for renewal in the summer of 1997 and, during the season, Martin had said that he would sit down and discuss it with me at the end of the season. I was expecting to sign a new deal, but then Aston Villa came in for me. Villa had just finished fifth in the Premier League and were, of course, managed by Brian Little, who I had enjoyed working with previously. It was too good an opportunity to turn down. I loved my five years at Filbert Street – I played at Wembley four times and won the Player of the Year Award twice. The fans were great and we achieved a lot of success. I still have friends at the club now."

The Foxes brought in Welsh international midfielder, Robbie Savage from Crewe, striker Graham Fenton from Blackburn and French goalkeeper, Pegguy Arphexad from Lens. O'Neill's final signing was the experienced striker, Tony Cottee, who joined from Malaysian club, Selangor.

To say the move came out of the blue to Cottee is a bit of an understatement. "I had been West Ham's top scorer for two seasons, but then I found myself way down the pecking order and I was given a free transfer. I didn't receive offers from any Premier League or Championship clubs, so I joined Selangor in Malaysia in October 1996.

At the end of the 1996/97 season, I had a young daughter, and twins on the way and I was ready to come home. I was hoping for an offer from a Championship club and was shocked when I heard that Leicester City had made an offer for me. I signed a two-year contract and was delighted to be back in the Premier League. The fact that they had also qualified for the UEFA Cup was the icing on the cake as I had never played in a European tie before."

Leicester were determined to prove that they were not just one-season-wonders and began the campaign in style. Ian Marshall scored the only goal of the game in the season curtain raiser, a home win over Aston Villa and the Foxes followed that with a superb win at Anfield, thanks to a winning goal by substitute, Graham Fenton.

Manchester United were next up and City held the Champions to a 0-0 draw before Arsenal visited Filbert Street in a match that Pontus Kamark describes as one of the best games he ever played in. "It was such a mad game. Dennis Bergkamp was phenomenal."

The Dutchman, Bergkamp, opened the scoring in the ninth minute and he doubled the Gunners' lead just after the hour mark. With just six minutes remaining, Arsenal were still winning 2-0 and it looked like City's unbeaten start was over. In fact, some fans had already left the ground. But Leicester refused to quit.

Emile Heskey pulled a goal back for the Foxes and, incredibly, two minutes into stoppage time Matt Elliot bagged an equaliser. The drama was not over yet, though. A minute later, David Platt lofted a ball into the City penalty area. Bergkamp controlled the ball exquisitely with his right foot, flicked it up with his left and then, with his right foot, he placed the ball beyond Keller to complete his hattrick. It was one of the greatest goals ever seen at Filbert Street.

At 3-2 and already deep into stoppage time, surely the game was all over? No, not this Leicester side. The Captain, Steve Walsh, popped up in injury time and smashed a bullet header into the Arsenal goal. An incredible match finished 3-3.

"What a game that was!" recalls Heskey. "I remember towards the end of the match, we had three corners on the spin and the fans were going crazy. They willed us on to snatch the draw. I recently watched the game with Ian Wright for Sky Sports. I'd forgotten that I'd scored because everyone talks about Bergkamp's hat-trick and Walshy's equaliser."

It was Geoff Peters' favourite game of the decade. "There were so many enjoyable games under Brian Little and then Martin O'Neill, but for pure rollercoaster emotion the 3-3 draw with Arsenal in 1997 is probably the one which gives me the most goosebumps when I think about Filbert Street."

Jersey Budd, who was among the jubilant fans sitting in the Kop that day, describes the sheer joy that he experienced when the ball hit the back of the net. "What a game. When Walshy scored the equaliser, I jumped up to celebrate, caught the person next to me with an elbow and almost knocked them out! I apologised as I helped them back up and they hugged me. That can only happen at a football game."

Steve Walsh retains fond memories of that match too. "That was a remarkable game. I was originally supposed to mark Bergkamp, but after a, shall we say, altercation, he did not like it and he went over to Matt Elliott's side. That match epitomised Leicester City and our ability to come back against all odds."

A couple of weeks later it was time for City to embark on their first European trip since 1961. That adventure had ended abruptly when Atletico Madrid defeated the Foxes over two legs. By a strange twist of fate, the Spaniards were again drawn to be Leicester's opponents.

One of the club's directors owned a travel firm, so he laid on travel for the fans – it was a huge fiasco. The coaches did not stop anywhere and supporters did not get the opportunity to enjoy the beautiful city of Madrid. The club were inundated with complaints when the fans returned to England.

Henry Doyle, and his wife, Karen, made the trip to Spain and were shocked at the experience. "It was our first European tie in many years, so it was an opportunity we didn't want to miss. When we landed in Madrid we were greeted by gun-toting Spanish Police who herded us through the terminal to the waiting coaches as if we belonged to a criminal gang.

We were not allowed anytime to enjoy Madrid; instead, we were kept waiting before being escorted, in convoy, to the Vicente Calderon Stadium – the home of Atletico Madrid. It is incredible to think that the ground stayed open until 2017 as it was in a severe state of disrepair back in 1997.

Inside the stadium things were no better. The few stewards we encountered were unable to speak English and we were surrounded by armed police.

The Leicester fans were well behaved and gave the eager

police no reason to use their batons. After the game, it was just the same. We were herded into coaches and driven straight back to the airport. Not a very nice experience for our first European match."

The Directors and key staff had a different experience in the Spanish capital as we were invited to attend a Gala dinner as guests of Atletico Madrid. Richard Hughes takes up the story. "Jesus Gill was the President of Atletico and also the Mayor of Marbella, a town on the Costa Del Sol, which was at the time, sometimes referred to as 'Costa Del Crime' by the British press. Gill was a controversial figure, but it was evident that he commanded respect. When he walked into the room almost two hours after everyone else, surrounded by security, everyone stood to attention. It was like being in a gangster movie!"

Thousands of Foxe's fans packed into the Vicente Calderon Stadium to watch their heroes in blue take on the mighty Atletico. Madrid were a formidable team at the time. They had

Leicester City line up for the tie against Atletico Madrid.
Back row: Steve Walsh, Kasey Keller, Emile Heskey, Matt Elliott, Garry Parker, Spencer Prior, Ian Marshall.
Front row: Steve Guppy, Muzzy Izzett, Neil Lennon, Pontus Kamark.

City fans enjoyed spectacular views at the Vicente Calderon Stadium.

won the Spanish League and Cup double, just a year prior and they had spent an incredible £45,000,000 during the summer of 1997 on Christian Vieri, Paulo Futre and, a familiar face to City fans, Juninho. To put this into context, Leicester had spent just £2,000,000 that same summer.

Steve Walsh was the proud Captain that evening. "It was a huge honour to lead Leicester out in a European tie. I didn't ever think I'd see it. We were up there with the established Premier League players and to compete against the best of Europe was amazing. It was a tough draw, though, and I sometimes wish we had played a lesser team.

Martin had won the European Cup as a player and he was desperate for us to do well in Europe. It would have been nice to have enjoyed a good run in Europe for him. He'd taken us to a different level and was the best manager I played for."

Ian Marshall stunned the Spaniards by giving Leicester the lead after just eleven minutes. In the seventieth minute, Juninho managed to lose his nemesis, Pontus Kamark, to score a deflected equaliser, before a disputed penalty was converted by Vieri to give Madrid a 2-1 lead to take back to Filbert Street. City had done themselves proud and were unlucky to lose.

Before the second leg, Leicester continued their fine league form and a 2-0 victory over Barnsley took the Foxes to third place in the Premier League. Martin O'Neill took home the September Manager of the Month award too.

Leicester were confident ahead of the return leg against Madrid, but sadly it was not meant to be. City had several valid penalty claims turned down and Garry Parker was bizarrely sent off for taking a free kick too quickly. Atletico scored two late goals on the counter as Leicester pressed for a goal and City's European adventure was over.

The questionable refereeing decisions were tough for Pontus Kamark to take. "We deserved to go though. There was something not right about that game. The referee gave us nothing and I couldn't believe it when Parker was shown a second yellow."

Defender, Julian Watts, who was a surprise inclusion in the line-up, was equally disappointed. "I went on a month's loan to Crewe at the start of the 1997/98 season and when I returned to Leicester, the lads were preparing for the home tie against Atletico Madrid. I did not expect to be playing and I do not think many people did. In fact, when we got to Filbert Street Steve Walford asked the kitman, Paul McAndrew, if he had brought my shirt because I was starting. Paul replied that he did not have it, so he had a mad dash through the traffic to the training ground and back to get my shirt.

It was a great experience for me to play in Europe. It was vastly different to English football. I remember Kiko – Madrid's Spanish International striker – whistled for the ball rather than call for it which was bemusing. It was a massive game for us against strong opponents, but I played myself into the game and really felt we were the stronger team. It was a bitter way to lose a game, especially a match of that magnitude."

The referee of that tie, Remi Harrel, was removed from UEFA's list of referees shortly after that match which tells its own story.

Kiko's shirt from the UEFA Cup tie at Filbert Street.

City fell at the first hurdle in their league cup defence, with Grimsby Town earning an unexpected 3-1 victory. Crystal Palace later ended the Foxes FA Cup dreams with a 3-0 win at Selhurst Park.

In December, Leicester began an eight-match run without a win that was ended in the unlikeliest of places. Following a short loan spell at Birmingham City, Tony Cottee was back at Leicester and determined to show City fans what he could do. "I was 32 when I joined Leicester and Martin O'Neill was always questioning whether I could still do it. I was questioning myself, too. When we arrived at Old Trafford to face the Champions, Manchester United, I discovered that I was playing. I scored the only goal of the game – a volley past Peter Schmeichel which was not easy to do – to give us a massive three points. It was my first league goal for Leicester and showed that I could still do it at the highest level.

Tony Cottee celebrates his goal that gave City a vital three points at Old Trafford in 1998.

I think the United fans were shocked that we had beaten them, certainly those fans who had witnessed our pre-match warm up! In the previous weeks, Steve Walford, the First Team coach, had us in a circle doing some exercises and a bit of one touch, but it was such a mess that we called it 'the shambles warm up'.

When we walked out onto the Old Trafford pitch at 14:30, we asked Wally if we could do the shambles. He knew what we meant and said, 'OK.' So, we got in a circle and Matt Elliott was doing Baloo the Bear, Muzzy was on the ground being a caterpillar and I was doing a silly Mick Channon celebration. I imagine the United fans were wondering, 'what are these idiots doing?' but it was great fun and it worked for us."

The Greece Captain, Theo Zagorakis, was signed for £750,000 in February and his lack of English led to an amusing moment as Kamark recalls. "I remember sitting in the dressing room at half time and we hadn't been playing well. Martin was not happy. He told Zagorakis what he wanted from him in the second half and asked him if he understood.

Theo replied, 'Yes.'

Martin then drew something on the board and asked Zagorakis if he could do that.

Theo replied, 'Yes, boss.'

Martin was not convinced that Zagorakis understood, so he asked him, 'Are you an idiot?' to which Theo replied, 'Yes, boss'.

Martin put down the pen, smiled and asked us, 'What chance do I have?'

The whole dressing room fell about laughing."

During the final few months of the season, City excelled against the bigger clubs but struggled against the lesser teams. Victories over Manchester United, Leeds United and Chelsea were followed by defeats to Blackburn Rovers, Wimbledon and Bolton Wanderers.

It was this inconsistency that prevented Leicester from qualifying for Europe via the league table. Still, it was another fine campaign and the Foxes finished the season in a respectable tenth place.

Behind the scenes

Leicester City were now an established Premier League team, playing European football for the first time in thirty years, so demand from fans was higher than ever before. During the 1997/98 season, all but four home matches were sold out.

The facilities within the Carling Stand were amongst the most profitable within the UK and there was scope for considerable expansion of these to meet the rising demand for our retail, conferencing, banqueting and catering facilities. The money we had raised by floating the company presented an opportunity for us to finally consider options for increasing our capacity and enhancing our facilities.

Our preference, like most fans, was to remain at Filbert Street. We evaluated several options, including redeveloping the East Stand and we even considered turning the pitch so that the Carling Stand would become a stand behind the goal and constructing three new stands. I'm sure you can imagine how impressive that stadium would have been. Sadly, it was not meant to be. The close proximity of the East Stand to residential dwellings meant that both options required us to acquire, and then bulldoze, up to ninety houses on Burnmoor Street. We met with the local residents, but many were reluctant to vacate their properties. Even if they were willing to sell, when you added on moving costs, professional fees and everything else on to the cost of buying the properties, it became unaffordable.

East Stand at Filbert Street was so close residential properties that it backed onto people's gardens!

Even if we had managed to purchase the properties for a reasonable price, development of the East and North stands would have only increased our capacity to around 30,000 this we felt was insufficient to meet our long-term demands and would mean that we'd also have to redevelop the South stand. When we considered the hoops that we would need to jump through to obtain the necessary planning permission, it became unfeasible.

We reluctantly concluded that it was time to say goodbye to Filbert Street.

We all know that Leicester City now play at the 32,000-seater King Power Stadium, but we were remarkably close to building another stadium in a different location. There were not many sites in Leicestershire that were large enough to house a football stadium, so we spoke to Leicester City Council to discuss the viability of various potential locations. We compiled a list and visited several sites, including Soar Valley Way in Aylestone, Hillcrest Farm which was just off junction 21a of the M1 and some council owned land in Beaumont Leys, near to the Walkers Crisps factory. Our preference – and the fans – was to remain close to the city centre, so we ruled these sites out. The remaining two options were the Powergen owned land at Freeman's Wharf and a site at Bede Island South, owned by Raab Karcher. Powergen were in discussions with Morrisons who wanted to build a new superstore at Freeman's Wharf, so we decided that our new stadium would be located at Bede Island South.

The Directors agreed to build the new stadium on this site at Bede Island South. You can see Filbert Street in the top right of this photo.

At the time Gimsons Timber Merchants and a host of scrapyards were situated on Bede Island south, but the owners had put the land up for sale and the directors agreed that the location was perfect for Leicester City for various reasons.

It was close to Leicester city centre, within walking distance, in fact, of Filbert Street – which is what the fans wanted – and, importantly, the price was right. Property developers, Goldwing Properties Ltd, were interested in purchasing the land and saw Leicester City's stadium as the centre piece of their new development. Keen to understand their thoughts some of the Directors and myself met them to discuss their plans.

We were extremely impressed. Goldwing wanted to completely redevelop the area and create a retail park surrounding our stadium. At the time we were modelling it on Chelsea Village. It would have been like the Ricoh Arena in Coventry is now, but much better. They also had plans to construct a marina on the banks of the River Soar and build a hotel and a themed pub, creating over three hundred jobs in the process. The main selling point for me was that the retailers would be contributing towards our new stadium costs because they would benefit from the matchday foot traffic that City would generate.

The Directors were satisfied that the stadium was affordable. Roy Parker was leading the development board and was determined that the stadium would be among the best in the UK, so before we drew up plans, I accompanied Tom Smeaton and Roy on a four-day trip to visit some of Holland's most up-to-date stadiums. We were shown around the impressive homes of PSV Eindhoven, Feyenoord and Ajax. The recently opened, Amsterdam Arena – now named the Johan Cruyff Arena – was particularly impressive.

It was a useful trip and gave us some good ideas. When we returned to Leicester, we asked architects to draw up plans for a magnificent state-of-the-art 40,000-seater, three storey stadium that would not only house top-level football, but also host other events, such as boxing matches and pop concerts. The concourse would be open so that fans could walk around the entire stadium, but we would close sections off for match days.

In addition to being the biggest stadium in the East Midlands, the venue would be the largest conference, banqueting, leisure and entertainment centre in the country. We would be open 365 days a year to take full advantage of the magnificent facilities.

Gilbert Kinch, Roy and I formed a team to work on the new stadium development. Gilbert picks up the story. "Roy Parker, Barrie and I worked tirelessly on the plans for the new stadium to be located at Bede Island, Roy especially. We took the plans to Leicester City Council and we were delighted when we eventually received planning permission."

Planning permission was also approved for a four-storey hotel, casino and restaurant, three food retail outlets and three non-food retail outlets. The plans were so impressive that the Football Association included our stadium on the A list for England's subsequently unsuccessful World Cup bid. We invited Gary Lineker to meet us and we presented the plans and a 3D model of the stadium to him. He was impressed.

I shared my ideas and our plans with the fans and took part in a live question and answer session on Radio Leicester as it was important to me that our supporters were involved and that they were listened to. I also gave fans regular updates in my programme notes and through our various Leicester City publications. We were still incredibly community focussed and planned to build a creche and gymnasium for the residents of Leicester.

**Gary Lineker and Richard Hughes with the model
of the proposed 40,000 seater stadium on Bede Island South.**

Cliff Ginnetta was pleased that the fans were a central part of the process. "Barrie, Roy and Gilbert made sure that we were involved in the new stadium plans. I had several meetings with the New Stadium Committee which kept me informed. I, in turn, relayed the details to the fans through the Supporters' Club. Things like this would not have happened had it not been for Barrie."

Our Filbert Street tours had always been incredibly popular as fans were able to access parts of the stadium normally closed off to the public. The highlight of the tour was the ever-expanding trophy room, displaying the many honours that Leicester City had won over the years. We were proud of our heritage, so we decided to include plans for a Leicester City museum to celebrate our former players and the club's history. The museum would display rare and unique memorabilia and have interactive features to appeal to fans of all ages.

Sadly, It was around this time that some of the Directors and myself began to face resistance from a minority of disruptive forces within the club. I had the vision of Leicester City regularly selling out a 40,000 stadium. The disruptive element, led by a couple of Directors, felt that 40,000 was too big for our club and they were concerned

The stadium that never was.

that the ground would be half empty on match days, but that was because they did not share my ambition. If I had suggested a 30,000 stadium, I am sure the same people would have said that it would be too small. I was confident that, had I stayed, we would have filled the stadium, and we would have also made more money off the pitch by making use of significantly better facilities than those that we had at Filbert Street. Leicester are now looking to expand the King Power stadium because the demand is clearly there.

Another attempt to scupper our plans was when some people objected to the fact that the road system would not be able to cope with the increased traffic. A public inquiry was called when the Deputy Prime Minister, John Prescott, raised concerns that the site would contain shops that were outside the city centre. Clearly, it was not all plain sailing, but I passionately believe that we would have overcome these obstacles and delivered one of the best stadiums in the country.

Gilbert shared my frustration. "Sadly, our stadium plans were thwarted by others who were jealous that Barrie and Roy would deservedly get the credit for the new stadium."

In January 2000, just weeks after I left Leicester, the disruptive elements within the Club who opposed the new stadium and capacity, scrapped plans for the stadium that Roy, Gilbert and I had helped to design. Prior to the start of the 2002/03 season, the 32,5000-seater Walkers Stadium was completed. Built on the nearby Freeman's Wharf at a cost of £37,000,000, this was significantly higher than the 40,000-seater stadium which we had been quoted for, around £32,000,000 – my team could have delivered. It was also disappointing when I read that the deal agreed with Walkers Crisps for the naming rights of the stadium was considerably less than the one that I had negotiated with them for the Bede Island South stadium. These two decisions, along with overspending and a lack of corporate governance at board level, were contributing factors in Leicester's fall into administration in 2002 – with debts quoted at around £30,000,000.

Chapter twelve - An award winning club - on and off the pitch

On the pitch - season 1998/99

The 1998 World Cup in France featured two Leicester City players for the first time; Matt Elliott was a member of the Scotland squad who narrowly lost to World Champions, Brazil, in the group stage, while Kasey Keller played twice for the USA.

It was two in and two out at Filbert Street during the summer of 1998. Defenders Julian Watts and Spencer Prior joined Bristol City and Derby County respectively and they were replaced by Gerry Taggart and Frank Sinclair, the latter becoming Leicester's £2,000,000 record signing.

Now an established Premier League manager, Martin O'Neill was attracting interest from other clubs. Before the season began, Everton made an approach for O'Neill, but that was immediately rejected by new City chairman, John Elsom.

Old Trafford was the venue for the season opener. Emile Heskey and Tony Cottee had given Leicester a 2-0 lead before Teddy Sheringham pegged a goal back for United and it took a last-minute free kick from David Beckham to deny the Foxes a win.

City recorded their first victory of the season in the following match which was at home to Everton, but they then went five games without a league win, by which time, there was further speculation around O'Neill's future.

In October 1998, former Arsenal manager, George Graham, stunned the Gunners when he left Leeds United and became the manager of their arch rivals, Tottenham Hotspurs. The chairman of Leeds, Peter Ridsdale, identified Martin O'Neill as his number one target.

A few days later, Leicester and Leeds faced each other; Tony Cottee gave the Foxes a 1-0 win. In City's next match, which was against Spurs, the blue army held aloft banners asking O'Neill to stay. Muzzy Izzet scored a wonder goal in a 2-1 victory and, after the game, O'Neill announced that he was staying at Leicester. Leeds appointed Graham's assistant, David O'Leary, instead.

Having already brushed aside Chesterfield and Charlton in the League Cup, City were drawn against Leeds in the fourth round. Another spectacular goal from Izzet helped Leicester to a 2-1 victory and earned them a place in the quarter final.

In November, winger Andy Impey was brought in from West Ham for £1,600,000 to provide some pace down the right-hand side and he slotted straight in at right wing back. Another player who made his debut in November was Stefan Oakes, a product of the City youth academy and brother of Scott who had turned out for the Foxes in the early nineties.

Stefan could not have asked for a tougher introduction to first team football. "I had been around the squad a few times and I travelled down to London for the match against West Ham United on 14th November. The team was usually announced on the day of the game. The manager came over to me and said, 'Stef, you've been tremendous in the reserves, but you're not starting or on the bench today!' The lads all started laughing and I got on with making the tea and doing the other jobs that us youngsters were expected to do.

Stefan Oakes, a left footed midfielder, made his City debut in 1998.

A week later, we were facing Chelsea at home and I was named as a sub. Chelsea were a class side with Frank Leboeuf and Marcel Desailly – both World Cup winners just a few months earlier – at the back and Gianfranco Zola up front. I remember warming up on the touchline when I heard my name called from the bench and I knew that I was about to play. I got excited and it was a dream come true when I replaced Graham Fenton in the sixty-eighth minute. Within minutes I won a crunching tackle against Desailly and the crowd loved it."

In the quarter final of the League Cup, a rare goal from Neil Lennon gave the Foxes a 1-0 win over Blackburn to set up a semi-final tie against Sunderland.

Back to the Premier League and, unlike the previous season, City were winning matches against the lesser teams, but struggling against the big boys. In January, Manchester United, on their way to the treble, hit the Foxes for six at Filbert Street, while February saw Arsenal bag five without reply at Highbury.

By the time the semi-final first leg came around, City were in twelfth place in the League and out of the FA Cup. The League Cup was Leicester's only chance of qualifying for Europe.

Tony Cottee had been enjoying a renaissance. Since his goal at Old Trafford the previous season, he had established himself as the club's first choice striker, alongside Emile Heskey. Cottee was enjoying the 1998/99 season; he scored his 200th league goal and won the Player of the Season Award at the end of the season. In an incredible career, the Londoner had scored close to three hundred goals, had played for England seven times and played in an FA Cup Final. All that he needed was to win a trophy.

Aged thirty-four, the League Cup was likely to be his last shot at gaining that elusive winner's medal. He hit a brace in the first leg at the Stadium of Light as City ran out 2-1 winners and he also scored in the second leg draw at Filbert Street that sent Leicester back to Wembley again.

Before the League Cup Final, City completed their transfer dealings for the season, with two players arriving and one departing. Sam McMahon had been on loan at Cambridge United and he made his move permanent. McMahon had been at Leicester for five years, but he had been unable to establish himself in the first team. "I loved my first few years at City. There were some great lads in that side and the social scene was fantastic. The fact that most of the players had joined us from lower league clubs meant there were no egos or big time Charlies. We were all mates and I still keep in touch with a lot of the lads.

I developed imposter syndrome towards the end of my time at Filbert Street as I remained on the periphery of the team and did not really feel like I belonged. I was a young lad with a family and I just wanted to play football. The problem I had was

was that I had Muzzy Izzet, Robbie Savage and Neil Lennon ahead of me, with Theo Zagorakis, the Captain of Greece, waiting in the wings, so it was hard to break into the first team.

The manager did not really communicate with me, so I did not know where I stood. At the end of each season, I waited anxiously to find out if I would be awarded a new contract. I inevitably got a one-year extension. In hindsight, I should have been more assertive and gone to see the manager to ask him to play me or sell me.

The team were doing great and were successful. It was a good time to be around the club, but I never really felt part of it and actually felt quite relieved when I joined Cambridge."

To add depth to the squad, Icelandic forward, Arnar Gunnlaugsson, signed for £2,000,000 from Bolton and Scottish midfielder, Charlie Miller, joined on loan.

On 21st March 1999, thousands of Leicester fans made the familiar journey to Wembley Stadium. The Foxes had come out on top in the league fixture earlier in the season, but Spurs were a good side with some fantastic players like David Ginola, Les Ferdinand and Darren Anderton.

City's plans were not helped by the fact that record signing, Frank Sinclair, missed the game because he had arrived late to a team meeting and was sent home just hours before the final.

The match itself was an ill-tempered affair. Rob Ullathorne was asked to stop Ginola from playing in much the same way that Kamark had stopped Juninho two years before. Ullathorne did his job well and the Frenchman hardly had a kick.

In the second half, Robbie Savage and Justin Edinburgh clashed and the Spurs man received a red card, which was the last ever sending off at the old Wembley. Tottenham's players and fans blamed Leicester's fiery Welshman. Tempers frayed and Savage was involved in a scuffle with Steffen Freund with the German attempting to get the City man sent off. When Savage was substituted in the ninetieth minute, boos rang out around the Spurs end. Leicester had scored last minute goals in their previous two matches at Wembley – against Crystal Palace and Middlesbrough – but they were on the receiving end this time.

Steffen Iversen's cross was parried by Kasey Keller into the path of Allan Nielsen who dived to head home the winner.

It was a crushing blow for City, especially for Cottee, who was so close to winning his first trophy. "I was devastated that we'd lost at Wembley. I remember the clock approached the ninetieth minute and I was thinking that we were going to win the game in extra time.

But then Allan Nielsen scored in the last minute and that was it. I had lost three Wembley finals with Everton and now one with Leicester. At the final whistle I stood on the pitch and cried my eyes out. Martin came over and told me that we would be back next year, but I didn't think so. It is so hard to get to a cup final and it was an amazing achievement but, at 33, I thought this had been my final chance."

Two weeks later, the two sides played again, this time at White Hart Lane. Robbie Savage was booed loudly by the home fans, but he had the last laugh. Goals from Matt Elliott and Tony Cottee gave Leicester a 2-0 win and three points.

With Filbert Street sold out for most home games, some fans watched the match from the roof on the nearby Bentley building.

Emile Heskey went on to play 62 times for England.

There was further good news before the season ended. Emile Heskey became the first City player to play for England since Gary Lineker when he came off the bench in a 1-1 draw against Hungary in April.

Heskey was delighted to represent his country. "I'd been involved with England at all youth levels and the Under 21s and I just expected to make the progression to the senior squad. The first team were getting older and I brought something different to the team. I was big and strong, but also mobile. Stan Collymore was probably the striker who was most similar to me, but I was younger.

I knew a lot of the players from the Under 21s and everyone was welcoming. It was a huge honour to play for England."

Cottee enjoyed playing alongside the talented Heskey. "Emile is right up there with the best strikers I've played with. I loved playing with him because he was such a team player. He was the star man and incredibly consistent. Emile made the runs and drew the players and I picked off the pieces. We complemented each other."

The Foxes finished the campaign in tenth place, their third successive top ten finish, proving that City were firmly established as one of the best teams in the country.

Behind the scenes

My days at Leicester City were the most enjoyable and successful of my career and I want to use this chapter to list some of the many, on and off pitch, accolades that Leicester City were fortunate to win, or almost win, between 1991 and 1999. Some of these have been mentioned already, but I think they are worth stating again.

Prince of Wales Accolade for the first 'environmentally friendly' football club in the UK – 1991

A great achievement for the club to receive royal recognition which really put Leicester City Football Club on the map.

Play-off Final – Runners up 1992

Brian Little's team performed heroics to reach the play-off final, just twelve months after narrowly avoiding relegation. It was heartbreak for the Foxes as a disputed penalty, scored by Mike Newell, was all that separated the two teams.

Investors in People Award – 1993

Recognition of the work that we were doing to train and develop our off the field staff to deliver a high-quality standard of service to our customers and fans.

Play-off Final – Runners Up 1993

Despite coming back from a three-goal deficit, City were cruelly defeated by a penalty.

Jewson Family Football Award for progress – Winner 1994

Credit to the hardworking staff in our commercial and community departments for the huge difference that they made to the community, particularly supporting families and making Leicester City an inclusive football club.

Play-off Final – Winners 1994

Brian Little's team produced heroics at Wembley when they beat Derby 2-1 to record Leicester's first victory at the famous stadium.

Programme of the Year – Winners in 1995 and 1996, runners up in 1992 and 1998

Awarded by Programme Monthly, Shoot magazine and Football Programmes Directory, this was national recognition for everyone who was involved in producing our match-day magazines, including the writers, photographers, editors and graphic designers.

Play-off Final – Winners 1996

History repeated itself as Martin O'Neill's side came from a goal down to win 2-1 and secure promotion back to the Premier League.

League Cup Final – Winners 1997

Most bookies had tipped Leicester for relegation, but the lads surprised everyone by defeating Middlesbrough to win the second major honour in the club's history.

Boss of the Year – Winner 1998

I was shocked and honoured to win the UK DHL Boss of the Year. There were thousands of nominees and I was delighted to win. My Personal Assistant, Michelle Newman, nominated me for the award, although she now claims that she thought she was putting me in for 'Tosser of the Year!'

Michelle explains why she nominated me. "When I told people that I worked for Leicester City they always assumed that it was a glamorous job. It did have its perks, but football is a very tough business and the pressure is intense. It is certainly not a nine-to-five job!

Barrie was not like a normal Chief Executive. He did not just sit behind his desk barking instructions, he got involved and was always prepared to roll his sleeves up and muck in. One example was the day before the start of the 1997/98 season. It was a Friday and we were due to face Aston Villa the next day. Due to no fault of the club, the new seating in the East Stand hadn't been prepared properly and we hadn't been granted a safety certificate. This meant that we would have to call the game off and no doubt incur a points deduction, as well as inconveniencing our supporters. This could not happen, so Barrie and forty dedicated members of staff turned up at 6am and worked hard to complete the maintenance and cleaning which meant that we were granted a safety certificate just hours before kick-off. Barrie mucked in and worked alongside the others and gained their respect. We all knew that he would never ask us to do anything that he would not be prepared to do himself.

As well as maintaining extremely high standards, Barrie was a lot of fun to be around and I nominated him for

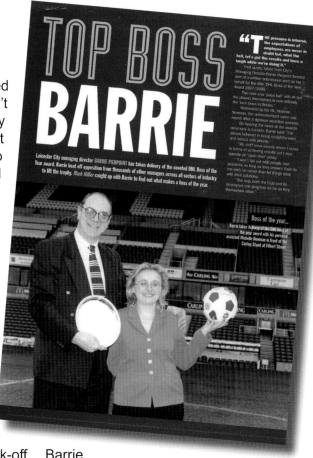

TOP BOSS
BARRIE

Leicester City managing director BARRIE PIERPOINT has taken delivery of the coveted DHL Boss of the Year award. Barrie beat off opposition from thousands of other managers across all sectors of industry to lift the trophy. *Mark Hillier* caught up with Barrie to find out what makes a boss of the year.

"THE pressure is intense, the expectations of employees are never in doubt but, what the hell, let's get the results and have a laugh while we're doing it."

That quote, taken from City's Managing Director Barrie Pierpoint formed part of a written submission sent on his behalf for the title DHL Boss of the Year Award 1997/1998.

The man who "plays ball" with all but the tenth boss in Britain.

Nominated by his PA, Michelle Newman, the announcement came last month after a rigorous selection process.

On hearing the news at the awards ceremony in London, Barrie said: "I've always believed in being straightforward and honest with people.

"My staff know exactly where I stand in terms of achieving results but I also operate an 'open door' policy.

"I won't fall out with people over problems as long as they present them to me early on rather than let things slow with their solutions.

"This way, both the Club and its employees can progress as far as they themselves allow."

Boss of the year...
Barrie takes delivery of the DHL boss of the year award with his personal assistant Michelle Newman in front of the Carling Stand at Filbert Street

The Boss of the Year award generated lots of good publicity for Leicester City and myself.

219

this award to give something back to him, a little thank you for all he had done for the club. He was known as a boss who looked after his people. He did so much for everyone else and never got the recognition he deserved."

It was kind of Michelle to nominate me, but I was no more or less important than anyone else at the club, we all had our roles to play and they were all important. I knew the names of everyone who worked at the club and I would speak to anyone. I do not mean this to sound disrespectful, but I learnt more from the staff on the 'shop floor', like the car park attendants and security guards, than I did from some of the Directors.

As well as winning an award I, along with Michelle, won a free holiday of our choice – separate holidays, of course – and Leicester City also benefitted as DHL – the award's sponsors – gave us £2000 worth of shipments. The award made the national and local press and the club and I gained excellent publicity.

Ease Awards – Winners in 1999 and runners up in 1998

Looking after our supporters was always a key priority for us and it was a pleasure to receive national recognition that we were doing the right things.

Leicestershire Business Sales and Marketing Award – Winner 1998/99

This award was credit to the entire commercial operation at Leicester City and testament to their hard work, dedication and results.

League Cup – Runners up 1999

Martin's side were unfortunate to lose to a last-minute goal at Wembley.

Turnaround Entrepreneur of the Year Award – Winner 1999

I was presented with this award at a lavish awards ceremony hosted by TV presenter, Eamonn Holmes. It was a huge honour to win such a prestigious honour that was sponsored by *The Times*, Ernst & Young and Citibank. The award was high praise for individuals who had been primarily responsible for turning around the financial or market fortunes of a business.

This was a fitting award that recognised that I had achieved the vision I'd had when I joined Leicester City. We had grown from a loss-making company in 1991 to a public company with a circa £20,000,000 turnover by 1999.

While I won the award, it was only possible because of the outstanding management and staff who worked with me to make it all happen. I thank them all for being part of our successful team.

John Aldridge believes the club's turnaround helped to launch the later success that Leicester City have enjoyed. "The Club has continued to develop and who could have dreamed that

It was a huge honour for me to win the Turnaround Entrepreneur of the Year Award in 1999.

years later the Club would win the Premiership trophy and be lauded around the world. I don't think it fanciful to suggest that this success had much to do with the legacy that Barrie Pierpoint left. 'Cometh the day, cometh the man.' This mantra certainly applied to Barrie's arrival at Leicester City; an inspired appointment."

Henry Doyle was also delighted to see me win the award. "Most fans judge success by the club's on field achievements and the performance of the team manager. However, it is equally important how a club is run behind the scenes. Barrie brought innovative marketing, not just to Leicester City, but also to many other football clubs who emulated his successful ideas.

As Sir Alf Ramsey said about the England World Cup Winner, Martin Peters, "He was 10 years ahead of his time" – that statement also applies to Barrie."

Executive of the Year Award – Runner up 1999

Acknowledgment of the off-field achievements at Leicester City.

Chapter thirteen - My final year at Filbert Street

On the pitch - season 1999/00

For the second successive summer, it was two in and two out at Filbert Street. Kasey Keller joined Spanish side, Rayo Vallecano, on a free transfer, while City fans also said goodbye to Swedish International, Pontus Kamark. Kamark's performances in the two League Cup final games against Middlesbrough will never be forgotten, but after five years in England, he felt that it was time to move back to his home country.

Pontus retains special memories of Leicester. "The whole club, players and staff, was like a family really. I enjoyed learning, so while I was at Leicester City, I took a degree in Marketing at De Montfort University. Barrie even let me spend some time with his marketing team so I could gain some experience. In the summer of 1999, I knew that it was time to return to Sweden, but Leicester was, and remains, an incredibly special club."

England International goalkeeper, Tim Flowers, joined from Blackburn for £1,100,000 and Phil Gilchrist made the move from Oxford United to Filbert Street.

Keen to shrug off the disappointment of the previous season's League Cup final defeat, the Foxes came back, firing out of the blocks. Emile Heskey and Muzzy Izzet both hit a rich vein of goalscoring form, with the latter becoming the first ever Leicester player to win the Carling Player of the Month award at the end of September.

Steve Guppy's consistent form on the left wing had not gone unnoticed by the England manager, Kevin Keegan. Guppy became the first, and to date only, player to represent England at under-21, semi-pro, B and senior level, when he made his full England debut against Belgium on 10th October 1999. Heskey also played in the 2-1 victory.

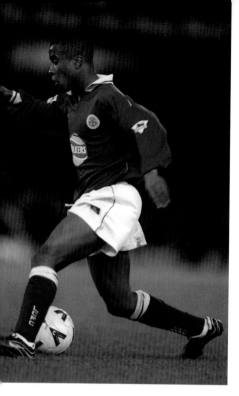

Danny Thomas became Leicester's last debutant of the millenium.

Three days after the international fixture, City faced Grimsby Town in the third round of the League Cup. Heskey and Izzet scored the goals in a 2-0 win for the Foxes.

By the time December 1999 came around, Leicester were fifth in the league. But they suffered an injury crisis and a 3-0 defeat against an exceptionally good Arsenal side kicked off a dismal run and City did not win another league match until February.

There was some good news during that period, though. Darren Eadie, a long-time target for Leicester, finally became a Fox in December when he signed for a club-record £3,000,000.

Another debutant that month – City's last debutant of the millennium in fact – was Danny Thomas. Thomas was a promising youngster who had attended the prestigious, Lilleshall, the Football Association's School of Excellence.

Thomas recalls the proud moment when he made his debut. "While attending Lilleshall as a fifteen year-old, I was part of an ITV documentary called *The World At Their Feet*. Shortly after joining Leicester City in 1998, ITV interviewed me for a follow up programme and I said that I intended to make my Premier League debut by the time I was eighteen. I was nowhere near the first team at that stage and I don't know why I said it, but it gave me a target.

I quickly made the progression to the reserve team and was playing really well. John Robertson, Martin O'Neill's assistant, had been an outstanding left winger during his playing days and he gave me lots of encouragement and advice.

During the 1999/00 season, Leicester had suffered with a lot of injuries and I remember getting changed in the youth team dressing room when Steve Walford, the first team coach, put his head around the door and said, 'I think the gaffer's going to play you soon.'

Shortly after that, we played Newcastle at home and I was named amongst the substitutes. On the hour mark, I was told that I would be going on. I was so excited. As I put my shirt on, I could hear the City fans sitting around the dug out shouting, 'Go on, Danny.' I wasn't nervous at all.

It was my dream to play in the Premier League at eighteen, but I wasn't happy with my performance and felt a bit deflated when I left the pitch. We were under pressure from a strong Newcastle side that featured Gary Speed, Alan Shearer and Duncan Ferguson and I just couldn't get into the game. I didn't play badly, it was just that I had been absolutely flying for the youth and reserve teams and I wanted to showcase my talents on the big stage.

I also played against Everton and West Ham and made the squad for several other games that season and I felt that I could push on the following year. But, sadly, it wasn't to be and I joined Bournemouth in 2002.

I enjoyed my years at Leicester – it was a real family club from the top down. There were some funny moments too. I owe a lot to Neville Hamilton and David Nish – the youth team coaches – who gave me so much encouragement and support. David was also involved in one of my funniest memories.

I was in the gym at Belvoir Drive with a couple of other youth team players when David Nish walked in and approached a treadmill that had been left on. I thought that he was going to switch it off, but he jumped up onto the treadmill to start a run. The running machine was going too fast and it tripped him up and sent him flying backwards. There was a wall behind the treadmill, so instead of him ending up on the floor, poor Nishy was trapped between the wall and the belt of the treadmill. He kept going round and round, like a hamster in a wheel! It was the funniest thing I have ever seen and I had to run out of the room before I burst out laughing. I daren't laugh in front of him because he was my manager and I was in my first year, but I couldn't hold it in either. If it had been captured on video it would have gone viral!"

In the cup competitions, City had formed a reputation as penalty kings. First, Leeds United were defeated 4-2 in a League Cup penalty shootout, then the Foxes knocked Arsenal out of the FA Cup, winning 6-5 on penalties. Stefan Oakes was one of City's penalty takers that day. "One of my favourite games for City was the FA Cup fifth round replay against Arsenal. They were a fantastic side with players like Thierry Henry, Robert Pires and Patrick Viera and they had given us the run around earlier in the season. In the FA Cup we were magnificent and took them to a penalty shootout. I did not really want to take one, but I'd had a good game and was asked, so I said I'd take one. Unfortunately, David Seaman saved it. But then Pegguy Arphexad stopped Lee Dixon and Gilles Grimandi's spot kicks and we went through to the quarter final."

Chelsea ended City's FA Cup hopes in the next round.

Leicester reached the semi-final of the League Cup after another penalty shootout victory, this time against Fulham. It was another astonishing game where City refused to be beaten. With five minutes remaining of the match, Leicester were trailing 2-0, but then Ian Marshall and Steve Walsh scored to take the game into extra-time. Chris Coleman put Fulham back in front, before Marshall's second of the game took the match to penalties. Arnar Gunnlaugsson, Robbie Savage and Graham Fenton scored their penalties, while Arphexad's heroics prevented the Londoners from scoring a single spot kick.

The semi-final first leg took place at Villa Park just two weeks later. A scoreless draw against Aston Villa led to their manager, the former City coach, John Gregory, labelling the Foxes 'boring.' The second leg was decided with a headed goal from defender-turned-striker, Matt Elliott, and Leicester were on their way to Wembley – again!

Jersey Budd was one of almost 22,000 fans celebrating at Filbert Street. "I had a season ticket in the Kop with my dad. When Elliott's goal took us to Wembley again it was brilliant.

The nineties were such a good decade to be a Fox. To share those moments with my dad was amazing. I still cannot comprehend it now. You were hugging and high-fiving strangers. The success that the club enjoyed brought the whole city together." First Division Tranmere Rovers overcame Bolton Wanderers in the other semi-final which meant that Leicester were the favourites to lift the trophy.

One of the few positives to come out of the injury situation was young Stefan Oakes, who was making a name for himself as a promising left-footed midfielder. "It was amazing to break into the first team during the 1999/00 season. Lenny, Sav, Theo and Muzzy were at the top of their game and I was learning so much from them. I worked hard in training and all the lads were great and gave me lots of help. I was playing well, and the gaffer was giving me lots of game time."

Just before the cup final, O'Neill signed Stan Collymore from Aston Villa. Collymore was a talented player who had held the English transfer record five years earlier when he joined Liverpool for £8,500,000. In 1997, Collymore joined Aston Villa. Two years later, he took a break from football as he was suffering from depression. When he returned, Collymore struggled to recapture the form that had promoted Villa to make him their record signing. As such, he was allowed to join Leicester on a free transfer. He made his City debut in a 1-1 draw away at Watford in the game preceding the League Cup final.

There was a huge demand for Wembley tickets, as Jersey Budd discovered. "I was seventeen and remember we had to queue all night for the cup final tickets, but it was great fun. We took a tent and a football and had a kickabout outside the ground. There were thousands of fans in line, but I managed to get my ticket around nine am. I couldn't wait to return to Wembley."

Several players were returning from injuries, so there was a lot of speculation around the team that O'Neill would pick for the final.

Stefan Oakes was hoping that he would be involved. "The night before the League Cup final we stayed in the Sketchley Grange hotel in Hinckley. Everyone was fit, so me, Sav, Lenny and Muzzy were vying for the midfield spots. I was desperate to play as I had missed out on the previous two League Cup finals. In 1997, I broke my leg in ten places so could not even travel to Hillsborough as a fan and, in 1999, I was part of the squad – but did not play – when we lost to Spurs.

I was rooming with Robbie Savage and he kept telling me that I was going to play because I had done well in the semi-final against Villa. When Martin told me that I would be starting I could not believe it.

The day flew by. I remember the coach ride down Wembley Way and seeing all the fans singing and waving flags. The excitement really kicked in when I saw the Twin Towers. Walking out onto the pitch I was hit with the noise from the supporters, it was unbelievable – the best day of my life."

The 2000 League Cup final was the last to be played at Wembley Stadium before it was demolished, so for many, it would be their last appearance at the famous ground. It was also the final chance for Tony Cottee to win the elusive winner's medal he so coveted.

As captain, Matt Elliott led the team onto the pitch and opened the scoring after half an hour. Former fox, David Kelly, equalised for Tranmere in the second half, but Elliott's second with ten minutes to go proved the decisive goal. Leicester had won the League Cup again!

Tony Cottee was overjoyed to finally break his Wembley hoodoo. "It was the crowning achievement on my career. Matty Elliott passed the cup down the line and when I finally got my hands on the trophy, I held it aloft. It was a special moment."

Stefan Oakes was at the beginning of his career but was equally delighted. "We were playing well in the league, had reached the quarter final of the

Tony Cottee was delighted to win the League Cup in 2000.

FA Cup and we were going into every game full of confidence. Winning a cup at Wembley was the icing on the cake."

A week after the final, Sunderland were the visitors for Stan Collymore's home debut. Collymore partnered Emile Heskey up front in one of the best games ever played at Filbert Street. Stefan Oakes describes the match. "That Sunderland game was incredible. The build-up was all about Stan. We were flying and playing really well. Emile and Stan just clicked up front and it was one of those matches where everything goes to plan. I came on as a sub when we were 3-2 up and got straight into it. I picked up the ball inside my own half and played a right footed pass out to Heskey on the right. He crossed the ball to Collymore who tapped in his hattrick goal.

I felt so confident, and the crowd were buzzing. On the stroke of full-time I scored a free-kick – my first League goal for Leicester – which made it 5-2."

Heskey explains that Collymore had been a player that he had looked up to. "Stan was a phenomenal player. He was playing for Nottingham Forest during the 1994/95 season when I made my debut. I can remember Mark McGhee telling me that Collymore was a player that I should watch and learn from.

We just clicked against Sunderland. That was match amazing and we played some exciting football. Filbert Street was rocking, as it was during most games in the late nineties. We had achieved so much in such a short space of time, but I think that if we had moved to a new stadium earlier, we could have gone to the next level."

City fans were on cloud nine but were brought back to earth days later with the news that Emile Heskey had played his last game for the Club. Shortly after the victory over Sunderland, he joined Liverpool for a club-record fee of £11,000,000.

It wasn't an easy choice for Heskey to make. "It was a tough decision as I had been at Leicester for so long. All my friends and family were in the city, but I knew that I needed to move to progress my career. I had already agreed to join Liverpool at the end of the season, but the deal was brought forward. It all happened so quickly. One minute I was at home and the next I was in Liverpool with nothing except the Puma tracksuit that I was wearing.

I loved my time at Leicester and I still love the Club. A few years later, when the club went into administration, I knew that I needed to do something to help. In my mind I was thinking, if there was no Leicester, there would be no me."

Stefan Oakes was sad to see his teammate go. "It was a shame that Emile left but I understood why he did as Liverpool were such a big club. He was great to play with. He got into great positions which made it easy to play balls over the top and he'd often turn a bad pass into a good one."

Leicester ended the season strongly and finished in eighth place which was their highest league position for twenty-four years. Tony Cottee, aged 34 years old, was the club's top scorer for the second year running. "My job was to score goals and from the time I broke into the West Ham side at 17, my aim was to be the top scorer for whichever club I was playing for. I scored 13 league goals during the 1999/00 season which was the most Premier League goals scored by a Leicester player in a single season. It remained a record until 2016 when Jamie Vardy took the record by scoring 24. I saw Jamie shortly after and joked, 'You didn't have to beat my record,' and he replied, 'Well, someone had to!'

I loved my three years at Leicester, it was an unexpected bonus. I appreciated every second and loved the thrill of the big games. We had great team spirit and the fans were fantastic."

Geoff Peters sums up what was a remarkable decade for Leicester City. "The contrast between the start and end of the nineties was enormous. The stadium was falling into disrepair, the squad under David Pleat was heading downwards while fan numbers and enthusiasm dwindled. Then in strode Brian Little on the football side and Barrie Pierpoint with his commercial clout and the whole place had a lift.

Imagine saying at the start of the decade that we would have seven trips to Wembley, two cup wins and four top ten finishes in the Premier League, plus a new stadium somewhere on the horizon. It's a bit like saying in 1990 that the all-conquering Liverpool wouldn't win a top division title for thirty years and that even Leicester would win it before them! It was a fascinating decade with way more ups than downs."

Behind the scenes

It was not a job; it was a way of life. And Leicester City was my life for almost nine years – I gave them everything I had.

The 18th September 1999 was one of the toughest days of my career. Leicester held Liverpool to a 2-2 draw, but it was not the result that I remember – it was the 'Pierpoint Out' campaign. When I took my usual seat in the Director's Box, the boos rang out and I was greeted with a sea of banners calling for my head.

How did it come to this? It is a question that I still ask myself today.

At the start of the 1999/00 season, Leicester City were at the peak of their powers, both on and off the pitch. But that was all about to change following a boardroom battle that even Jeffrey Archer would have struggled to conjure.

I enjoyed eight and a half successful years at a fantastic club, but the final few months were the hardest of my life. When I first sat down to write my story, it was because I wanted to take the opportunity to tell fans how hard my team and I worked and to give them a rare insight into the inner workings of Leicester City during the nineties. To celebrate the achievements of the many dedicated, often unsung heroes, who had helped to transform Leicester City from a struggling, loss-making Division Two club, into a profitable top ten Premier League side with a circa £20,000,000 turnover.

So, while I am not going to use this book as a vehicle to attack the few disruptive forces – some of whom were directors, managers and staff – that I encountered, I do want to explain what I was never allowed to say, or what the press were instructed not to print and how it affected me and my family at the time. To do that it is important to give some context to the events leading up to my public departure from the club.

There was a popular misconception that I wanted to control the football side. That was not correct. Why would I want to do that when we had one of the best managers in the game in Martin O'Neill? Brian Little and Mark McGhee had made it very clear that I didn't want to control, nor interfere in, the football side when they were the team managers. I knew that my role was to be responsible for ensuring that the club was being run as a profitable business. The more money that we made, the more Martin would be given to invest into the playing side.

Until we relocated to our new stadium, our match-day income was constrained by Filbert Street's capacity, so we had to carefully budget and live within our means. So many clubs were stretching themselves financially and creating budgets that assumed ambitious league positions and cup runs. That was an incredibly dangerous strategy and I was not prepared to risk Leicester City's future by spending money that we did not have. When you look at teams like Leeds United, Charlton, Bolton, and even Leicester after I left, I was proved right.

This is where some of the problems began. The board set, and delegated, budgets to each department – including the football team – which were based on our income. When you are spending millions of pounds a year on players' wages, having a laundry allowance may seem trivial, but the adage 'look after the pennies and the pounds will look after themselves' is so true.

It is hard for the supporters because they are not privy to everything that occurs off the pitch. They just want to see a successful football team, winning trophies. Martin had shown what he could do with limited funds and he wanted more money to see if he could take Leicester to the next level. Everyone at the club wanted to help him to do that.

There was another misconception that I prioritised the business side to the detriment of the football team but, again, that is not true. I always had the club's best interests at heart. In a boardroom full of passionate football people, someone had to be the voice of reason and not let emotions take over – i.e. let their hearts rule their heads – and that someone was me. There are too many 'yes men' in football who are afraid to offer an opposing view. It is sad that after I left, no one had the courage to challenge the board and ask, 'Hold on, can we afford this?' Just six months after I left, players were signing new contracts with huge, unsustainable pay rises.

Rather than holding the club back, I was hugely responsible for its growth. When I joined Leicester in 1991, we were in the financial doldrums with under-utilised, poor facilities and we were trapped in a cycle of having to sell our best players to break even. The various initiatives that my team and I introduced brought in millions of pounds for the football club and that helped to enable Brian, Mark, and Martin to smash the Leicester's transfer record several times and to achieve success on the pitch. That was why we worked so hard, to make money for the managers to build a successful team. My staff and I wanted exactly the same things that the fans wanted.

Our on and off pitch achievements attracted attention from other clubs who were envious of our success. Everyone knows that players and managers are targeted by other teams, but executives are very often sought after too, including me.

I remained very loyal to Leicester City, even though I was offered better financial packages elsewhere. Derby County were the first team to make an approach. I knew Lionel Pickering, the Derby owner and he made me a good offer in May 1995. It was not long into my time at Leicester though and I felt that I still had unfinished business, so I signed a new contract at City instead.

Coventry were the next club to offer me a role in August 1998. They had seen what I had achieved with the Carling Stand and they offered me a CEO role to help them to develop their club in readiness for their longer term move into a new stadium. It was another attractive offer, but Leicester wanted to keep me and offered me a new deal, so I signed that and committed my future to Leicester City. Luton also made me an offer, again on better terms, but I remained faithful to City despite being constantly undermined by some of the media, a couple of disruptive directors and a few senior managers within the Club.

When we floated in 1997, we restructured the club and had two different boards: a Football Board and a PLC Board.

**Coventry City was one of several clubs that I
turned down to stay at Leicester.**

Football chief executive to stay at City

"They recognise other people are after me. I am a 'doer', and my standards are very high." *Barrie Pierpoint*

LEICESTER City FC chief executive Barrie Pierpoint turned down the chance to spearhead the building of Coventry City's new £60 million stadium after City matched their rival's lucrative offer.

In an interview with the Mail, Mr Pierpoint revealed he was wooed by the Highfield Road club, which offered him a lead role in the construction of a new state-of-the-art stadium with a sliding roof.

Appointed recently as Leicester City chief executive, Mr Pierpoint said the Filbert Street club's board moved swiftly to improve his terms, persuading him to stay and 'finish the job' at Leicester – a task which includes the building of a new 40,000-seater stadium for the Foxes.

By: **TIM WALSH**

He told the Mail: "I like Leicester but, like anybody, I sometimes take stock of my career and ask myself if I want to move on to something else. Derby approached me before and now Coventry.

"They recognise other people are after me. I am a 'doer' and my standards are very high.

Coventry's task is massive and they were more than impressed with what I had to say, but Leicester made sure they matched their offer. I have delivered here a business befitting a Premiership club."

He would not reveal what his new deal is worth – hammered out by the Leicester City board last month – but said he was looking forward to his challenge at Leicester and the move to a new site.

The move is two years down the road, he said, although the club has received enquiries from a number of interested parties.

He added: "There are a lot of people talking to us at the moment. Whether the site becomes houses or factories, I don't know. Whatever we are going to do will involve consultation."

PLANS: Pictured during the Leicester City roadshow, which went to Loughborough and Hugglescote, organised to show fans the new stadium plans, is (top left) City director Gilbert Kinch, (top right) Mr Pierpoint, (bottom left) Market Harborough Conservative Club chairman Gordon Spence and (bottom right) Bass key account manager and sponsorship manager Richard Perry

Roy Parker remembers how this ultimately split the board into two factions. "The two sets of Directors should have worked together, but the football side often did things without consulting the rest of us and were acting in isolation to the main board, particularly in relation to transfers. This lack of control resulted in one of our players being sold without the entire PLC Board's knowledge. As a public company we had neglected our fiduciary duty by not informing the auditors."

Gilbert agrees with Roy's assessment. "It soon became clear that the PLC board was split. We had three Directors on one side, with Barrie, Philip Smith, Roy Parker and myself on the other. This meant that we had the upper hand on voting which ultimately blocked their whims and demands and helped ease concerns from my investors."

Football is rife with egos and some people within the club resented my success. Turning around a business does not win you many friends. Twice, I was offered a payoff to leave.

'Barrie. You know I don't like you,' one disruptive Director told me after he had pulled me into a room.

'Yes. And I do not like you either,' I replied

'Well, I'd like to offer you some money to **** off,' he said.

'I've just signed a three-year contract. If you want to pay me that in full then I will leave. But if not, I am not going anywhere,' I replied forcefully. Why should I leave a job that I enjoyed and was good at, and be out of pocket, too, just because some disruptive senior people within the club did not like me?

When I did not take a pay off and leave voluntarily, certain members of my staff, under instruction from a couple of disruptive forces from above, made a false allegation about me in a bid to force me out of the club. They claimed that I had used a club contractor to build a conservatory at my home which was nonsense. Sir Rodney Walker, the PLC Chairman, conducted an investigation, and during a board meeting, he informed the Directors that the allegations were completely without foundation and he vindicated me of any suspicion of wrongdoing.

The boardroom animosity grew and it all came to a head at a board meeting as Gilbert explains. "There was a vendetta to get rid of us, the so-called 'Gang of Four,' which began shortly after a very awkward board meeting held on 10th September 1999, during which the PLC Chairman and Football Club Chairman both resigned."

As they left the room, they gave their verbal resignations.

The Finance Director then left the meeting as he was not feeling well, although he did not resign. The remaining Directors appointed Phil Smith as the new PLC Chairman and released a press statement to announce the changes. The duo later denied resigning and turned the public against four other directors – Gilbert Kinch, Roy Parker, Phillip Smith and myself.

I learnt a lot about the media during this period and the fact that they will print whatever they want and put their own spin on facts to create the story that they think will sell papers, even if that story is not the truth. I now understand the phrase, 'Don't let the facts get in the way of a good story.' I tried to get my side across and spoke to several journalists, but they either misquoted or ignored me because the truth did not fit their narrative.

One example that springs to mind is when the *Leicester Mercury*'s Bill Anderson penned an article questioning why Leicester City had spent £3,500,000 on non-football wages the previous season. There was no context to the question and the implication was that I was diverting money away from the football side to fund the commercial operation. The attack was against me, but my team were caught in the crossfire and became collateral damage. I was incensed. I wrote to the Mercury to explain that the £3,500,000 that we had invested in wages had generated £4,600,000 which had been ploughed back into the club. I suppose the article would not have had the same impact had the headline read, "Non-footballing staff make £1,100,000 profit last year!"

The press created an unfair, one-sided view of the story and labelled us as the 'Gang of Four.' We were not a 'Gang of Four.' We were four hard-working Directors who cared deeply about the club.

John Sharp, although not a Director at the time, was still a passionate supporter and he could see where this was all going. "The Club had been poorly managed between the flotation and the administration and was clearly running into financial trouble. To their credit, Directors like Roy Parker, Gilbert Kinch and Phillip Smith realised this and attempted to change the direction of policy. Together with Barrie, they became, unfairly, known as the 'Gang of Four.'"

The boardroom dispute should not have played out in public. We should have resolved it privately, but some Directors, along with others within the club, were only too happy to feed the media vultures who were circling Filbert Street. This was not in the best interests of Leicester City, but they had an agenda to turn the fans and public against me and it worked. It was a smear campaign that was orchestrated by the two who had walked out, along with others within the club, against three other Directors and myself. They used the manager's popularity to support their actions. It was reported in many newspapers that O'Neill would resign if Gilbert, Roy, Phillip and I remained at the club. It was a catastrophe.

Someone leaked a story to the *Leicester Mercury* saying that I had voted against Martin becoming our new manager. This is false as I was not even a board member at that time, so I was not given a vote. It is true that three board members did vote against Martin's appointment and it was ironic that one of those was the Director who had leaked this story!

I do not know why, but Martin did not like me from day one. When I approached him to welcome him to the Club, Martin made it very clear that he wanted nothing to do with me. I think that some disruptive people at the club had spoken to him before he arrived and they blackened my character before I even had a chance to meet him. This immediately turned him against me, which was such a shame because working together, like I had worked with Brian and Mark, we would have become an enormously powerful force which would have greatly benefitted Leicester City.

On the eve of the Premier League match at home to Liverpool, one of the disruptive Directors and some of those working against me appealed to fans to "express their feelings" during the game. Someone printed 'Pierpoint Out' banners and handed them out to supporters before the game. It was incitement.

It was a far cry from when I became the Leicester City PLC Group Chief Executive, almost 18 months earlier. Upon my promotion Gary Silke, who wrote the Club's Fanzine, told the *Leicester Mercury*, "It all seems like a step forward. I am glad to see Pierpoint with more power. He's brought us a long way."

Suddenly I was public enemy number one as the story dominated the back pages of the local and even the national press. The boos, the banners and the publicity were one thing and I could handle that, but some people took it much further.

I received multiple death threats. The abuse became so frightening that I had to have a police escort to matches and I could not go into a shop without being abused and threatened. When I had a brick thrown through a window at my house, the police insisted that I needed protection, so I had armed guards

City 2 Liverpool 2

Fans air views on board bust-up

CITY REPORT
PAGES 2 & 3

HAVING THEIR SAY ... City supporters make their feelings known about the boardroom bust-up in no uncertain terms, while (right) City chairman John Elsom gets the thumbs-up from former chairman Martin George

SPORT OF THE 28 PAGES WORLD

FOUR-PAGE RYDER CUP SPECIAL STARTS ON PAGE 70

SEAMAN BOSS SHOCK SEE PAGES 80-81

They're trying to tell you something Barrie

Leicester fans had a clear message for chief executive Barrie Pierpoint yesterday — GO NOW.

Thousands of supporters waved banners and called for his head during the 2-2 draw with Liverpool at Filbert Street.

There were more demonstrations at the main entrance after the game. Pierpoint, blamed for a boardroom split, watched the match in the directors' box.

Match Report – Pages 92-93

■ POINTS OF VIEW — Leicester fans hold banners calling for the sacking of chief executive Barrie Pierpoint over his dispute with manager Martin O'Neill during a demonstration at yesterday's game

PEOPLE SPORT

EVERY NATIONWIDE MATCH!

(20) SPORTS PAGES BECAUSE WE'RE MAD FOR FOOTBALL

...makes ...an late

BY ANDY DUNN

a vital pre-match training because of a practical joker.
...obson had chalked up the time

ITV bid to nick Match of Day

BY STEVE BOKE

★ ITV want to steal Match of the Day from the BBC just weeks after snatching presenter Des Lynam. ITV sports chief Brian Barwick said they would bid for the Saturday night show when the rights came up for renewal in 2001.

END OF THE PIERPOINT SHOW ... Leicester fans angrily demonstrate against chief executive Barrie Pierpoint during the 2-2 draw with Liverpool after a week of bitter boardroom wrangling involving O'Neill at Filbert Street

237

living at my house. The worst part was how all of this affected my 80-year-old mother. It caused me a lot of health problems due to the stress of the situation and the constant harassment.

Rustie Lee, who had become a close friend, was saddened by the events. "When people went against him, it was hard to take. I think the fans had only received one side of the story and many didn't realise how much he had done for their club – he had supported them through thick and thin and had had such a positive impact on Leicester City."

Michelle Newman, my PA, could see a difference in me. "You could tell that he was badly affected by it. It was horrible what happened, the fans and the shareholders didn't know the real Barrie or what he had done for the Club."

I do not care how passionate you are; there are no excuses for physical abuse and threatening behaviour. They were not real fans. I was just doing my job and it really hurt me. It was horrible, but I carried on being determined, focussed, passionate and motivated to help Leicester City.

I wasn't the only one who suffered either, as Gilbert Kinch explains. "While the dispute raged on, Barrie provided security at our homes to protect us from irate fans calling for our heads. The 'Gang of Four' stigma remains and will live with me forever. It was the worst period of my life to date.

None of us deserved it, not least Barrie, who achieved more than anyone else for the Club off the pitch. Barrie was innocent and, as I am a man of principle, I was happy to stand by him, even if it meant me losing my directorship."

One Saturday when we were playing away at Leeds United, I was driving up to the match with Richard Hughes when we were stopped on the M1 by the West Yorkshire Police Force. I had been obeying the speed limits, so could not understand why I had been pulled over.

'Are you Barrie Pierpoint, CEO of Leicester City Football Club?' one officer asked.

'Yes officer,' I replied. 'Is everything ok?'

'I'm afraid not, sir. We have been tipped off by the Leicestershire Constabulary that there has been a credible threat to your life. We will have to escort you to the game.'

I could not believe it. I received a police escort – one in front and one behind – all the way to Elland Road. It was a terrifying time.

It was not just the Directors who were affected. It was a

difficult working environment for all the staff as the club was being ripped apart. The support that I received from my colleagues was invaluable for me and kept me going.

Charles Rayner feels that I inspired him while this was going on. "Barrie is such an enigmatic character and it was always such a joy to go into work. He was incredibly supportive, caring and fiercely loyal to his team. Certain characters within the Club tried to make it extremely uncomfortable for him, but he always rose above it.

I have worked for many bosses in my time, but Barrie was head and shoulders above all of them and by far the best. In turn, he always made me want to achieve the absolute best I could."

In the end, an Extraordinary General Meeting (EGM) was called, where shareholders would vote on a resolution to remove Gilbert, Roy, Phillip and myself off the board. Ahead of the EGM Philip Smith wrote to shareholders to present the facts, but it was too late. Fans and shareholders had already made up their minds as Gilbert explains. "Sadly, the fans never grasped the severity of the situation and they did not realise that our club was heading for financial disaster if things did not change for the better. The unrest at the club was evident and it meant that I had been unable to sign up more than eight investors to the President's Club.

The fans got their wish – Roy, Phillip and I resigned on 20th December 1999, two days before the EGM."

I did not have the option of resigning from the board as I was a paid officer, as well as a Director and I was legally advised to stay on at the club.

On 22nd December 1999, Richard Hughes drove me to the EGM at Donnington Park to hear the inevitable news. I was sadly voted off the board by the shareholders, while John Elsom and Sir Rodney Walker were voted back onto the board. I was put on gardening leave until January 2000 while the club agreed a settlement with me.

Cliff Ginnetta, like others, had expected me to leave the club following the EGM. "There was a clear divide between the football club board and the PLC Board towards the end. Barrie's success had attracted jealousy from

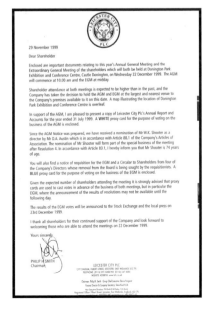

239

IMPORTANT NOTICE FROM THE CHAIRMAN OF THE BOARD
(Page 1 of 4)

Dear Shareholder,

Mr John Elsom and Sir Rodney Walker have, together with their promoters, filed a requisition which requires that the Company in an Extraordinary General Meeting consider a resolution to remove four Directors from the Board. (They are, Messrs. Pierpoint, Kinch, Parker, and Smith.)

It would be reasonable to expect that proposals to remove 80% of a Public Limited Company's Board would be in response to a matter or matters so serious that the removal of the relevant Directors was necessary either to prevent continuing fraud or other illegal activity or to allow the business of the Company or any part of it to function properly.

PERSONALLY MOTIVATED REQUISITION

In fact, the reasons and purposes behind the requisition made by Mr Elsom and Sir Rodney Walker are personally motivated and the dispute which has occasioned the requisition has absolutely nothing to do with either football or the management of the Company's business.

Both before and after a Board Meeting on 10th September 1999, during which both Mr Elsom and Sir Rodney Walker resigned, we have considered that the reasons for those resignations and matters relating to them should properly be kept confidential. Each Director and employee of the Company has an enduring duty of confidence, particularly in respect of matters discussed at Board Meetings.

Sir Rodney Walker and Mr John Elsom have not felt similarly constrained by their duties of trust and confidence and have in fact directly sought publicity for their own personal objectives.

In the circumstances of the requisition, I feel we have no alternative other than to explain the circumstances of Sir Rodney Walker's and Mr John Elsom's resignation from the Board and their conduct prior to their resignations.

CONSPIRACY AGAINST BOARD

The Board Meeting on 10th September was called to discuss two issues, firstly,

1

matters surrounding the Worthington Cup Final ticket inquiry by the Football Association and, secondly, to consider appropriate action to be taken in respect of conspiratorial accusations made by certain members of staff against the Company's Chief Executive, Mr Barrie Pierpoint.

As a result of the accusations made by members of staff, investigations were carried out by both the Company's internal auditors and the Company itself, under the supervision of Sir Rodney Walker as Chairman. Both investigations found that the accusations against Mr Pierpoint were entirely groundless, and concluded that the staff involved had been encouraged in a conspiracy to discredit the Chief Executive and thereby the Board of Directors, the Club and the Company.

Evidence was also brought to light showing that both Sir Rodney Walker and Mr John Elsom either colluded or allowed the attempts to discredit the Chief Executive to continue in clear breach of their duties and responsibilities and Company Procedure.

Sir Rodney Walker initially declined to confirm that Mr Elsom had been involved in the attempt to discredit Mr Pierpoint until Mr Elsom himself confirmed that this was the case. When the Board expressed its dissatisfaction as to Sir Rodney's conduct of his investigation and his failure to recommend or endorse an appropriate response, he stated that he considered that he should be allowed to carry out his investigations and reach such conclusions as he saw fit. If he wasn't able to do so he would resign.

The Board continued, quite properly, to maintain that the manner in which Sir Rodney Walker had conducted the inquiry and his unwillingness to be forthright in respect of its findings were inappropriate. In response, Sir Rodney clearly and unequivocally resigned from the Board and left the meeting.

The Board considered that it was Mr Elsom's admitted involvement in the conspiracy against Mr Pierpoint which caused Sir Rodney Walker to resign and that he had further brought the Club into disrepute with the Football Association and the Club's supporters in respect of his personal conduct relating to the Worthington Cup tickets investigation. In response, Mr Elsom clearly and unequivocally resigned from the Board and left the room.

RESIGNATIONS

Mr Elsom and Sir Rodney Walker resigned because they were placed in an untenable position as a direct result of their own improper conduct. They now seek to remove the four Directors, despite the fact that no allegations whatsoever have been made in respect of their own conduct or indeed of their management of the Company.

2

The dispute between the Requisitionists and the four Directors was not of the latter's making nor occasioned by their wrong doing. They did not seek to remove the Requisitionists from the Board or indeed ask for their resignations. The Requisitionists resigned because, by their own conduct, they found themselves in an untenable position.

Following the Board Meeting on 10th September, Sir Rodney Walker and Mr John Elsom have publicly denied that they resigned. This is simply untrue and raises further questions as to both Mr Elsom's and Sir Rodney Walker's suitability to hold the office of Director in a Public Limited Company. Nevertheless, it is the four Directors, and only they, who have attempted a reconciliation and, for the benefit of the Club, they remain willing, even at this late stage, to consider any proposals Sir Rodney Walker or Mr Elsom may put forward. Indeed, in the event that the resolutions proposed by the Requisitionists are rejected the four Directors are prepared to invite Mr Elsom to return to the Board provided he undertakes to observe the fiduciary and other duties incumbent on a Director.

PASSIONATE ABOUT LEICESTER CITY FOOTBALL CLUB

The Directors are as passionate as the supporters and shareholders about Leicester City Football Club playing football at the highest level in the Premiership in appropriate surroundings and enjoying proper facilities. All these objectives, to be realised or sustained depend on the sound management of the Company's business and this can only be achieved by way of a strong, independent and professional Board of Directors.

The Board has overseen the commercial success of the Company, which has never been questioned by the Requisitionists, and has provided the framework and the finances necessary for the acquisition and retention of players and the Team Manager and the other essentials for the Club's continued success on and off the field.

NO INTERFERENCE IN FOOTBALL

The four Directors wish to make it absolutely clear that they have no interest whatsoever in interfering with the day to day running of the football team or its operations. They are the first to acknowledge Martin O'Neill's enormous achievements on the pitch and all recognise that he is a key asset to the Club. They have no intention of interfering in any way with his activities as Team Manager and will do everything possible to ensure he stays with the Club. The Company has already secured his services until June 2002.

It is widely understood that Mr Elsom, as Chairman of the Football Board, has represented team interests at Board Meetings of the Plc. In the event that Mr Elsom declines the Board's invitation to return to the Board, it is happy to repeat its invitation to Martin O'Neill to join the Board as Director of Football.

3

NEW STADIUM WORK WILL BE WASTED

The Board has devoted enormous time and resources into the new stadium project. The Company's medium and long term future depends on the acquisition of a new stadium, not only to allow for necessary commercial expansion, but also to ensure that we retain our manager and players and our status in the Premier League.

In the event that the resolutions proposed are approved at the EGM, the time and resources devoted to the new stadium by the current board will be wasted and the resultant delay is likely to be detrimental.

NO CREDIBLE ALTERNATIVE

It is ironic that the 'alternative Board' should be proposing Mr Martin George as a Director when Sir Rodney Walker removed him from office during 1998. These are not the plans of credible alternative management who will balance the needs of football and commercial activities.

It is imperative that the present Board be allowed to continue to manage and develop the Company's business independently and responsibly on behalf of the shareholders and to pursue the Company's medium and long term plans in a sound and positive manner.

The appointment of an additional number of well-qualified non-executive directors and the introduction of a clear media strategy are the Board's immediate objectives.

We are all committed to the continued success of our Club. However, that success will depend not only on our Manager and our Players, but on the retention of a professional and independent Board which adheres to the highest standards of corporate governance. It is with regret that two former Directors have chosen to depart from these standards and have sought to personalise the issues in the way that they have. In so doing they have done a great disservice to the Club and its many Members and Shareholders.

NO SINGLE PERSONALITY IS BIGGER THAN THE CLUB. IF YOU AGREE WITH THIS STATEMENT, IN THE BEST INTERESTS OF THE CLUB I URGE YOU TO VOTE AGAINST EACH OF THE RESOLUTIONS.

WHY CHANGE A WINNING TEAM?

PHILIP SMITH
CHAIRMAN OF LEICESTER CITY PLC

4

some of the other Directors. Once it became 'Pierpoint versus O'Neill' there was only ever going to be one winner. It was a real shame that it ended the way it did for Barrie. After the EGM, I shook his hand and Barrie said, 'I know it is only business, Cliff. I hope that we remain friends.' He was magnanimous in defeat and it showed the character of the man.

I always got on well with Barrie and he did some really good things for the club. It just went wrong at the end and it wasn't really his fault. Without Barrie we would have struggled and wouldn't have made it to the Premier League as quickly. In fact, we might even have gone the other way! A lot of the success that we have enjoyed since he left is down to the foundations that Barrie laid."

Supporter, Ashley Barratt was sad to see Barrie leave. "As fans, we aren't privy to the internal wranglings within the football club, so we didn't know what was really going on behind the scenes, though it was clear that something wasn't right. Barrie's acrimonious departure was very sad. It was a forced end to one of the most successful periods in Leicester City's history. I felt that it was a poor way to treat someone who had been so instrumental in reviving the fortunes of the club. We took a step backward after he left."

The day after the EGM, the *Independent* reported that, "O'Neill insisted after Monday's resignations that he would now be honouring his contract, which runs until 2002." However, O'Neill resigned in May 2000 to take over at Celtic.

Leicester appointed Peter Taylor as the new manager. In July 2000, when Leicester City posted their 1999/00 annual report and accounts, I was disappointed to see that there was already a 6% reduction in our commercial department's income. I can't say that I was surprised, though. Shortly before the EGM, I had told the Daily Mail, "I fear the worst if these people get control. We are trying to protect the long-term interests of this club. We do not work in the short term. They seem to work on the back of a fag packet and this club will be dragged back twenty years." And I was proved right.

With the benefit of hindsight, many fans now realise that the outcome of the boardroom battle (i.e. my head) marked the beginning of Leicester's downfall. With no one to say, 'no,' the club's spending was out of control.

In a speech that I delivered at Leicester University during the summer of 1999, I finished with these prophetic words.

"The new football economy has undeniably created enormous opportunities for those fortunate enough to be close to the top. But there are risks ahead.

Unless clubs begin to take action by limiting their dependence on revenue streams outside of their direct control – and in particular, unless they begin to adopt a more market-led and professional approach towards their customers and trading activities – many professional clubs risk becoming severely exposed and ill-equipped to compete in a changing environment."

Though no longer Directors, Gilbert and Roy attended the next AGM. "Despite not sitting on the board, Roy Parker and I remained major shareholders, Gilbert says. "When we attended the next Leicester City PLC Annual General Meeting, we had our say in front of the other shareholders. The PLC Chairman, Sir Rodney Walker, subsequently apologised to us both for the hurt that we had experienced, thanked us for the service we had given to the club and exonerated us both from any wrongdoing.

Shortly after the club opened the new stadium in 2002, its shares were suspended and Leicester City entered administration. Roy, the investors I had attracted, and I all lost a substantial amount of money as our shares became worthless."

I was also saddened when Leicester City entered administration. I was not surprised, though and I know that it would not have happened had I still been CEO. Both Boards of Directors were to blame. Everything that I had worked so hard for had gone within three years. A lot of people, including local businessmen and fans, lost substantial amounts of money because of the way the company had been run since Gilbert, Roy, Phillip and myself left. It was devastating.

John Sharp agrees with me. "When the Club went into administration this really proved that the so-called 'Gang of Four' (and those like myself who counted themselves as their supporters) were correct after all."

I do not have any bitterness and there are no hard feelings towards anyone involved. I was as delighted as anyone to see Leicester crowned Premier League Champions. I have been welcomed back at the Club many times and I have always received a good reception from the fans.

For lots of supporters I will always be considered the villain, but at least now, I have had my say and you have the chance to make up your own mind about the part that I played in Leicester's success during the nineties.

Chapter fourteen - A man in demand

Life after Leicester City

I agreed a settlement with Leicester City in January 2000 and, for the first time in years, I was unemployed. But not for long . . .

Just days after I was 'persona non grata' at Filbert Street, I started to receive phone calls from other football clubs. So many, in fact, that I had to take my phone off the hook! They were offering me roles as Chief Executive. I met with some clubs and decided to accept an offer from Bristol City. After what had been a turbulent few months, I needed to take some time off to rest, so we verbally agreed that I would start working at Ashton Gate in March 2000.Well, that was the plan. . .

In February 2000, I was driving when I received a phone call on my mobile. I pulled over to answer and was greeted by an American sounding voice with the hint of a European accent.

'Are you Barrie Pierpoint?' the voice asked.

'Yes,' I replied

'Have you recently left your role as CEO of Leicester?'

'Yes,' I answered again, wondering where this was going.

'Can we meet?'

'I'm sorry, but who is this?' I asked.

'Don't you know who I am?' the voice challenged.

'No, sorry. Should I?' I was becoming more confused by the minute.

'I'm surprised'

'What are you trying to sell me?' I asked, eventually becoming frustrated.

'I am Milan Mandaric,' the voice replied proudly.

I was still none the wiser, so I said, 'I'm sorry, but I still don't know who you are.' I was met with silence. After a few moments I asked, 'Are you still there?'

'Yes, I am still here,' Milan replied before introducing himself. 'I am the Chairman, and owner, of Portsmouth Football Club and I want you to work for me.'

'I have already agreed to join Bristol City.' I said.

'Have you signed anything?' he asked.

'No, but –'

'Then forget them,' he interrupted. 'I will pay you more than they will and, whatever terms you have agreed, I will better them. Meet me first.' I was intrigued, so we arranged to meet at a hotel in London a few days later.

Milan began the meeting by explaining his vision for Portsmouth and then I told him what I had achieved at Leicester – although he already knew that, hence his offer – before I stated what I felt I could deliver for Portsmouth. Milan then left to visit the lavatory. Twenty minutes later he had not returned and I was starting to get worried. Eventually I saw him walking back to the table with a piece of paper in his hand. Milan had been drawing up a contract of employment on hotel headed notepaper! He put it in front of me and said, 'Sign that.' I did.

The first thing I did when I left the hotel was contact Bristol City to tell them that I would not be joining them. I felt bad as I knew that I had let them down, but I had to do what I felt was right for me.

In April 2000 I moved to Portsmouth to begin the next chapter in my career. The club was in a mess.

Milan Mandaric was born in Yugoslavia in 1938. Having transformed his father's machine shop into one of the most successful companies in the country, he was concerned with the socialist nature of the Yugoslav government, so he packed his bags and moved to the United States.

He made his fortune in the land of opportunity, within the computer industry, and in the seventies, he decided to invest some of his money into football. The North American Soccer League was attracting the world's best players, albeit they were in the twilight of their careers. Pele and Franz Beckenbauer were playing for New York Cosmos and Johan Cruyff had signed for Washington Diplomats. Mandaric created a new team, the San Jose Earthquakes and, not to be outdone, he recruited his own superstars – George

Milan Mandaric later became the owner of Leicester City and was responsible for appointing Nigel Pearson as manager.

Best and Alan Birchenall were two of his signings. The NASL model, however, was not sustainable and the league eventually folded. Keen to remain in football, Milan bought a Belgian club, R Charleroi and, later, French Ligue One side, Nice.

In May 1999, Mandaric sold Nice and bought his first English club, Portsmouth. At the time, Pompey were experiencing a financial crisis and had entered administration. Milan saved the club from possible extinction. Portsmouth were struggling at the bottom of the Championship and Milan wanted a Premier League club, on and off the field.

My first day at Portsmouth was like my first day Leicester. I am sure there was something going on somewhere, as the club was haemorrhaging money. There was little infrastructure within the club, and it was clear that there had been minimal investment during the past thirty years. I spent the first ten weeks working typical 14-hour days as I threw myself into turning the club around.

I learnt that some staff, management and directors from Leicester City Football Club – the same people who had caused all the trouble at Filbert Street for some of the directors and myself – had contacted some of the Portsmouth directors to try and turn them against me, but it did not work. I met with all the staff – full and part time – and laid out my vision. I was also blunt that if they did not share that vision, there was no room for them at Fratton Park, Portsmouth's home ground.

I was concerned about the reception that I would receive from the Pompey fans and the local media following my high-profile departure from Leicester, but I need not have worried – they were great to me. I got the supporters on board immediately

Fratton Park- the home of Portsmouth F.C.

by stage managing it. The fans loved Milan which was not surprising since he had saved the club, but I discovered that the supporters had been kept at arm's length by the previous owners and directors and that there was no love lost between the fans and Milan's predecessor.

I arranged an early meeting with the fans to introduce myself, explain my vision and to give them an opportunity to tell me what changes they wanted made to their club. They welcomed me straight away and were delighted to be invited inside the club and allowed to have their say. They told me the problems and I explained that I would fix them and reminded them that they could come to me at any time. It did not take me long to make things happen and the supporters knew that I was genuine.

It was very reminiscent of my early days at Leicester. We did not have a Director of Marketing for a start – that brought back memories! I returned to Filbert Street to sign Richard Hughes (he did not have to undergo the same rigorous recruitment campaign that I did to get the same job at Leicester City, though!) and together we began to make changes.

I am a firm believer in not reinventing the wheel, so we replicated a lot of the initiatives that had proved successful at

I shared my vision for the Club with the Pompey fans.

246

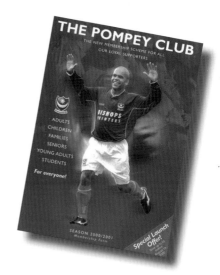

Leicester, many of which further bridged the gap between the club and the fans. I introduced Fans' Forums at Pompey, not just to agree the retail products they wanted us to stock, but to discuss the matchday experience, kit designs – the whole club really.

We quickly redesigned and refurbished the club shop and launched a new ticket office within the shop. I introduced a new membership scheme and Richard rolled out Family Night Football which saw attendances for our reserve games increase from five hundred to around three thousand for some games.

I was making so many changes and it was obvious to everyone that Portsmouth were on an upward trajectory. The fans were happy, but Milan was hard to please. He expected me to achieve everything I had at Leicester in one year, despite the fact that it had taken me eight at Filbert Street.

Tony Pulis was the team manager when I joined, and he was wary of me initially. I worked hard on that relationship and eventually Tony brought me in to his confidence. Ironically, Milan had poached Tony from Bristol City, too! Pulis took over from World Cup Winner, Alan Ball, in January 2000 with the team sitting in the relegation zone. He was tasked with ensuring that Portsmouth did not drop into England's third tier and he guided the team to eighteenth place, four places and five points away from the drop.

Early in the 2000/01 season, Tony left and was replaced by Steve Claridge – Pompey's top scorer the previous season – who took on the role of player-manager. I knew Steve from Leicester, of course. It was his first managerial role and he got off to a good start, winning his first three matches and scoring in each too.

I enjoyed my spell at Portsmouth, but it was very odd at times. One afternoon I popped out to the local Co-op to buy some lunch. While I was in the queue my phone rang. 'Hello,' I answered.

'Barrie, it's Milan. What are you doing in the Co-op?' he asked.

'I'm buying a sandwich,' I replied.

'It's half past two, Barrie. A bit late for lunch isn't it?' Milan said accusingly.

'I've been busy and not had chance to get out before now,' I responded. 'Anyway, I thought you were in America?'

I enjoyed a good relationship with the Pompey fans who were sad to see me leave.

'I am,' he replied.

'Then how do you know where I am?' I asked.

'I have my sources, Barrie.' Milan said before hanging up the phone. It was bizarre.

I had only signed a short-term contract and as it neared its end, I made the decision to leave Portsmouth when it expired and move closer to home. In total contrast to my final days at Leicester, the fans were devastated as they could see the progress we had made and they did not want me to go.

I may have only been there for almost a year, but I developed a close relationship with the Pompey supporters and I enjoyed watching them celebrating their later FA Cup success, although I was also saddened to see the club's demise a few years later. I truly hope that they have now turned a corner and are heading back to the top flight.

POMPEY: Supporters' Club issue 11th-hour appeal

DON'T LET PIERPOINT QUIT NOW, SAY FANS

POMPEY supporters have sent an impassioned 11th-hour appeal to Milan Mandaric: Don't let Barrie Pierpoint leave the club.

On the eve of the chairman's crunch meeting with the Fratton chief executive, fans have taken the unusual step of formally backing a club employee.

Paddy Thomas, the vice-chairman of the Pompey Supporters' Club, said:

'Mr Pierpoint has made the world of difference since he arrived at Fratton Park. He listens to fans and acts.

'He has worked as hard as Mr Mandaric in giving Pompey back to the fans.

'Under Mr Pierpoint, we have had a glimpse of the promised land. The threat of having that taken away is too horrific to contemplate.'

Pierpoint has been disturbed by an 'inner clique' at Fratton which he feels is undermining his attempts to bring Pompey into the 21st century.

His six-month contract expires at the end of the year, and this weekend is expected to sit down with Mandaric to discuss the way ahead.

There are fears that Pierpoint's frustrations at the 'faction' of people inside and outside the club' who are trying to prevent his plans from bearing fruit will be enough to force him out of Fratton.

Thomas, a vehement critic of the Gregory regime, is convinced Pierpoint is the man who can lead Pompey into a brighter future.

'In the past, trying to get a point of view across to the owners of the club was like

by Colin Channon
The News

banging your head against a brick wall.

'But Pierpoint has set up a series of meetings with supporters – and, more than that, he actually listens to what the fans have to say.

'He then goes away and acts immediately – some of the improvements he has made after receiving advice have been very rapid indeed.

'He is a big believer in customer rights, and thinks that, generally, football fans get a raw deal. He has tried to give all Fratton supporters a better deal.

'He is acting out all the promises Mr Mandaric made when he came to the club. You just have to go to Fratton Park – the ground is much improved, the ticket office is now unrecognisable from before, the catering is better – everything is user-friendly now.

'I know Mr Mandaric is worried about the amount of money that has been spent, but sometimes you have to invest some to get some.

'We have written to Mr Mandaric telling him all this. We want him to know that supporters appreciate what has happened, and that we do not want to return to the bad old days.

'Mr Mandaric has proved in the past that he listens to fans. I hope he does now, too.'

■ What has happened to the Pompey noise? Why have fans decided to launch their own Christmas CD? And what is the best goal ever scored at Fratton? Turn to Pages 86 & 87 to find out.

I was looking forward to a break, but within days, Geoffrey Richmond, Chairman of Bradford City, invited me to Yorkshire for a chat. He told me that he had been impressed by the success I had brought to Leicester and Portsmouth and he asked me if I wanted to see the new stand that he was building. He was as proud as if he were showing off his baby.

'What do you think?' he asked me.

'Can I be honest?'

'Yes, please,' he replied.

'Who designed this stand? It is not a good design.' I said.

'Why?'

'The logistics aren't right. It does not flow. There are lots of things that need correcting,' I told him.

'I designed it,' he said, glumly. I thought I had upset him so I asked if I should go.

'No,' he replied. 'I want you to stay and fix it. Can you do it?'

'Yes, I can, but it will be difficult,' I said.

'Can you start tomorrow?' he asked.

'No, I can't start tomorrow,' I replied.

'What about the day after?' he suggested. He was desperate for me to join and we sat down and discussed terms. I presented the financial package that I was looking for and said that I could work three days a week. He countered that by offering me double my daily rate and said that I could work as many days as I needed! I accepted – how could I refuse? – and began work in May 20001. I brought Richard Hughes (again!) to Valley Parade, Bradford's ground, as my first signing.

The impressive Sunwin Stand at Valley Parade was opened in 2001.

Richard was not the only familiar face. When Jamie Lawrence left Leicester, he joined Bradford and helped to guide the club to the Premier League, becoming a club legend, and fans' favourite, in the process. Jamie explains that the feeling was mutual. "I loved them, and they liked me too. When fans are paying a lot of money for a ticket, they want to see the players working their bollocks off. No one could ever say that I did not leave it all out on the pitch. I used to have a beer with the fans, and I sat with them at away matches, too.

Barrie was top draw and it was good to see him again when he joined Bradford. He always had time for me – probably because I was a bit of a wide boy! He introduced a lot of community stuff and I loved getting involved with that. I was out and about all the time, meeting fans and coaching kids. Football gave a lot to me and this was an opportunity for me to give back. You could make someone's day by signing an autograph or posing for a photo. I loved my time at Bradford, it is my spiritual home."

My main objective was to fully utilise the new Sunwin Stand so that we could make some money. It was a huge challenge.

Some of the streets around the stadium were a mess. There was the odd burnt out car, rubbish piled high in some front gardens and there was even an old bed and sofa left to rot outside one house. The new stand helped to tidy up and attract new business to the area.

We began by launching the 'Scoring for Schools' campaign. Bradford City teamed up with local schools to offer discounted and free tickets to students and teachers. For every order the schools placed with us, we gave them cash back – £1 for every kid's ticket and £4 for every adult's ticket purchased. We also gave them free tickets for the teachers to supervise the students at the matches. The schools used the tickets as an incentive for attendance, improved grades and general good behaviour.

It helped to increase attendances at home games and improved our standing within the community, but I needed to attract new customers and generate non-football revenue. We started to perform wedding ceremonies at the stadium and I introduced top-class conference and banqueting. In the evenings, we were popular with businesses, couples and families.

I borrowed another idea from my Leicester days – Sportsman's Dinners. Our first event was in November 2001 and Chelsea legends, Peter Osgood and Ron 'Chopper' Harris, regaled us with their tales from the Swinging Sixties. It was a

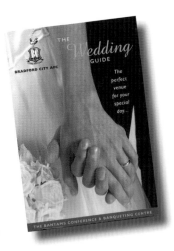

hit and they became a regular event. It was hard work, but we brought in a lot of new business to Bradford.

My contract was up for renewal towards the end of the 2001/02 season, but I decided not to renew. After eleven years of eating, sleeping and working in football I needed a break. I enjoyed my time in football, but the hours I had to work meant it became my life. I had fully immersed myself in the game for over a decade and I wanted to do something different.

However, the lure of the game proved too much and I returned to football a few years later, albeit for a brief time.

In 2006 I was approached by a Leeds-based law firm; they were contacting me on behalf of their client who had formed a consortium and were in talks to take over the League Two side, Boston United, who were on the brink of insolvency. I was asked to join the club, examine the books and undertake due diligence for the potential buyer.

I spent a year working as their Chief Executive and, although the takeover fell through, I had such affinity to the club that I arranged for a public meeting to be held at their York Street stadium. I invited many potential investors and, during the meeting, I, and the Club Secretary, John Blackwell, explained the desperate situation and appealed to investors to save the club. David Newton, a property developer, was in attendance and, shortly after the meeting, he took the club over and is now their owner and chairman. The financial crisis meant that Boston slid down the leagues, but they are now making their way back up to the Football League and are shortly due to move into a new stadium. Good luck to them.

York Street, home of Boston United.

I look back on my career with pride. I am fortunate to have worked at some fantastic football clubs, Leicester City, Portsmouth, Bradford City and Boston United, and I was also in demand from other clubs too, including Bristol City, Luton Town, Derby County and Coventry City. I have worked with thousands of hardworking, dedicated people and have made some life-long friends. Those football years – especially those spent at Leicester – were the best days of my life.

It is thirty-odd years since I walked through the door at Filbert Street. While a lot has changed in football during that time, in some respects, things are the same. I see so many clubs experiencing financial difficulty and clubs who are not fully maximising their commercial potential. The answer seems to be to try and attract a billionaire investor, but this does not always work. Leicester City's current owners have been fantastic to the club and its supporters, but for every set of owners like the King Power group, there are a hundred awful ones who do not have the club's, or fans' interests at heart. For clubs who do not have the luxury of wealthy benefactors, an excellent marketing and business development professional could make a huge difference.

If the right club approached me would I do it again? Of course, I would!

Postscript - About Barrie Pierpoint

In 1951, Arthur Rowley was enjoying the first of eight successful seasons as Leicester City's star striker. I was born that same year, just thirty miles away from Filbert Street in Clifton – a suburb in the south west area of Nottingham. Clifton was later the birthplace of Olympic gold medallist, Jane Torvill and England international footballers, Viv Anderson and Jermaine Jenas. My parents were hard working, caring and loving. My father worked in a textile factory and my mother at the local Co-op store.

I was not actually born a Pierpoint. My family name was Pierrepont, but my father changed it to Pierpoint as he didn't want our family name to be associated with the UK's Official Executioner, Albert Pierrepont, who we were told was a distant relative. The rest of my father's side of the family kept their name, so I had to remember which spelling to use when sending Christmas and birthday cards to my aunties, uncles and cousins.

I was eight when I experienced live football for the first time. My father took me to Meadow Lane to watch Notts County. I don't remember who they played, or the score, but I do remember him buying me a wooden rattle and a scarf. Like many Nottingham based football fans in those days, we then alternated between County and Nottingham Forest. While I always enjoyed the day out with my father, I was not ever a huge football fan, although in my late teens I did assist various local football clubs and even did some refereeing too.

I have always been creative. When I was a child, I did not sleep much because I had so many ideas swimming around in my head. My mind was always buzzing. I used to wake early and sit in the dining room writing down my thoughts and ideas.

Two of my mother's brothers drove buses and they used to let me ride with them on their journeys through Nottingham. Thus, as a kid I dreamed of following in my uncle's footsteps and becoming a bus driver.

Sadly, my parents separated before my eleventh birthday and I had to step up to be the man of the house. It was tough and made me grow up fast. With my mother working full time, I was responsible at weekends for cleaning the house, gardening and other chores.

My working-class parents did not attach much importance to education and although I inherited their work ethic, I was never really encouraged in my academic abilities. So, I left school at fifteen with no qualifications. My first job was working as an office junior which meant that I was basically licking stamps and filing all week.

During my teenage years I suffered from a lack of confidence and struggled with the social aspect of working life. I hated being in large crowds which meant that it was difficult to even get to work as the crowded bus made me claustrophobic. I became slightly depressed and anxious. I suffered with my nerves for a few years in my mid to late teens, relying on medication to keep me calm. My mother was a very strong-willed person and her support really helped me to turn my life around.

I now consider my bout of depression to be a positive thing as it led me to a revelation; there could be a more exciting life out there for me. I decided to push myself and see what I could achieve so I took night classes at Nottingham Trent Polytechnic and then I found my calling – marketing and management.

My desire to embark on running my own business began when my confidence had been re-established, so I started working as a Commission Operator, self-employed at a Jet Petrol station in Nottingham at the age of 21. By the age of 23 I had six petrol stations and about 30 staff.

A few years later having worked long hours and weekends in petrol retailing I decided to give that all up and try my hand in a 'real job' as my mother would call it, with the Nottingham Chamber of Commerce. I was to sell memberships to join the Chamber and advertising space within their business magazine. The Chamber gave businesses training services, legal and business advice, guidance on legislation, seminars and many other benefits.

I met lots of businessmen and entrepreneurs and through them, I developed my business acumen.

At twenty-eight I set up my own publishing business with two friends which was eventually bought out by Robert Maxwell's empire. I walked out there and then!

Over the next ten years I sharpened my skills and continued to make a lot of money for many businesses.

As stated, I became the first Director of Marketing and the first Chief Executive of Premier League football club, Leicester City. I also had spells at fellow football clubs, Portsmouth, Bradford City and Boston United.

In 2002, I bought a struggling Advertising Agency in Leicester with Richard Hughes and we helped, and turned around, many other businesses.

I have been involved with numerous charities; during my time at Leicester City I was an ambassador of Leicestershire Children's Hospice, Rainbows, and I have continued to work with and support many charities ever since.

I was a non-executive Director at Leicester Sound commercial radio station and a non-executive Director at Glenfield hospital.

I have also been a governor of Loughborough College. I have mentored graduate students and provided advice and guidance to start up and small businesses. I have been elected as a local Boston Borough Councillor where I live in Lincolnshire, was the Deputy Mayor of Boston for a year and became Non-Executive Director of many businesses, assisting them to develop and grow.

I also remained involved in professional sports from 2000 to 2008, assisting sports and football clubs such as Peterborough United, Watford, Boston United, Leicester Riders, Leicester Tigers, Leicestershire County Cricket Club and Leicester Racecourse, where I have helped as an interim CEO or in consultancy roles.

In 2008, I moved to rural Lincolnshire where I continue to live. I am now a business and management consultant with various clients within the Midlands.

Not bad for a shy lad from Nottingham who dreamt of becoming a bus driver!

Contributors

This book would not have been possible without the contributions and involvement of the following people:

Former Leicester City Players
Alan Birchenall
Gary Coatsworth
Tony Cottee
Mark Draper
Simon Grayson
Matt Heath
Emile Heskey
Colin Hill
Pontus Kamark
Jamie Lawrence
Sam McMahon
Gary Mills
Carl Muggleton
Stefan Oakes
Ian Ormondroyd
Lee Philpott
Richard Smith
Danny Thomas
Steve Walsh
Julian Watts
Mike Whitlow

Former Leicester City Team Managers
Brian Little
Mark McGhee

Former Leicester City Directors
Gilbert Kinch
Roy Parker
John Sharp

Former Leicester City Employees
Trevor Dempsey, Promotions' Manager
Richard Hughes, Business Development Manager
Alex Irving, Conference and Banqueting Manager
Michelle Newman, Personal Assistant to the Chief Executive
Charles Rayner, Retail Operations Manager

Former Leicester City Partners
John Aldridge OBE, DL. Managing Director of the Leicester Mercury Media Group
Keith Beaumont, Chief Executive of Leicester City Challenge Limited
Henry Doyle, Partner in Edge & Ellison Solicitors
Rustie Lee, Television Personality and Celebrity Chef

Former Leicester City Corporate Clients
Martin Page, Owner and Director of Walkers Tyres
Jim Mutton, Chief Executive of Loughborough College

Leicester City Supporters
Ashley Barrett, CEO of Barratt Smith & Brown Legal Services
Jersey Budd, Singer/Songwriter
Ian Stringer, BBC Radio Leicester Sports Presenter
Cliff Ginnetta, Leicester City Supporters' Club Chairman
Geoff Peters, TalkSport Radio Presenter

The following sources were incredibly valuable in our research for the book:

Of Fossils and Foxes - Dave Smith & Paul Taylor
Farewell to Filbert Street - Neville Foulger
Starting a Wave - Brian Little
The *Leicester Mercury* Archives at the Record Office for Leicestershire, Leicester and Rutland.

Acknowledgements

There are many people whom I would like to thank for their help in creating this book.

Firstly, John Hayes and Matthew Hayes from Champions(UK)plc for sponsoring the printing of this book, creating and delivering the marketing and publicity campaigns and for providing all the support to make this book a success.

Geoff Sanders, of Champions (UK) plc, for designing the cover.

Scott Giles and Amy Coleman, of Champions (UK) plc, for organising and managing the marketing and publicity campaigns.

Simon Atherley from Simply Page 1 for sponsoring and developing the promotional book website.

Steve Walsh for writing the foreword.

Lois Hide for proofreading the book.

Michelle Hawksworth (previously Newman), Charles Rayner and Richard Hughes who shared their memories, provided material for the book and for all their support during my time at Leicester City.

Trevor Dempsey and Alex Irving for their contributions for the book and for their support when working with me at the Club.

Former Leicester City Team Managers, Brian Little and Mark McGhee, for their contributions and full support when working with me at the Club.

Roy Parker, Gilbert Kinch and John Sharpe, former Leicester City Directors, for their contributions to the book and for their support during my time at Leicester City.

Philip Smith, former Leicester City PLC Chairman, for his support during my time at Leicester City.

All of the former players, former employees, corporate clients, fans and all the many other special people for your contributions and support over the years.

Neville Chadwick Photography and the Leicester Mercury for sourcing and allowing us to use some great City photos.

Mathew Mann - for approaching and persuading me to produce the new book and especially for his research, interviewing all the contributors, writing all the editorials and producing the book in its entirety.

Thank you to everyone who buys the book, I hope that you enjoy the stories from the nineties.

Finally, thank you to Rainbows, hospice for children and young people, for allowing us to donate money for each copy sold to their very valuable and worthy cause.

Barrie Pierpoint has collaborated with Mathew Mann to write this story. Mathew would like to thank . . .

Barrie, for taking me into your confidence and allowing me to be a part of this project.

Everyone involved in the success that Leicester City enjoyed during the nineties - thank you for the wonderful memories.

All the contributors for being so accommodating and for sharing their stories.

Everyone who reads this book. I hope you have enjoyed the story.

My wife, Holly, for her support and encouragement.

And, finally, to my wonderful children, Dylan and Eve, who inspire me every single day.

Photograph Credits

supporting rainbows
hospice for children and young people

Rainbows Hospice for Children and Young People is based in Loughborough, Leicestershire, and is the only hospice of its kind in in the East Midlands. The charity delivers a comprehensive range of support services, nursing and care for children and young people with life-limiting conditions. Its incredible team of people help with end of life care, symptom management and respite care and in addition, provide support to parents and siblings through their bereavement.

Since opening its doors over 25 years ago, it is recognised as a centre of excellence in paediatric palliative medicine and has a specialist team of dedicated doctors, nurses, health professionals and carers.

Rainbows currently supports over 450 families. With your help, it can do even more to ensure it brings care and happiness to those, and more, children, young people and their families.

www.rainbows.co.uk